TO BE AN AMERICAN

CRITICAL AMERICA
General Editors: Richard Delgado and Jean Stefancic

TO BE AN AMERICAN ★

Cultural
Pluralism
and the
Rhetoric of
Assimilation

Bill Ong Hing

NEW YORK UNIVERSITY PRESS
New York and London

NEW YORK UNIVERSITY PRESS
New York and London

Library of Congress Cataloging-in-Publication Data
Hing, Bill Ong.
To be an American : cultural pluralism and the rhetoric of
assimilation / Bill Ong Hing.
p.   cm. — (Critical America)
Includes bibliographical references (p.   ) and index.
ISBN 0-8147-3523-1 (acid-free paper)
1. Pluralism (Social sciences)—United States.   2. Immigrants—
United States.   3. Acculturation—United States.   4. United States—
Ethnic relations.   I. Title.   II. Series.
E184.A1H54   1997
305.8'00973—dc20   96-35678
                                          CIP

New York University Press books are printed on acid-free paper,
and their binding materials are chosen for strength and durability.

Manufactured in the United States of America

10 9 8 7 6 5 4 3 2 1

For my children, Eric, Sharon, and Julianne

Contents

Acknowledgments

The countless immigrant clients and families with whom I have worked over the past 25 years provided the primary impetus for the writing of this book. They are inspirational people who have taught me volumes about life. Most have been hard-working, decent, and law-abiding. Relatively few were criminals. I appreciate the opportunities I have had to get to know them; they have made my professional life worthwhile. I have encountered them in a variety of places: law offices, legal clinics, community presentations, the immigration court, and in detention facilities. They do not deserve the negative image that dominates much of today's media.

I think of my clients often. I thought of them a few years back when I read that the most common name given to newborn boys in Los Angeles County was José. Given what we know about the demographic development in certain parts of the country like California, that fact was enlightening but no surprise. I was quite happy that the parents of all the new Josés born in Los Angeles County sought to record the name as José rather than as Joseph or Joe. Their action was a departure from what I experienced generations earlier.

When I was born in a small, predominantly Mexican American town in Arizona in 1949, my immigrant parents named me Billy—not William, or even Bill, but Billy. They chose this name because they had been told by doctors and others in the community that since they were in America they had to give their children American names and record our births with those names. They chose Billy for me because they had heard of other boys called Billy. Little did they know that most Billys had birth certificates under the name of William. Growing up, I had Mexican American friends whom I called Pancho, Pedro, Leonardo, María, and Reynaldo, whose birth certificates bore the names Frank,

Peter, Leonard, Mary, and Ray. Although my birth certificate reads "Billy," my parents, like all Chinese immigrants, gave me a Chinese name: Sun Yuen. Chinese names, like Native American names, have an intended meaning. Stupidly, on my part, I never bothered learning the meaning of my Chinese name until I was in high school. I found out that it means "new source"—a name that I rather like. We have come some distance since that era. Today, recording a child's birth as José or Tseming or Kwame is not unusual.

I think of my clients when I drive around the state. Ironically, immigration authorities deport Latinos in California from places named Modesto, Salinas, San Francisco, San José, Los Angeles, Fresno, and San Diego.

Of course I think of my clients when I hear the rhetoric of today's restrictionists. When neo-nativists think of refugees and immigrants the words that come to their minds are economic drain, welfare recipients, public school costs, non-English speakers, crime, separatism, conflict, and non-assimilation. But to those of us who know and work with, or who are ourselves, immigrants and refugees, thinking of refugees and immigrants conjures images of family, hard work, courage, cultural enrichment, and innovation.

When I first started working in immigration as a legal services immigration attorney in 1974, most of my clients were either Mexican or Chinese. Their names were Cabral, Ayalde, Lau, Chan and occasionally an oddity like my Cuban-Chinese client, Jacinto Cuan. But by the end of the 1970's and into the 1980's, the client list included Salvadorans, Guatemalans, Nigerians, Liberians, Iranians, Egyptians, Filipinos, Koreans, Vietnamese, Haitians, and South Africans. The names were different. Atanacio, Pineda, Mattoto, Ibrahim, Patel, Balian. Of course during this period, in addition to the Cardoza-Fonsecas and the Wongs that I represented, I also counselled the Walls and the McMullens and others from Canada and Europe including teenagers and young adults from places like Great Britain, France, Ireland, and Scandinavian countries looking for a free deportation ticket back home after money had run out here.

Many friends and colleagues have encouraged me to think about my clients and their impact on our society as I have proceeded on this project. I am deeply grateful for their counsel: Roberta Achtenberg, Ian Ayres, John Barton, John Burton, John Hart Ely, Ed Epstein, Lawrence Friedman, Tom Grey, J. D. Hokoyama, Kevin Johnson, Jerry López,

Shauna Marshall, Bill McGowan, Joyce Hing McGowan, Miguel Méndez, Mary Morgan, Rose Matsui Ochi, José Padilla, Eva Jefferson Patterson, Nancy Pelosi, Drucilla Ramey, Cruz Reynoso, Bill Rojas, Bill Simon, John Tateishi, Kim Taylor-Thompson, Michael Wald, Patricia Williams, Lucie White, and Diane Wong. Friends at the Immigrant Legal Resource Center have continued to inspire my work: Kathy Brady, Eric Cohen, Sister Martha Garcia, Susan Lydon, Nancy Mowery, Rebecca Rivera, Anaya Rose, and Mark Silverman. Several students helped along the way: Michelle Alvarez, Jon Blazer, Stephen Carpenter, Daina Chiu, Selena Dong, Shubha Ghosh, David Kazanjian, Margaret Lin, Stephanie Martz, John Russ, Eric Talley, and Rufus Whitley. My administrative assistant, Yvonne Yazzie, has been a constant resource. And I am sincerely indebted to the New York University Press editor-in-chief, Niko Pfund, and the series editors, Richard Delgado and Jean Stefancic, for their trust and confidence in me.

Of course none of my work is possible or worthwhile without the love, support, encouragement, example, and understanding of my wife, Lenora, and our children, Eric, Sharon, and Julianne. They are my spirit, bringing perspective, balance, sanity, and sustenance to my life.

Introduction

Proposition 187, an initiative to exclude undocumented children from public schools and bar their families from medical care, passes overwhelmingly in California. Congressional proposals that would reduce legal immigration by a third and preclude legal immigrants from receiving public assistance receive strong bipartisan support. The Immigration and Naturalization Service imposes strict asylum rules: applicants—even the poorest and most sympathetic—are prohibited from working, and any would-be refugee who misses the filing deadline is forever barred from applying.

Is there any doubt that we are experiencing one of the most potent periods of anti-immigrant fervor in the United States? Nativists, xenophobes, and exclusionists have long been a part of the American landscape. From time to time their rituals influence immigration policies.[1] We are in the middle of such a time. If we listen closely, today's fears echo those of other eras: job loss, shrinking resources, a fracturing national culture, all due to a flood of immigrants. Much of the public as well as policymakers are listening indeed.

Much of America is hurting economically, insecure about its economic future. Much of America looks around and sees declining city services, failing public schools, and an inequitable tax system. And much of America looks around and senses change in its surroundings—change that is puzzling or worrisome, rather than natural or enlightening. To many who make up this part of America, the explanation that restrictionists (those who would severely reduce immigrant visas) offer up—the immigrant as culprit—makes sense. Immigrants in the workforce are easily picked out. Immigrants on the street not speaking English or dressed differently are impossible to miss. The traditional image of the immigrant as vital to the economy and to society, as a contributor of new energy and innovation, is facilely cast aside as outdated and wrong.

Since 1965, America has experienced significant demographic changes. The African American population has increased by more than a third, while Latino and Asian Pacific American growth has been even more dramatic. The Latino population has almost tripled; today, more than one in ten Americans are Latino. The Asian Pacific American population which numbered under a million in 1965 is estimated at almost 9 million today—some 3.3 percent of the total population. One of four Americans is a person of color, and the proportion is even greater in states like California, Texas, New York, Florida, and Illinois.

Immigration has accounted for much of the growth in the Latino and Asian American communities. From 1971 to 1990, nearly 9 million immigrants entered from Asian and Latin American countries.[2] Today, more than half a million immigrants are entering annually, and Asian and Latino immigrants make up 75 percent of that number. If current trends continue, the U.S. census projects that by the year 2050, the population will be almost evenly divided between Anglos and people of color (53 percent Anglo, 14 percent African American, 25 percent Latino, and 8 percent Asian Pacific American). Of the projected population of 390 million in the year 2050, one-third will be post-1970 immigrants and their descendants. In certain parts of the United States, the impact will be felt even sooner. For example, by the year 2020 non-Hispanic whites will be a minority in California, a mere 34 percent of the population; Latinos will be 36 percent, followed by Asians at 20 percent and African Americans at 8 percent. Not since the first decade of the twentieth century—when southern and eastern Europeans entered in large numbers for the first time—has there been such a dramatic change in the ethnic composition of the nation.

These demographic trends, altering the ethnic composition of America, have defined the debate for many modern-day restrictionists on what it means to become an American. For them, allegations that immigrants harm the economy become pretextual, secondary, or unnecessary. They are troubled by the increasing numbers of Asian and Latino faces that have appeared seemingly overnight. They are more troubled by the cultural and social impact of these immigrants than by their economic influence. Disturbed by so many non-English-speaking foreigners, they construe much of the behavior of these newcomers as a lack of loyalty to the nation.

The current cycle of nativism comes at a time when immigration is dominated by Asians and Latinos. As a result, the discussion of who is and who is not American, who can and cannot become American, goes beyond the technicalities of citizenship and residency requirements; it strikes at the very heart of our nation's long and troubled legacy of race relations. Underlying the debate over immigrants and American identity is a concern about the interaction, or lack of interaction, among different racial groups.

Because some oppose immigration on the basis that "immigrants hurt the economy," a rational look at what economists have to say on the topic is essential. As this book will demonstrate, the allegations of the negative economic impact of immigrants are clearly overblown and largely unsupported by the weight of evidence. The current level of anti-immigrant rhetoric is simply not justified on economic grounds.

Contextualizing the impact of immigrants is also important. Until we can understand the *real* causes of our fears about job loss and public bankruptcy, we cannot evaluate immigrants' actual collective role in our economy. Since California seems to be the hotbed for much contemporary anti-immigrant fervor, I examine the genesis of such hostility: the state's ailing economy and strained budgets. Another crucial factor is the loss of jobs that the country experienced in recent years and the globalization of the economy. I also take up the question of how, in using low-wage immigrant workers, we may simply be exploiting poor workers both domestically and globally. I counter arguments from immigration opponents who say that like Japan, we can operate our economy quite well without immigrant workers. Since many restrictionists, including the proponents of Proposition 187,[3] argue that efforts to curb immigration should be supported because immigrants compete directly for jobs with African Americans, I investigate some of the real issues facing the African-American community.

Because the principal complaint of restrictionists today is culturally and socially premised, the primary purpose of my efforts here is to analyze the positions of two broad groups: first, the assimilationists, whose opposition to current immigration is chiefly grounded in cultural or social complaints, and second, the cultural pluralists, the counterpart to the assimilationists, who promote diversity or multiculturalism. The debate between these two groups not only influences our views toward immigration policies, but also encompasses the very nature of American culture and our normative visions of society. The objections that cultural assimilationists and Euro-immigrationists express about today's immigrants generally consist of overlapping race-based and culture-based complaints. And two points that assimilationists seem to overlook must also be considered—that the United States is *already* a multiracial, multicultural country whose culture is constantly evolving, and that today's immigrants actually *do* acculturate. I set forth some modern-day justifications for a pluralistic approach related to visions of democracy, the economy, and social benefits. We must all be encouraged to consider a new approach to cultural pluralism which respects diverse views and cultures, which is constantly attentive to race relations, and which shares a common core set of values. In confronting these difficult issues, we need to go beyond the rhetoric of assimilation and cultural pluralism and think seriously about what it means to become an American in an increasingly diverse society.

In their current attack on the influx of Asian and Latino immigrants and criticism of interethnic group conflict and separatism, assimilationists essentially posit two solutions: terminate or drastically curtail immigration; and Americanize those who are here. In response to these proposals that are couched in a rhetoric of culture, I set forth my own constantly evolving notions of cultural pluralism and what it means to be an American.

The concept of a common unifying core set of values holding different groups together must be considered. This core would include respect for laws, the democratic political and economic system, equal opportunity, and human rights. This concept does not, however, imply a lack of support for ethnic communities. Indeed, diversity must be the basis for an "American" identity. Ethnic communities are critical to providing a sense of identity, fulfillment, and self-confidence for many. Society should respect those who hold separatist views and prefer to live and work among others of the same background. At the same time, society should strive to eradicate the harmful situations that lead to separatist sentiment. We cannot expect those at the margins to buy into a core without the commitment of the power structure. Immigrant adaptation, and the creation of a common core, must be viewed as the dual responsibility of the immigrant and the mainstream.

As I consider these issues, my experiences growing up in a multicultural community and working with immigrants seem relevant. Certainly no one's personal experiences should be used to generalize for all others. But we should listen to each others' anecdotes and views, for it is from these stories that we understand the perspectives of others. My own stories are shared not to elevate anecdote to theory, but in the hope that others may benefit—as I believe I have—from these experiences.

Restrictionists and pro-immigrant advocates do agree on one critical point: we face a defining moment in the nation's history. The course we choose will tell us much about ourselves.

chapter 1

A *Superior* Multicultural Experience

Our experiences, from childhood through adolescence, young adulthood, and beyond, inevitably shape our views of race, assimilation, and a multiracial society. I grew up in Superior, Arizona, a copper-mining town of about five thousand people in the east-central part of the state. The youngest of ten children in one of three Chinese American families (or one extended family, since their members were my uncles, aunts, and cousins), I spoke mainly Cantonese to my immigrant parents,[1] and English to my American-born siblings. We had a small grocery adjacent to our house. Since Superior was predominantly Mexican American, I spoke Spanish to our older customers and a combination of Spanish and English to the other children in the neighborhood and at school. Speaking Spanish on school grounds was prohibited. Some of our customers and my classmates were Native American, mostly Navajo and Apache. With them I spoke English.

I learned a lot about Mexican American culture growing up in Superior. I spent a good deal of time at my friend Leonard Martinez's house, eating and talking with Leonard and his grandmother, who was from Mexico. I learned about hunting from his grandfather and uncles by listening to their stories and sharing in the celebration when they returned from trips with deer, rabbit, wild boar, or quail. The father of my friend and next-door neighbor Ray Ramirez taught me how to sing and play several Mexican *corridos* (folk ballads) on the guitar. My friend Diana Viramontes was great at sandlot baseball and at cracking open *piñatas* (candy-filled figurines) blindfolded at birthday parties. She once even introduced me to her Girl Scout friend Mary Rose Garrido, on whom I had a crush for several years afterward. It was not uncommon for some Mexican children to taunt me because I was Chinese. But I was good at defending myself, and often my Mexican friends joined in on my side.

Growing up, I was especially close to a Navajo classmate, Margie Curley, and an Apache, Joe Thomas. Both read everything they could find, wrote interesting stories, and had beautiful handwriting. Margie was soft-spoken and we often had long conversations about our families and interests. Joe, one of my Little League teammates for four years, was one of the most popular children in school. I lost track of Joe and Margie after high school, although I heard later that Margie settled on a reservation and makes jewelry; neither had the funds to go on to college. I came to know another Navajo family that traded at our store, the Bendles. The parents were terrific with the children—always exercising the right amount of discipline, but spoiling them with candy on occasion and consistently assigning responsibility and displaying trust. Hugh Bendle, Jr., became a fine tennis player, and with the help of loans, grants, and Mr. Bendle's savings from his wages as a copper miner, all three of the Bendle children went to college.

After school each day, I played games with Mexican, Anglo, and Native American schoolmates and friends: baseball, basketball, football, marbles, tops, and yo-yos. From the ages of seven to fourteen, I played Little League and Senior League baseball in the summer. When I was fifteen, I decided to spend the summer in California with one of my older sisters, and was quite envious of the fact that Superior's Senior League All Star team, comprised of many of my friends, won its way to the Senior League World Series in Louisville, Kentucky. In Kentucky, local families provided housing for the team. One of my Anglo friends, Billy Joe Walker, told me that when the team arrived in Louisville, the family that was assigned to him was chuckling on the drive to their house. He asked them why, and they explained that with a name like "Billy Joe," they were expecting him to be African American.

Little League baseball meant ballpark food. Even before I played Little League, much of the fun of going to the games as a kid was in the small concession stand where I could buy hot dogs, corn-on-the-cob, burritos, and tacos. End of the season all-star games were particularly rewarding because our local Little League parents' group always budgeted money for meals after regional and state games. After one Little League all-star game played twenty miles away in Miami, Arizona, we returned home victorious to feast at my favorite restaurant in town, the Triple X Café, a Mexican restaurant. Coincidentally, the Senior League all-star team that my brother Johnny was on was also celebrating a victory at the Triple X. I recall a friendly argument between our coaches over which Hing kid was the better ball player. The Triple X was owned by the Nuñez family and one of the sons in the family, David, was one of my best friends. Whenever I ate there, I got the royal treatment.

Summer also meant horseback riding for my brother Johnny and me. Although we never owned a horse, Johnny had a knack for talking horse-owning neighbors and local ranchers into lending us theirs. One of my mother's store customers—Tony Banda—used to ride his pinto horse to the store when he needed to pick up a few items. He gave me my first real horseback ride when I was two or three years old. My brother Johnny was a great rider. After we moved into a bigger home, on the main highway through town, he often rode in our yard and in front of our house. I remember coming out the front door one hot summer afternoon to find four carloads of vacationers parked in front of our house (probably traveling to or from Phoenix). Cameras were clicking and the kids were screaming, "A real cowboy! A real cowboy!" The subject of their excitement was my brother Johnny, with a cowboy hat, grinning widely, horn-rimmed glasses and all, showing off on one of our neighbor's horses.

I received the best lesson in how to present a book report from another of my Little League baseball teammates, Manuel Silvas. Manuel had a tough-guy side but was always very nice to me. Until our freshman year in high school, he was a mediocre student. But our freshman English teacher, Rudy Burrola, and Manuel seemed to make a connection. Burrola recommended *Catcher in the Rye* to Manuel for an assigned book report. When it was Manuel's turn to present an oral presentation in class, he absolutely blew everyone away. He read a moving passage from the book as part of his presentation, and acted out another scene. In the end, the entire class understood Manuel's interpretation and we were all quite affected. This was a stressful time in Manuel's life, to say the least. A year earlier, his father—who had murdered his former girlfriend—was executed in the Arizona gas chamber (the last death sentence execution in Arizona in almost thirty years). I can never forget Manuel's grief. He is now a lawyer in the Phoenix area.

High school also provided opportunities for a number of extracurricular activities. I played freshman basketball and four years of tennis. At the beginning of my sophomore year, there was a good deal of excitement over the fact that the girls' tennis team was getting two new members, both immigrants. Both were attractive and blue-eyed, with light brown hair, one from Canada, the other from Spain. While the hair of most of my Mexican friends was dark brown or black, many also had light brown hair. Among them were Marcella Rodríguez, whose father Leo also owned a grocery store, and Carol Woods, who had sisters with dark brown hair.

I also played the guitar in a couple of rock-and-roll bands in high school. One band, which we named "The UNs" for the United Nations, became quite popular in Superior and a couple of other little towns in the area. We decided on the "UNs" because of our composition: a Chinese American lead guitarist, a Mexican American singer and saxophonist, a rhythm guitarist of Scandinavian descent, and a drummer of German extraction. Our music ranged from Chuck Berry and the Beatles, to some Motown, Richie Valens, and many Spanish-language Mexican songs. We performed mostly at high school dances, but also got hired at weddings, birthday parties, and civic and social club dances. After high school, the lead singer Armor Gomez performed as a lounge singer in Las Vegas for many years.

Most families in Superior had someone who worked for the copper mine, then owned by Magma Copper Company. The mine was open twenty-four hours, with three eight-hour shifts a day. The work was dangerous, containing the deepest shaft mine in North America. People were killed; there were fires. You could hear the loud whistle blow once, long and steady, at the end of each shift. When the whistle blew differently, my classmates would look worriedly at one another. This sound meant that an accident had occurred; friends and classmates who realized that their father was not working that particular shift looked relieved; the others could not calm down until they went home to see if things were all right. The mine-mill labor union was active. My parents extended grocery store credit to union members during lengthy strikes, thus earning their loyalty, even though my parents also traded with wealthier management families.

One of my brothers was an elementary schoolteacher for a while in a small agricultural town in Arizona named Eloy. He was also the school's track coach. But he gave up teaching after a few years in order to manage a small grocery store in another small town nearby named Coolidge. When he went on vacation he needed someone to help run the store in his absence. I did this a couple of times for him when I was in high school, and I recall these occasions with great fondness. His customers were mostly agricultural workers: Mexicans, Native Americans, African Americans, as well as Anglos. His three or four employees were generally Mexicans, African Americans, and Anglos. They were a lot of fun to be around; after-hours I met their families and they showed me around Coolidge and took me to parties.

My whole family was exposed to and embraced these multiple cultures. My mother ran the grocery store, and spoke with customers, employees, salesmen, deliverymen, and repairmen in both English and Spanish. Unlike my mother, neither of my two aunts was fluent in Spanish or English; yet both worked in their own family stores and interacted with our non-Chinese neighbors and customers.

My family celebrated a variety of holidays—American, Chinese, and Mexican—and sometimes even traveled to Flagstaff for summertime Native American festivals. Similarly, we ate a variety of foods at home, mainly Chinese, American, and Mexican. My sisters still cook great Mexican cuisine. Our Mexican customers and neighbors often brought us dishes to sample and my mother reciprocated with some of her own. Every day with dinner, we ate Texas Long Grain rice especially ordered from a distributor. Another of our customers, a Syrian American family, did the same. A German immigrant couple who were also customers often spoke of their native culture and foods. When I was in high school, they even offered me their own homemade concoction for acne. Occasionally we would drive to Phoenix (about sixty miles away) for Chinese wedding banquets or Ong Family Association get-togethers. (As a child I learned that my family surname is Ong, not Hing. When my father immigrated, he stated his name in customary Chinese fashion— last name first—as Ong Chun Hing. The clueless immigration official wrote down Hing as the family name.)

Many of my high school classmates went to college. Others stayed in Superior and mined copper like their parents. Two of my nephews did not go to college, instead staying in Superior to run a large grocery store. The support of my parents (my father completed high school in China, my mother a few years of grammar school), my siblings, and our next-door neighbor Mr. Gonzales, motivated me to go to college. Mr. Gonzales was the most distinguished person I knew. He lived in Washington, D.C., where he worked for Senator Carl Hayden, but he came home a few times a year to visit his Mexican-born mother. When in Superior, he took the time to tell me about his work and encourage me to study hard and go to college.

Superior was in many regards a typical close-knit small town. High school sports were a central focus. The American Legion, Veterans of Foreign Wars, Knights of Columbus, and Rotary Club all had active chapters. My father was the first president of the Superior Rotary Club and during World War II served as the town sheriff. There was an active union. We attended the predominantly Anglo Presbyterian Church (without my Buddhist mother), although most of our friends and customers were Catholic. In fact, two of my sisters were christened as Catholics. Superior had other churches as well: Baptist, Episcopalian, Spanish-service Presbyterian, Jehovah's Witnesses, and Mormon. At nineteen my brother Johnny married his high school sweetheart, a Mormon.

Although I left Superior after graduating from high school to attend college at U.C. Berkeley, my early life in Superior has profoundly influenced my thinking on multicultural, multiracial, and multireligious communities, class distinctions, and social values. Although life was not without strife, my family was part of a larger community that respected our Chinese American identity and culture. We learned about and respected other cultures and languages. I learned values and approaches to life from people of all backgrounds, from my Catholic Mexican American playmates to my Jewish high school history teacher, from Navajo and German customers to the chief administrator of the local mine. In retrospect, the opportunity to hear different perspectives was clearly an advantage.

My life after high school—at U.C. Berkeley, in law school, in Chinatown, at the Buddhist church, as a legal services attorney, immigration lawyer, academic, participant in community activities, spouse, and parent—has reinforced the values I began to develop in Superior. How could I not be influenced by my African American college roommate from Texas, the jazz band we formed, People's Park, or the all-Asian American fraternity I initially spurned but ultimately joined? Or my experience as the president of a fledgling Asian American law student group in law school? Or the Chinese immigrant children to whom I taught American folks songs at the Chinatown YWCA? Or my wife's five-generation Chinese American family and its eleven-year struggle to build a Buddhist church? Or the diverse group of clients I've represented beginning at a legal aid office?[2] Or the community activists I've met and worked with for over twenty-five years? My early life in Superior and all of these subsequent life experiences have created impressions—some would say biases—that lead to views about America and being an American that one might loosely call cultural pluralism. Since recognition of the potential biases created by one's background is a necessary first step to wrestling with the challenge of a multiracial society, I continue to try to make sense of how that past affects my thinking today.

chapter 2

A Nation of Immigrants, a History of Nativism

"We are a nation of immigrants." How many times do we hear this phrase? Most of us encounter it in positive terms beginning in elementary school. Take my daughter's Fifth Grade social studies textbook *America Will Be.*[1] Chapter 1 is entitled "A Nation of Many Peoples," and the first paragraph contains this passage: "From the earliest time, America has been a land of many peoples. This rich mix of cultures has shaped every part of life in the United States today." The authors continue, as a "pluralistic culture, life is exciting. People work, join together, struggle, learn, and grow."

Today the phrase—"we are a nation of immigrants"—is invoked on both sides of the immigration debate. On one side we are told, "We are a nation of immigrants, immigrants are our strength, they invigorate our economy, they stimulate our culture, they add to our society." On the other, "We are a nation of immigrants, but times have changed; they take away jobs, they are costly, the non-English speakers make life complicated, new immigrants don't have our values."

As early as 1751, Benjamin Franklin opposed the influx of German immigrants, warning that "Pennsylvania will in a few years become a German colony; instead of their learning our language, we must learn theirs, or live as in a foreign country." A couple of years later, he expanded this thought:

> [T]hose who came hither are generally the most stupid of their own nation, and as ignorance is often attended with great credulity, when knavery would mislead it, and with suspicion when honesty would set it right; and few of the English understand the German language, and so cannot address them either from the press or pulpit, it is almost impossible to remove any prejudices they may entertain. . . . Not being used to liberty, they know not how to make modest use of it.

Responding to dramatic increases in German and Irish immigration in the first half of the 1800s, the Kentucky Senator Garrett Davis spoke out against further immigration and proposed a twenty-one-year residency requirement for naturalization. In his view,

> [M]ost of those European immigrants, having been born and having lived in the ignorance and degradation of despotisms, without mental or moral culture, with but a vague consciousness of human rights, and no knowledge whatever of the principles of popular constitutional government, their interference in the political administration of our affairs, even when honestly intended, would be about as successful as that of the Indian in the arts and business of civilized private life. . . . The system inevitably and in the end will fatally depreciate, degrade, and demoralize the power which governs and rules our destinies.[2]

The Undesirable Asian

These social and cultural exclusionist views were accompanied by economic concerns. For example, job and wage competition provided an early impetus for the anti-Chinese crusade of the mid-1800s. The Chinese worked for lower wages and seemed to make do with less; they were criticized for being thrifty—for spending little and saving most of their meager wages. At the Oregon constitutional convention in 1857, a proposal was made to exclude the Chinese because whites "could not compete" with Chinese working for $1.50 to $2.00 a day. The Chinese had frequently been politically exploited on labor issues. Mine owners threatened to let the Chinese take over the entire industry because white miners demanded $3 a day while Chinese workers asked only $1.50. During the construction of the transcontinental railroad, Chinese workers were paid two-thirds the rate for white workers.[3]

The influence of economic nativism was quite apparent by 1870. Labor organizations—including plumbers, carpenters, and unemployed shoemakers—led a massive anti-Chinese demonstration in San Francisco that drew national attention. Labor groups held anti-Chinese rallies in Boston and New York as well.[4]

The hostile reception given the Chinese was of course due to race as well as to economic competition. Some parallels between the treatment of Chinese and African Americans can be drawn. For example, one of the earliest efforts to exclude the Chinese from California by state law was passed in the assembly as a companion to a measure barring entry to those of African descent. And certainly the major political parties stressed concepts of race superiority which excluded African Americans and by implication other people of color from the meaning of the Declaration of Independence. But in Congress's 1870 deliberations over whether to liberalize the naturalization laws by extending them to all aliens irrespective of origin or color, the right to naturalize was extended to aliens of African descent and denied to Chinese because of their "undesirable qualities."[5]

Republicans and Democrats alike tended toward nativism. In California, the antagonism between old stock and European immigrants subsided and coalesced. By 1876, both major political parties had adopted anti-Chinese planks in their national platforms, and the Workingman's Party of California emerged as a leading force against Chinese immigration.[6]

An important element in the anti-Chinese crusade was doubt that they could successfully assimilate into American society. The assumption was that Chinese were infusible elements—an assumption that would trouble melting-pot assimilationists and certainly the more extreme supporters of Anglo-conformity. Until the coming of the Chinese, no immigrant group had differed sufficiently from the Anglo-American root stock to compromise basic social institutions such as Christian religion and ethics, monogamy, or natural rights theory. Social foundations were not negotiable to advocates of "Americanization." The immigrant had to convert and shed foreign, heathen ways. The alternative was total exclusion of culturally distant groups. American opinion leaders may have had a real melting pot in mind prior to the arrival of the Chinese, albeit one which already excluded Native Americans and African Americans, but the idea of adding Chinese to the mix was not acceptable.

As immigrants, the Chinese posed the first serious threat to the melting pot concept. They were believed to be immutable, tenaciously clinging to old customs, and recalcitrantly opposing progress and moral improvement. Nonwhite and non-Christian at a time when either trait alone was a serious handicap, the Chinese looked different, dressed differently, ate differently, and followed customs wholly unfamiliar to Americans.[7]

Racist beliefs that evolved during the three decades of unrestricted Chinese immigration added a biological dimension to Chinese exclusion. Oriental blood supposedly determined the oriental thoughts and oriental habits that precluded any possibility that the Chinese could be Americanized. The failure to extend the naturalization laws in 1870 officially recognized this in denying citizenship to Chinese immigrants. Even supporters of unrestricted Chinese immigration made it clear that they could not conceive of the Chinese as a permanent part of American society. An 1876 congressional commission report concluded that the denial of naturalization to Chinese was necessary to preserve republican institutions. Irish newspapers noted that "degraded races" such as "Niggers and Chinamen" were incapable of understanding the democratic principles for which the Irish had continually fought.[8]

Anti-immigrant sentiment was initially legitimized at state and local levels. Chinese immigrants were barred from operating laundries and testifying at trials. Latin miners were targeted for special taxes. All aliens were barred from owning land. Antimiscegenation laws prevented the marriage of whites to people of color. The rights of non-English speakers were trashed in public schools. But after the 1875 Supreme Court ruling in *Chy Lung v. Freeman* that states could not pass laws regulating immigration,[9] greater pressure was placed on Congress to exclude.

The Chinese were the first ethnic group to be targeted in sweeping federal legislation. Although Chinese laborers were at first encouraged and welcomed, they soon encountered fierce racial animosity in the 1840s, as did miners from Mexico, South America, Hawaii, and even France. Irish Roman Catholics in California, replicating the racial prejudice they had suffered on the East Coast, rallied against the brown, black, and yellow foreigners in the mines. This racial prejudice, exacerbated by fear of competition from aliens, prompted calls for restrictive federal immigration laws.

California's foreign miners' tax of 1850 effectively forced out Latino miners who refused to pay the $20 per month license fee. But the Chinese remained, thereby standing out as the largest body of foreigners in California and eventually feeling the full weight of prejudice upon them. "Anticoolie" clubs (low-wage Chinese laborers were referred to as "coolies") surfaced in the early 1850s, and sporadic boycotts of Chinese-made goods soon followed. By 1853 anti-Chinese editorials were common in San Francisco newspapers.

For a time this sentiment gained powerful political backing from the newly formed Know-Nothing Party. Organized in the 1850s to exclude all foreign-born citizens from office, to discourage immigration, and to "keep America pure," the Know-Nothing Party demanded a twenty-one-year naturalization period. On the East Coast it fought against Irish Catholic immigration, while on the West Coast the target was usually the Chinese.[10]

By the late 1860s the Chinese question became a major issue in California and Oregon politics. Many white workers felt threatened by the competition they perceived from the Chinese, while many employers continued to seek them as inexpensive laborers and subservient domestics. Employment of Chinese by the Central Pacific Railroad was by this time at its peak. Anticoolie clubs increased in number, and mob attacks against Chinese became frequent. Seldom outdone in such matters, many newly organized labor unions were by then demanding legislation against Chinese immigration. The Chinese were at once resented for their resourcefulness in turning a profit on abandoned mines and for their reputed frugality. Much of this resentment was transformed into or sustained by a need to preserve "racial purity" and "Western civilization."

In 1879 a measure was placed on the California ballot to determine public sentiment: 900 favored the Chinese, while 150,000 were opposed. During the 1881 session of Congress, twenty-five anti-Chinese petitions were presented by a number of civic groups from many states. The California legislature declared a legal holiday to facilitate anti-Chinese public rallies that attracted thousands of demonstrators.

Responding to this national clamor, the forty-seventh Congress enacted the Chinese Exclusion Act on May 6, 1882. The law excluded laborers for ten years. But leaders of the anti-Chinese movement were not satisfied. After pressing for a series of treaties and new laws, they succeeded in securing an indefinite ban on Chinese immigration in 1904.

Similar reactions eventually led to the exclusion of other Asian immigrants. Japanese immigration was first curtailed in 1907, then permanently barred in 1924. An Asiatic Barred Zone was established in 1917 partly in response to negative reactions to immigrants from India. But the Zone excluded immigrants from Arabia to Indochina, and included Burma, Thailand, the Malay States, Indian Islands, Asiatic Russia, the Polynesian Islands, parts of Arabia and Afghanistan, as well as India. Filipinos, who were regarded as nationals of the United States after the U.S. takeover of the islands in 1898, were given an annual immigration quota of only fifty after Philippine independence was finalized in 1946.

MAKING AMERICANS OUT OF MEXICANS AND NATIVE AMERICANS

The Mexican immigration experience shares commonalities with that of the various Asian groups, including the exploitation of workers and a challenge to family reunification. Immigration from Mexico to the United States, even well into the twentieth century, was largely unrestricted. But as soon as economic, social, and political pressures in the United States rose to certain levels, the restrictions quickly fell into place. In 1821 Mexico took control of California, Texas, New Mexico, and Arizona, and parts of Colorado, Utah, and Nevada when it declared its independence from Spain. Within twenty-five years, however, Texas was annexed by the United States. And by the end of the Mexican-American War in 1849, the Treaty of Guadalupe Hidalgo gave all Mexicans living in these areas the option of becoming U.S. citizens or of relocating within the new Mexican borders. Although some Mexicans moved to Mexico, most remained in what became U.S. territory. In the years following the treaty, Mexicans and Americans paid little attention to the newly created international border. Miners, shepherds, and seasonal workers traveled in both directions to fill fluctuating labor demands in what was essentially one economic region.[11]

While many states engaged in active recruitment of Mexican immigrants through the late 1800s, nativist sentiment was also conspicuous.

s and class status, notwithstanding their "American-
ho returned to the reservation found themselves in a
iliar cultural landscape.[22]

ivate access to Native American lands declined and the
milation correspondingly diminished. The movement
art because of the emergence of a racist perspective that
ns could not attain the level of accomplishment of the
er factors which led to the termination of the assimilation
ded the fading of religious and scientific transcendent
easing secularization of society, and studies by anthropol-
nologists which contributed to the public's awareness of
mplexity, and uniqueness of the Native American cultures.
s, white artists and intellectuals from Taos and Santa Fe
d the Pueblo tribes to oppose legislation that would have
squatters in their land claims against the Pueblos; their
akened much of the country to the values of Native American
d to the threat posed by the ongoing policies of assimilation.[23]
st sentiment eventually caught up with Mexicans by the time
at Depression. Not surprisingly, the popular criticism of Mexi-
nals was economic in tone—their high-paying jobs would be
for native workers if they were removed. Thousands of Mexi-
re deported and thousands more were pressured to leave. Be-
930 and 1940, the Mexican-born population in the United States
d from 639,000 to 377,000. The protection-of-the-labor-market
ing was used against Mexicans again in 1954, when "Operation
ck" was implemented by the Immigration and Naturalization Ser-
n the midst of the post-Korean War recession and over a million
cumented Mexicans were deported.[24]

URNING CATHOLICS AND OTHER SOUTHERN AND
STERN EUROPEANS

economic conditions in western Europe improved in the late nine-
th and early twentieth centuries, immigration from Germany, the
ted Kingdom, and Ireland declined. But at the same time, immigra-
from southern and eastern Europe rapidly increased. During the
decade of the twentieth century, which remains the decade that
essed the greatest immigration to the United States, 1.5 million

Mexican immigrants may have been welcomed as workers, but they
occupied an inferior position in the social structure. Eventually old labor
began to attack new labor for its reluctance to enter unions.[12] This
mixture of demand for cheap Mexican labor and resistance to massive
Mexican migration has continued throughout much of the twentieth
century leading to enigmatic combinations of guestworker/temporary
worker programs (e.g., the Bracero Program), and massive raids and
Proposition 187 movements.

While Mexicans were also subject to cultural, social, and racial
complaints from the Anglo-oriented power structure, for some time in
the early part of this century at least they were not regarded as unassimi-
lable as had been the Chinese. But Mexicans definitely had to be assimilated. From 1915 to 1921, one government-sponsored Americanization
program was aimed directly at Mexican immigrants. In 1900, about a
hundred thousand persons of Mexican descent or birth resided in the
United States. By 1930, the figure was 1.5 million. While restrictionists
and employers who claimed a need for cheap labor battled over future
Mexican immigration, a third group of "Americanists" sought to assimilate Mexican immigrants. By 1913, California Governor Hiram Johnson
was able to establish a Commission on Immigration and Housing, which
directed efforts to teach English to immigrants and involve them in
Americanization programs. The Commission focused its attention on
Mexican immigrant women, in the belief that they were primarily responsible for the transmission of values in the home. School districts
employed special classes and "home teachers," hoping that Mexican
women would pass on their newfound values to children and their
husbands.[13]

The Americanization program cast a broad net over many aspects
of the immigrants' lives, with much of the program based on insidious
stereotypical beliefs about Mexicans. The Commission regarded developing English-speaking ability the fundamental goal, not simply for
facilitating a common language, but because it would help imbue immigrants with the values of American society by helping them see "the
relation between a unified working force, speaking a common language,
and industrial prosperity." Family planning was a key ingredient because
progressives and nativists alike feared that uncontrolled Mexican immigrant population growth would contribute to Anglo "race suicide." The
development of a work ethic outside the home was considered important
so that Mexican women could fill the labor need for domestic servants,

seamstresses, laundresses, and service workers in the Southwest; it would also contribute to " 'curing' the habits of the stereotypical 'lazy Mexican.' "[14] Getting the Mexican woman out of the home was also considered necessary to alter her values because at home her intellectual ability would not be stimulated by her husband.

Americanization programs taught food and diet management because a healthy diet was viewed as fundamental to creating productive members of society. Mexicans were to give up their penchant for fried foods; tortillas would be replaced with bread, and lettuce served instead of beans. The typical noon lunch for the Mexican child, thought to consist of a folded tortilla with no filling, was supposedly the first step in a life of crime, since the child would be tempted to steal from the other children. Furthermore, health and cleanliness were emphasized since program directors felt that Mexicans could not easily learn sanitation and hygiene because they found it less strenuous "to remain dirty than to clean up."[15]

In the end, the Americanization program aimed at Mexican women had little impact on cultural practices. Certainly, an increase in female employment in factories, laundries, hotels, and bakeries may have been facilitated by these efforts, but in the home, little cultural change among the Mexican population was evident. While the Mexican immigrants' material possessions changed, their values, cultural practices, and loyalty to Mexico remained largely unaffected. By the time of the Great Depression in the 1930s, the Americanization program stopped, restrictionist sentiment carried the day, and about half a million Mexicans were coerced by U.S. officials to return to Mexico.[16]

Anglo-conformity assimilation programs were not limited to immigrants. From the 1870s to the 1930s, the Americanization movement implemented a complete assault on every facet of Native American life: language, appearance, religion, economic structure, political models, values, and philosophy. The removal of most of the eastern and southern Native American tribes to the trans-Mississippi region by the 1840s was designed not only to secure state jurisdiction over Native American lands, but also to inculcate the essentials of the white man's civilization into the people. Reservations were designed not only to remove Native Americans from the path of advancing whites, but also as a tool of control.[17] The purported purpose of assimilation was to encourage Native Americans to modify their traditional lifestyle by emulating superior white civilization and striving for agrarian self-sufficiency. But many of

the methods use‌d annihilation."[18]

Assimilation sou‌ with Western Europe‌ ers sought to instill the Americans, supplanting reformers stressed respe‌ Gates, the leader of the 1896, "We have, to begin savage Indian broader desi‌ savagery into citizenship we selfish before we can make awaken in him wants." The a rected by Christian reformers, f‌ with the Christian God.[19]

Tribal culture was suppressed of Native American behavior. Rese‌ Affairs administrators restricted ha‌ meat slaughtering techniques, dancin‌ observances.[20] Like Americanization p‌ grants, Native American Americanizatio‌ values. While Mexican women were th‌ tactic was used with Native Americans. young Native Americans for a thorough re the hope that the inferior Native American be destroyed at their roots. By 1870, the feder‌ off-reservation schools under the auspices o‌ American parents were pressured and coerced i‌ away to these schools under threat of withhol‌ money. Reluctant children were hunted down and to schools against their will. Once there, they we‌ eight years and not permitted to see their families. native clothing, speak their own tongues, practice retain their own names. The philosophy was, to quote founder and head of the Carlisle School for Indians in "kill the Indian in him, and save the man."[21]

In the end, the isolation and transformation shattere‌ can cultural values and left the young Native Americans d‌ ostracized. Sent out into the white world, they were spurne‌

immigrants entered from Russia and another 2 million from Italy and Austria-Hungary. The constant flow of Italians, Russians, and Hungarians fueled racial nativism and anti-Catholicism. This culminated in passage of the Act of February 5, 1917, which contained a controversial literacy requirement that excluded aliens who could not "read and understand some language or dialect."

The reactionary, isolationist political climate that followed World War I, manifested in the Red Scare of 1919–20, led to even greater exclusionist demands. The landmark Immigration Act of 1924, opposed by only six senators, once again took direct aim at southern and eastern Europeans whom the Protestant majority in the United States viewed with dogmatic disapproval. The arguments advanced in support of the bill stressed recurring themes: racial superiority of Anglo-Saxons, the fact that immigrants would cause the lowering of wages, and the unassimilability of foreigners, while citing the usual threats to the nation's social unity and order posed by immigration.

The act restructured criteria for admission to respond to nativist demands and represented a general selection policy that remained in place until 1952. It provided that immigrants of any particular country be limited to 2 percent of their nationality in 1890. The law struck most deeply at Jews, Italians, Slavs, and Greeks, who had immigrated in great numbers after 1890, and who would be most disfavored by such a quota system.

RENEWING THE ATTACK ON MEXICANS

The national origins quota system and statutory vestiges of Asian exclusion laws were abolished in the 1965 amendments to the immigration laws. But by the time I started practicing immigration law as a legal services attorney ten years later, the rise of anti-immigrant sentiment particularly directed at Mexicans was conspicuous. I went to the local INS office in San Francisco on a daily basis to represent people in custody, most of whom were Mexican. Although INS employees acknowledged that Mexicans did not make up the majority of undocumented aliens in the country, Mexicans were targeted by INS sweeps. Even in the mid-1970s, exclusionists were advancing a labor displacement theory, and Congress was considering an employer sanction law that was referred to as the Rodino Bill. Exclusionists constantly complained about undocumented workers coming across the U.S.-Mexico border, and the Commissioner of the INS routinely alleged that 12 million undocumented aliens were in the United States. INS agents and officers whined about how we were all going to have to learn Spanish unless something was done.

In truth, restrictions on Mexican immigration were initiated even in 1965. Between 1965 and 1976, while the rest of the world enjoyed an expansion of numerical limitations and a definite preference system, Mexico and the Western Hemisphere were suddenly faced with numerical restrictions for the first time. Additionally, while the first-come, first-served basis for immigration sounded fair, applicants had to meet strict labor certification requirements. Of course, waivers of the labor certification requirement were obtainable for certain applicants, such as parents of U.S. citizen children. As one might expect given the new numerical limitations, by 1976 the procedure resulted in a severe backlog of approximately three years and a waiting list with nearly 300,000 names.[25]

During the 1965–76 experience, two noteworthy things happened. First, Mexicans used about 40,000 of the Western Hemisphere's allocation of 120,000 visas annually. Second, during this eleven-year period, the State Department wrongfully subtracted about 150,000 visas from the Western Hemisphere quota and gave them to Cuban refugees.[26]

In 1977, Congress imposed the preference system on Mexico and the Western Hemisphere along with a 20,000 visa per country numerical limitation. Thus, Mexico's annual visa usage rate was virtually cut in half overnight, and thousands were left stranded on the old system's waiting list.[27] The eleven-year misallocation of visas to Cuba eventually led to a permanent injunction and a "recapturing" of the wrongfully issued visas in *Silva v. Levi*.[28] However, Mexicans again received the short end of the stick when the State Department's formula for reallocation, which failed to provide sufficient visas for thousands of Mexicans on the *Silva* waiting list, was upheld. As a result, in February 1982 INS authorities began to round up those *Silva* letter recipients who had not been accorded immigrant visa numbers in order to advise them of the termination of the *Silva* injunction against their deportation and the end of their work authorization derived from their *Silva* letter class status. The recipients were further informed that unless provisions of the existing immigration law qualified them to remain in the United States, they would have thirty days for voluntary departure. Because of the public outrage, as of August 20, 1982, the INS ceased to enforce departure in cases involving former *Silva* letter recipients subject to deportation or exclusion proceedings. However on February 1, 1983, the Enforcement Branch of the INS ordered that the processing of *Silva* letter recipients be resumed.[29]

To make matters worse, in the first year of the preference system and the 20,000 limitation on countries of the Western Hemisphere, Mexico lost 14,000 visas due to a congressional mistake. The effective date of the new law was January 1, 1977. Since the government's fiscal year runs from October 1 to September 30, by January 1, one full quarter of fiscal year 1977 had expired. During that first quarter, 14,203 visas were issued to Mexicans pursuant to the immigration system which prevailed in the Western Hemisphere before the new law became effective. The State Department nevertheless charged those visas against the newly imposed national quota of 20,000, leaving only 5,797 visas available for Mexican immigrants between January 1 and September 30, 1977. In *De Avila v. Civiletti*,[30] the Seventh Circuit Court of Appeals sustained the State Department's approach even though it was "obvious that Congress . . . through inadvertence failed to inform the State Department how to administer during a fraction of the fiscal year a statute designed to apply on a full fiscal year basis."

The effect on Mexican immigration of the 1977 imposition of the preference system and 20,000 visa limitation (modified in 1990) is not surprising. Mexico and Asian countries share the largest backlogs in family reunification categories.[31] For example, the category for married sons and daughters of U.S. citizens (Third Preference) for Mexico is backlogged more than eight years. Brothers and sisters of U.S. citizens (Fourth Preference), a category which has been under constant attack by retiring Senator Alan Simpson, must wait at least eleven years if they are from Mexico and eighteen years if from the Philippines.

Mexicans continue to be victims of highly publicized INS raids. Dubbed "Operation Jobs" or "Operation Cooperation," they are reminiscent of "Operation Wetback" and raids directed at Asian immigrants in the past. In what the INS labeled "Operation Jobs" in April 1982, five thousand people of primarily Latin appearance were arrested in nine metropolitan areas across the country.[32] Critics of the raids charged that the operation was directed at Mexicans, whipped up antialien hysteria, and caused much fear in the Latino community, while providing no jobs for native-born citizens.[33] Curiously, "Operation Jobs" was launched during the same week that restrictive legislation (the Simpson-Mazzoli Bill) was being marked up in the senate subcommittee on immigration. The raids also coincided with Congress's consideration of additional funds for the INS.

"Operation Jobs" merely highlighted what had been going on for many years. A review of litigation initiated long before the 1982 operation indicates that the INS had long focused its sweeps on persons of Latino descent.[34] In fiscal year 1977, for example, of the deportable aliens arrested, more than 90 percent were Mexican.[35]

As the INS enforcement budget grew larger and larger during this period, the Supreme Court, swayed by arguments that the undocumented alien problem was worsening, gave more flexibility to INS enforcement strategies. First, in 1975, in *United States v. Brignoni-Ponce*,[36] the Court held that under certain circumstances, roving Border Patrol officers could stop motorists in the general area of the Mexican border for brief inquiry into their residence status if there was reasonable suspicion that passengers were undocumented. Next in 1976 in *United States v. Martinez-Fuerte*,[37] the Court carved an exception to the Fourth Amendment's protection against unreasonable search and seizure, by allowing the Border Patrol to set up fixed checkpoints located on major highways away from the Mexican border for purposes of stopping and questioning individuals suspected of being undocumented aliens. Then in 1984 in *INS v. Lopez-Mendoza*,[38] the Court held that even if the INS violated the Fourth Amendment's protection against illegal search and seizure in its apprehension of undocumented aliens, illegally obtained evidence could still be used against the aliens in deportation proceedings.

THE HAMMER FALLS AGAIN ON OTHER IMMIGRANTS

The history of anti-immigrant sentiment that was manifested in local and state laws directed against documented immigrants such as alien land laws and foreign miners' taxes has modern corollaries that attempt to limit certain occupations and professions to citizens. As a general rule, such state restrictions have been deemed unconstitutional by the Supreme Court. For example, in *In re Griffiths*,[39] the exclusion of lawful permanent residents from the practice of law in Connecticut was invalidated, and in *Sugarman v. Dougall*,[40] a New York law providing that only U.S. citizens could hold permanent state civil service positions was struck down. However, the protection that the Court had provided in this area began to erode around the time that more flexibility was being given to INS enforcement activities. Beginning with *Folie v. Connelie*[41] in 1978, the Supreme Court has deferred to the states requiring U.S. citizenship when the government job entails a public function, or involves the "formulation, execution, or review of broad public policy." Thus, in *Folie,* the Court held that New York could bar aliens from holding state law enforcement positions. A year later in *Ambach v. Norwick,*[42] the Court ruled that public schoolteaching (even teaching French in high school!) fell within the public functions exception and could be limited to citizens as well.[43]

The clamoring and complaining about immigration has not only been about Mexicans, of course. Consider the reaction to Southeast Asians on refugee policy. The 1952 overhaul of the immigration laws granted the attorney general discretionary authority to "parole" into the United States any alien for "emergent reasons or for reasons deemed strictly in the public interest." Although the original intent was to apply this parole authority on an individual basis, the 1956 Hungarian refugee crisis led to its expanded use to accommodate those fleeing communist oppression. The parole authority was also used to admit more than 15,000 Chinese who fled mainland China after the 1949 communist takeover and more than 145,000 Cubans who sought refuge after Fidel Castro's 1959 coup.

The satisfaction of policymakers with the status quo began to evaporate with the upsurge in Asian entrants that started in the mid-1970s. The watershed event was the fall of Saigon in April 1975. Initially, the United States merely wanted to evacuate fewer than 20,000 American dependents and government employees. However, to invoke numerical restrictions in the midst of a controversial and devastating war would have been unconscionable, and evacuees soon also included former employees, some 4,000 orphans, 75,000 relatives of American citizens and residents, and 50,000 Vietnamese government employees and officials. Between April and December 1975, the United States thus admitted 130,400 Southeast Asian refugees, 125,000 of whom were Vietnamese.

The exodus did not stop there. By 1978 thousands more were admitted under a series of Indochinese Parole Programs authorized by the attorney general. Following the tightening of Vietnam's grip on

Cambodia, several hundred thousand "boat people" and many Cambodian and Laotian refugees entered. In fact, annual arrivals of Southeast Asian refugees increased almost exponentially: 20,400 in 1978, 80,700 in 1979, and 166,700 in 1980.

The unpredictable numbers of Southeast Asian refugees provided the impetus for reform and ultimately, the passage of the 1980 Refugee Act. The new law provided two tracks for refugee admission into the United States. The first provides the President with the power to admit refugees who are outside the United States only after consultation with Congress, while the second relates to procedures by which aliens in the United States or at ports of entry may apply for asylum. And while the United States has allowed in more than a million refugees under the first track since 1980, the numbers have been much more regulated than under the previous parole authority.

In contrast, only between five and ten thousand asylum applications have been approved per year. To say the least, the United States has not reacted warmly to notable groups who have reached our borders seeking asylum under the second track. When Haitians, El Salvadorans, Guatemalans, and Chinese boat people began arriving in significant numbers, the powers-that-be were quick to label them economic rather than political refugees.

This response has manifested itself in humiliating ways. In the early 1980s, the INS implemented an efficiency plan in Miami by which Haitian asylum hearings were often limited to fifteen minutes, immigration judges were ordered to increase productivity and hear at least eighteen cases per day, and some attorneys were scheduled for hearings at the same time for different clients in different parts of the city. The federal court of appeals chastised immigration officials for violating due process and ordered a new plan for the reprocessing of asylum claims.[44] A similar suit concluded with the INS agreeing to reevaluate potentially up to half a million Salvadoran and Guatemalan asylum cases from the 1980s, due to strong evidence of INS political bias and discrimination against these applicants.[45]

The rise in anti-immigrant sentiment in the 1980s was apparent in other ways. In 1982 as part of a major legislative package, Republican Senator Alan Simpson from Wyoming initiated a crusade to eliminate the immigration category allowing U.S. citizens to be reunited with siblings. He persisted in his efforts to abolish the category until he retired in 1996. These efforts have constituted a rather transparent attack on Asian and Mexican immigrants. Combined, Asian and Mexican immigrants make up the vast majority of sibling-of-citizen immigrants. Eliminating the category would therefore curtail Asian and Mexican immigrants who might eventually petition for even more relatives. Nativism toward immigrants was manifested in rabid support for English-only initiatives across the country, as was a rise in hate crimes directed at Asian Americans.

Casual observers of immigration policy in the 1980s might cite the Immigration Reform and Control Act of 1986 as an example of a congressional swing toward a pro-immigration position because of its legalization (amnesty) provisions that led to the legalization of about 3 million undocumented aliens. The truth is that the employer sanctions provisions in the law (making it unlawful for employers to hire undocumented workers) was the main part of the law, and received overwhelming legislative support. The amnesty provision just barely eked through the House of Representatives.[46]

One explanation of the great influence that anti-immigrant groups have today is rooted in the exposure of the INS's illegal actions against Haitian, Guatemalan, and El Salvadoran asylum applicants. The illegal actions of the INS in processing their applications was the agency's response to complaints that the asylum system was too generous or manipulable. But once the agency's illegal actions were exposed, exclusionist whining about the asylum system dramatically spiraled.

When boatloads of Chinese began arriving in 1992 and 1993, the exclusionists were given new fuel. At first, this created a dissonant situation for the INS. After all, the Chinese were fleeing communism, weren't they? But the situation seemed somehow different. Two incidents that occurred in late 1992 only days apart demonstrated the dilemma. In one, a Cuban commercial pilot commandeered a flight and landed in Miami. All aboard who wanted asylum, including the pilot, were welcomed with open arms, and none were taken into custody. Yet, a few days later, a boatload of Chinese seeking asylum landed in San Francisco Bay, and every single person on board who could be rounded up was incarcerated. Many applied for asylum arguing that they feared persecution because of their opposition to China's one-child-per-family birth policy or because they had supported the protesting students at Tiennanmen Square in 1989. It was the nature of these claims that exclusionists labeled outrageous, citing the Chinese as perfect examples of how the asylum system was being exploited. After several Chinese boats arrived—particularly the highly publicized Golden Venture in New York Harbor in 1993—exclusionists were able to rally great public and political support for their cause, and asylum and undocumented immigration has been on the front page ever since.

Facing a severe budget problem, California's Governor Pete Wilson added a good deal of fuel to the fire in 1992 by blaming many of the state's fiscal woes on immigrants. His charge was that immigrants were costing state taxpayers billions in public assistance, medical care, and education. Armed with gubernatorial support, the main lobbyist for the Federation for American Immigration Reform (FAIR) in California, the former national INS Commissioner Alan Nelson, and a former INS regional official, Harold Ezell, joined forces with other neonativists in California to place Proposition 187 on the 1994 ballot. Targeting undocumented immigrants in Proposition 187 proved to be a smart political tactic which enabled its proponents to attract supporters who might otherwise not have been opposed to immigration per se.

Throughout the Proposition 187 debates, its major proponents claimed that they were motivated only by a concern with undocumented immigrants, and that documented immigrants were beneficial to the country. They lied, of course. As soon as Proposition 187 passed, neonativists immediately set their sights on reducing the flow of legal immigrants. Thus, responding to political pressure, the Commission on Legal Immigration Reform, chaired by the late former Congresswoman Barbara Jordan, recommended reducing legal immigration by a third. Congressman Lamar Smith and Senator Alan Simpson also introduced proposals that would make cuts. Even before Proposition 187, Republicans in Congress attacked legal immigrants by proposing to reduce spending by eliminating lawful permanent residents from benefits that ranged from Supplemental Security Income to school lunch programs for their children. The welfare cuts were enacted by President Clinton in 1996.

Clearly, the historical cycles of anti-immigrant backlash can successfully sway political opinion that gets manifested in the form of exclusionist legislation. Demographic changes across the country over the last couple of decades and predictions for the future provide the impetus for much of the nativist sentiment today, especially for those uncomfortable with notions of diversity and change.

Refugees, immigrants, and their advocates have come to rely upon the final and most famous lines of the American Jewish poet Emma Lazarus's sonnet engraved at the base of the Statue of Liberty:

Give me your tired, your poor,
Your huddled masses yearning to breathe free,
The wretched refuse of your teeming shore.
Send these, the homeless, tempest-tost to me.
I lift my lamp beside the golden door!

The problem is that long before this gift from the French people was even dedicated by President Grover Cleveland in May 1886, the United States had adopted policies antithetical to the spirit of the Lazarus poem. Her sentiment is simply not embodied in the constitution and has no legal meaning. Nativists and xenophobes have graffitied over the verse time and time again. And time and time again, the Supreme Court has found nothing in the constitution to nullify federal immigration laws related to admissions criteria, exclusion grounds, or deportation.

The kinds of anti-immigrant statements we hear today from Pete Wilson, Patrick Buchanan, Peter Brimelow, Alan Simpson, FAIR, and others are simply not new. When their words begin to carry weight and get implemented into immigration policies, we know that the nativist-taggers have struck again, and that the powers-that-be have once more become uncomfortable with what is becoming of the definition of an American.

chapter 3

Mi Cliente y Amigo
Rodolfo Martinez Padilla

I am often asked by students and friends, especially those who work with community-based organizations, why I decided to specialize in immigration law. My sense is that they are seeking a romanticized answer about how I was moved by my parents' struggles with the immigration process, or that I was inspired by the plight of migrants and refugees seeking freedom or a better life, or that perhaps the inequities of the immigration laws or enforcement procedures sparked my interest. Indeed any of these explanations could be plausible. But the truth is that I fell into the field because the only opening available in the office where I wanted to work was in immigration law.

Upon entering law school, specializing in immigration law was not the plan. During the summer after my first year of law school, I volunteered as a law clerk in the Chinatown/North Beach Office of the San Francisco Neighborhood Legal Assistance Foundation (SFNLAF). A variety of cases were assigned to me, but most pertained to landlord-tenant disputes or consumer issues. The work was so rewarding and stimulating that I continued to clerk there until I graduated in 1974. Clearly, law school would have been a miserable time but for my concurrent work at SFNLAF that provided context and meaning for my training as a lawyer. By bar exam time, SFNLAF was unequivocally the place I wanted to work. Since the only opening was in immigration, I grabbed it and soon found myself immersed in a workload of over a hundred open cases.

In retrospect, becoming an immigration lawyer made sense for me. As it turns out, practicing any kind of law in or near Chinatown in the mid-1970s would have meant working with immigrants, given the changing demographics of the community. Although the 1970 census counted more U.S.-born than foreign-born Chinese Americans, by 1980 the reverse was true. But as the son of an immigrant, with many immigrant relatives, and growing up in a town with numerous immigrant residents, becoming an immigration lawyer has meant something special, as it would for anyone with a similar background.

Stories from my own family's immigration history provide plenty of fuel for my interest in the field. My father was born in Oong On Lei Village in Canton Province, China in 1893, and entered the United States on a false claim to U.S. citizenship. He admitted that he was born in China in 1893. But his father, who had been a cook during the construction of the Southern Pacific Railroad, claimed that his birth certificate was destroyed in the 1906 San Francisco earthquake and that he had traveled to China around the time that my father was conceived. Therefore, my father entered as the son of a U.S. citizen. My mother was born in Scranton, Pennsylvania in 1901, and was therefore a U.S. citizen at birth. When she was three, she accompanied her mother, a native of China, to China so that her mother could care for her own ailing mother. My parents met in 1920 through a marriage broker who escorted my father to my mother's village, Ngan Voo. My mother was not one of the women in the village looking for a husband, but my father spotted her at a distance and insisted on meeting her. My mother eventually immigrated as the spouse of a U.S. citizen. Although she was a citizen at birth, she could not reenter as a citizen for two reasons. First, she did not have her birth records to prove her place of birth. And second, technically she had lost her citizenship by marrying a foreign national at a time when the law stripped women of U.S. citizenship for marrying foreign men. Of course my father was making a false claim to citizenship, so their situation presented a messy picture to say the least.

Before my mother could reenter the United States in 1926 as the spouse of a U.S. citizen, she had to pass inspection at Angel Island in San Francisco Bay. Between 1910 and 1940, about fifty thousand Chinese were confined—often for months and years at a time—in Angel Island's bleak wooden barracks, where inspectors would conduct grueling interrogations. In a sense, my mother was lucky because her detention on Angel Island lasted only a week. Months earlier, she had received coaching instructions from my father (who had returned to the United States soon after their marriage) on how to answer certain questions. This was typical of the Chinese immigrants of the time. The strict exclusion laws forced distortions of family trees and histories if immigration was to succeed. The schemes devised to thwart the racist immigration laws were ingenious. For both the successful and unsuccessful, however, it was agonizing to be compelled to lie and cheat in order to reunite with family members.

The directions to my mother were more unusual than most because she had been born in the United States. She was to assert birth in China and marriage to my father, the son of a purported U.S. native. A claim to U.S. citizenship by my mother would likely result in serious delay; records in Scranton would have to be obtained and a call for my mother's alienated brothers on the eastern seaboard to come testify would have been probable. So when my mother was called in for interrogation a week after arriving at Angel Island, she was questioned for about thirty minutes and was deemed admissible as the spouse of a citizen.

Growing up in Superior, I also had a sense of the gender imbalance that plagued the Chinese American community for decades after the enactment of the Chinese exclusion laws. I grew up in a small house attached to my mother's small grocery store. The store and house were on the poorest street in Pinal County, a rural part of south-central Arizona. The store consisted of three small aisles of food, a small butcher area, and an area with dry goods—shoes, fabric, hurricane lamps, and the like. The small second floor of the back storeroom contained six narrow rooms with little headroom that we used for storage. As a child, I learned that during the 1920s and 1930s these rooms were actually used as sleeping quarters by men who came from China without their wives to work for my father. They cooked and ate in one of the slightly larger rooms of the musty, dank second floor.

Two of the men who worked for my father were an uncle and a cousin whom I grew up knowing. They were Geen Hong Go (Uncle Art) and Cherng Goo Cherng (Uncle Charlie). Having entered the United

States with false papers, they were always introduced to the townspeople as my father's brothers. Although both had lived in the United States since the 1920s or 1930s, their wives and children did not join them until the early 1960s. Uncle Charlie's wife (Cherng Goo) was my father's sister. But because of my family's disordered history, she immigrated as my father's sister-in-law.

The memory of my aunt Cherng Goo's arrival is a stark reminder of the effects of years of exclusion. As a kid, I wanted to be a basketball star. So when my parents told me that my aunt had been a champion basketball player in her youth, I was beside myself with excitement. I practiced diligently for weeks in anticipation of our first encounter, expecting a great shooting and dribbling display from her upon her arrival. But by the time her metaphorical boat came in, she was an elderly woman whose basketball-playing days had long since passed. We had all been victimized by the exclusion laws.

My immigration memories span a continuum from my family to my clients. A distant older cousin fled to Mexico after being indicted for selling false green cards. My mother underwent intensive preparation to testify at an immigration hearing on behalf of another relative. Years later, when I practiced in Chinatown, I met hundreds of clients who had similar stories of false papers and family histories to gain entry into the United States during the exclusionary era. Throughout my life, and especially after I became a lawyer, I have often marveled at the ingenious schemes my ancestors and other Chinese devised to thwart the immigration policymaker "ghosts," as they were called. For decades, the authorities were determined to exclude the "Yellow Peril," yet many Chinese were able to overcome the racist laws by inventing families, occupations, backgrounds, and birth certificates destroyed in earthquakes.

Over the years, the questions related to immigration directed to my parents' generation did not rekindle fond memories. The historical prejudices codified against my uncles and aunts, grandfathers and grandmothers resulted in pain. They were forced to lie and to cheat because of the oppressive racial biases of others. Thus, my veneration for their creative schemes inevitably turns to anger after the sobering realization that, despite the anecdotal successes of many in evading discriminatory immigration policies, my ancestors unnecessarily bore tremendous hardships.

Most of my Chinese cases have pertained to visa matters. But over the years I have represented several hundred clients—of myriad nationalities—in deportation proceedings. In the late 1970s, part of my function as a legal services attorney was to provide public defender-type representation to aliens who had been arrested by the INS in the San Francisco region. I visited the detention branch on a daily basis to interview detainees, and cooperated with the Immigration Court when they needed an attorney to provide representation. Nationals of Canada, Nigeria, the Philippines, Iran, Ireland, Great Britain, and other parts of Europe were often in the detention area. In fact, every month or so I would encounter young European tourists in their twenties who turned themselves in for deportation because they had run out of spending money. I recall a Caucasian man who was born in China to Portuguese parents, who was being deported to Portugal even though he had never lived there. And there was a Greek client who immigrated at the age of three, but was being deported at the age of twenty-seven for possession of marijuana. In the 1980s, I represented many Central Americans seeking asylum in the United States, including one Nicaraguan whose case became a precedent-setting decision in the Supreme Court. I also helped to represent a black South African who was granted asylum because of apartheid.

But over the years, most of those I have represented in deportation proceedings have been Mexican nationals. Representing Mexicans in deportation proceedings always came naturally. The vast majority of my Mexican clients reminded me of neighbors, friends, and grocery store customers from Superior. They were gracious, honest, hardworking, friendly, grateful, and committed to their families. They appreciated my limited Spanish-speaking ability.

I recall introducing my wife, a Chinese American raised in San Francisco Chinatown, to a Mexican family I was representing shortly after our marriage in 1976. The family had been subjected to a harrowing, abusive raid by INS agents at 5 a.m. one morning, and I needed to get a better idea of what had transpired by visiting them at their home in San Jose, California. So on a Sunday afternoon, my wife and I drove to San Jose to call on the family. My wife had had little contact with Mexicans—or any Latinos for that matter—growing up. She was aware of my legal work conceptually, but had never met any of my clients. Over the course of the afternoon, as she experienced my clients' warmth, generosity, and hospitality, my wife became their strongest advocate for resisting deportation. How in the world, she asked, could they be hurting anyone; and why in the world would the INS want to deport such a decent family? After a struggle that took almost a decade, I was able to obtain lawful permanent residence status for the entire family.

Most of my clients have been Mexican because Mexicans have long been the focus of INS enforcement priorities. Of the 1,327,259 deportable aliens located by the INS in 1993, 95.6 percent (1,269,294) were Mexican nationals,[1] in spite of the fact that by all estimates Mexicans make up less than half of the undocumented population in the United States. So anyone willing to represent low-income immigrants as I have over the years will naturally have a caseload that is substantially Mexican.

Take the case of Rodolfo Martinez Padilla.[2] Rodolfo was a client of the Immigration Law Clinic which I directed at the Stanford Law School. In the fall of 1993, with the assistance of students enrolled in the clinic, Rodolfo, who was in deportation proceedings, succeeded in having those proceedings suspended and was granted lawful permanent resident status. To qualify, Rodolfo had to establish continuous physical presence in the United States for at least seven years, good moral character, and extreme hardship if deportation had been ordered.[3]

I first met Rodolfo in 1987, and found his work record, his worldview, and his attitudes about the United States typical of the thousands of immigrants—especially Mexicans—I have represented, been consulted about, or grew up with in Superior. His story and those of other Mexican immigrants are important because much of the current debate over immigration is about Mexican immigration.

Rodolfo's family and circumstances surrounding his migration to the United States are not unusual. Born in 1963 in a small town in the state of Michoacan in northern Mexico, Rodolfo, accompanied by his uncles, first crossed the border at the age of ten. He returned to Mexico but came back to the United States in 1979 with his parents and siblings. Since then they have lived in the East Palo Alto/Redwood City area, which is about thirty miles south of San Francisco. Rodolfo attended one year of public high school in 1980. His entire immediate family— his father, mother, two older brothers, one older sister, two younger sisters, and a younger brother—resides in the United States. Most of the family became lawful permanent residents through the legalization (amnesty) program of the Immigration Reform and Control Act of 1986 (IRCA). Rodolfo is married and has two U.S. citizen children (one from a prior relationship); he sees and cares for both of them regularly. He acts as a constant mentor and "big brother" to his nephews and nieces. The entire family has regular get-togethers, picnics, and barbecues. Except for his mother, all the adults in Rodolfo's family have paying jobs. None has ever received public assistance.

Rodolfo's employment history may be of particular interest to people concerned with the impact that immigrants such as Rodolfo have on the labor market. As with many immigrants, the family's primary method of finding jobs is through word of mouth and mutual help. Rodolfo and his family have a very strong and active network of friends and family that they rely on to hear about and to get work. At just about every place Rodolfo has worked, some family member has been employed at some point in time. Rodolfo always has his ears open for new opportunities, and the community is a vitally active highway of information. If someone loses a job, friends help with loans and a new job search.

Rodolfo has done a fair amount of "pavement pounding," going from business to business and filling out applications. He says that when he was young he would get on a bus and go to San Jose (about fifty miles south of San Francisco). He would apply for work in establishments along the main boulevard—El Camino Road—the entire route home. Sometimes he would fill out six applications a day. Although he reads the newspaper, he has not used it to get information about jobs. Current and former employers always gave Rodolfo a good reference for prospective new employers. Often Rodolfo has held two jobs at the same time in order to better support his family.

A chronicle of Rodolfo's jobs and job-finding methods is illuminating:

1. He secured his first job at a restaurant, Le Lumiere in Menlo Park, through his father and his uncle who both worked there. His father got the Le Lumiere job from his brother (Rodolfo's uncle) who was working there previously. When his uncle quit, his job was given to Rodolfo's father. Rodolfo initially started working there to help his father for free.[4] He was working as a dishwasher when the owners noticed and liked his work more than they liked his father's work. Although Rodolfo was young and still in high school, they fired his father and gave him the job. The wife of the owner of Le Lumiere owned another restaurant, Carol's, and she asked Rodolfo to work there as

well. Rodolfo would work at Carol's in the morning and Le Lumiere in the afternoons and evening. Rodolfo dropped out of high school when he was eighteen because he was working very long hours (sixteen hours a day) and felt that he could not go to school at the same time. He started working at the age of seventeen in 1980. He left these jobs because of the long hours and he felt that he was not earning enough money. Each place paid about $100 per week. His bosses offered to pay him more money, but he felt that the raise was not enough to compensate him for the number of hours he was working. His departure was amicable; later when he needed a recommendation for his job at the Discount Club, these employers were happy to provide it. Rodolfo also knew that he could make more money working in the kitchen of a restaurant rather than just washing dishes. He looked for and found jobs in restaurants where he would start out as a dishwasher, but eventually have the opportunity to work in the kitchen.

2. Rodolfo found the job at Wata, a drug manufacturer, by going to an unemployment office in San Mateo where jobs are posted. He had no problem getting access to these listings in spite of the fact that he was asked for a green card, by providing proof that he and his family had been in the United States for a long time and that he had attended school here. His mastery of English was very helpful in this situation. Rodolfo worked at Wata inspecting pills, but had to leave because he became allergic to the chemicals. He was paid about $150 per week at Wata.

3. Between his job at Wata and his job at Spiral, Rodolfo worked at Andre's Restaurant. This was one of the restaurants where he worked up to helping in the kitchen. He eventually left Andre's because they were not paying him enough money. He was paid about $150 per week. In general, he usually left restaurant jobs because a better opportunity made itself available. For some time he worked at Spiral in the morning and at Andre's at night.

4. Spiral Engineering hired Rodolfo first as a janitor then as a machine operator because his sister worked there as a supervisor. Other family members were already working there: his aunt, mother, and father. His boss regarded Rodolfo as one of his best and most conscientious workers, and was sorry to see Rodolfo leave for a better job later. Spiral was paying him $4.20 an hour. During some of the time that Rodolfo worked at Star, he also worked at the Elks Club part-time as a janitor. The Elks Club paid $4.50 an hour. Rodolfo's brother worked

at the Elks Club for eleven years as a janitor. His brother got the job through a friend. His brother was looking for work by applying to businesses near his family's residence. One day when he was visiting various businesses, he saw a friend working outside the Elks Club building and asked him if he would help him submit his application. Rodolfo's brother stopped working at the Elks Club because he wanted to make more money. He now works in a pet food business, and got that job through Rodolfo. Rodolfo was working at the Discount Club and one of his coworkers was the son of the owner of the pet food business. Rodolfo asked his friend to help his brother get a job there.

5. Rodolfo got a job at Splashmaster, a swimming pool company, through a different sister who was working there. Apparently she found out that they needed someone to cut pipes, and she told him to apply. Rodolfo also left Splashmaster because of the low pay (about $100 per week).

6. For a while, Rodolfo worked for an industrial janitorial service as an employee (as opposed to an independent contractor). He only stayed for two months because it was "a heavy job." The hours were very long, he had to operate heavy machinery, and he was paid $4.50 an hour.

7. Rodolfo got his job with the Discount Club through an uncle who was working there (the same one who was working for Le Lumiere). His uncle told Rodolfo that they were looking for janitors. He applied and got the job. He worked there steadily and once received the Employee of the Month award. He got bonuses every month. As a steady employee, he accumulated vacation and sick leave time, and also donated money to the United Way through regular payroll deductions (he also does that at his current place of employment). He started at $5.85 an hour and when he left was receiving $7.66 an hour. During his time at the Discount Club, Rodolfo also worked a second job, about two or three hours a day, at Sandwood Market. He was a stock boy and bagger and was in charge of reloading the soft drink machine and carrying out bottles. Unfortunately, Rodolfo injured his back on the job at the Discount Club, because of heavy lifting and running a large floor scrubbing machine. He received disability compensation for two years, and is now working at a less strenuous job. Rodolfo was a well-regarded employee at the Discount Club. At his deportation hearing, his supervisor submitted a letter of support.

8. Rodolfo got his current job at Star Products, where he is a

machine operator assembling electronic and computer parts, through his sister-in-law who works there. She encouraged him to apply for the job and put in a good word for him. When he first started working at Star Products he was working on the assembly line, putting together electronic parts. One Saturday he was asked if he would be able to work overtime in another department where workers operated machines and conducted much more complex and detailed work. Based on his performance that day, the supervisor of the department took Rodolfo off the assembly lines and added him permanently to the machine operator department. This job entailed more responsibility and required extensive training. Today he operates delicate machinery that assembles wiring and other computer and electronics parts, and earns a higher wage than he did in his previous position. Some months ago, Rodolfo had to be hospitalized for a hernia. Company officials valued and trusted him enough to lend him $1,000 for his medical bills. He repaid the entire amount within four months. He's been there almost one year and is paid $5.00 an hour.

Except for his injury at the Discount Club, Rodolfo's primary reason for leaving jobs has been a desire to earn more money or because a new and better opportunity presented itself. After working long days— sometimes sixteen hours—and discovering at the end of the week that his earnings totaled under $300, he looked for better opportunities. Through his network of friends and relatives, he kept his eyes and ears open for any available opportunities, either for himself or for others.

As an ambitious and independent person, Rodolfo has demonstrated entrepreneurial skills as well. When he was on disability, he was quite concerned that he would be unable to make a living. He approached his father and proposed that they work together to make extra money. Since his father is an excellent mechanic, they bought and fixed used cars, and then sold the cars for a profit. For example, they bought one truck body for $300, and after they had fixed it, sold it for $4,000. At his father's suggestion, Rodolfo also moved back in with the family during his recovery so that Rodolfo could cut down on living expenses. Today Rodolfo's father continues to buy and repair used cars, but Rodolfo cannot help him because he is busy with his job at Star Products and with setting up his business.

Rodolfo has made an agreement with the president of Star Products about becoming an independent contractor to provide the company with janitorial services. The way this came about is that Rodolfo noticed that the president often complained about the regular janitorial service. Apparently, they are very sloppy in their work, sometimes leaving the offices in a worse state than when they arrived. Rodolfo started picking up after them because he thought that the mess they left reflected poorly on the company. Customers frequent this establishment and he believed that it was important to have a clean work environment. Eventually the president noticed and suggested that he contract with the company independently to clean the place up after-hours. Rodolfo took this suggestion seriously and decided that this would be an important business opportunity for himself and his family.

Since he spoke with the president of the company, he has been slowly buying pieces of cleaning equipment, some costing as much as $1,600. Initially Rodolfo plans to work his regular day hours at the company and then have his wife help him clean the Star Products facilities at night. He figures that the president of Star Products has other business connections that Rodolfo's business can benefit from. In time, he hopes to expand his business with these connections and looks forward to owning his own business. He has thought out, planned, and negotiated all the details very carefully. At first, he will be working on a probationary basis in order to allow his employer to examine his work to make sure it is satisfactory. During this time, the president has agreed to pay him a regular wage (as if he were doing his regular job), but at an overtime rate. After one month, if his work is satisfactory, he will go on contract status and finally be independent. He will be securing a worker's compensation package for himself and his wife, and he has applied for a business license. He learned what he needed to do to start his independent janitorial contract business by helping and observing a friend who owns his own janitorial contracting service. He helped his friend finish jobs out of friendship and without compensation. Now this friend is advising Rodolfo and helping him start his own business.

Allegations about the economic "impact" of immigrants brings to mind acquaintances and former clients like Rodolfo and his family. They are not representative of all immigrants. But they are also not atypical. Most of my Mexican clients have been more like Rodolfo than unlike him. They defy the stereotype of the poor immigrant lured across the border by the ease of life on welfare. They are hardworking, honest, very family oriented, and not criminals. As Rodolfo's job history reveals, they may take low-paying jobs, but they keep an eye open for better-paying positions. The twin economic arguments—job and wage displacement, and net fiscal burdens in the public sector—appear to involve contradictory stereotypes of the hardworking immigrant willing to take any job, and the pathologically welfare-dependent or costly immigrant.

Anticipating that some will be skeptical of an anecdotal approach centered around the experiences of one individual, I now turn to hard economic realities.

chapter 4

Searching for the Truth about Immigrants and Jobs

We are young and we come to the United States to work. And [using government services] looks bad. If I know I can pay my doctor, I don't need to go to the government. I don't need food stamps. That's for the old people, for the children that don't have no fathers. I don't feel good if I go over there and I can be working. You can find a job in the United States anywhere you go. Especially if you can speak a little bit of English. If you don't speak no English, you get your green card. If you don't get your green card, you work in the fields, you work dishwash[-ing], everywhere. There's a lot of work.

— RODOLFO MARTINEZ PADILLA, age 31
native of Michoacan, Mexico

Negative images of immigrants and their purported impact on the U.S. economy have permeated the airwaves and print media headlines of late. These images largely revolve around two anti-immigrant arguments, broadly conceived of as "economic" in nature. The first argument posits that immigrants have a negative effect on the labor market, displacing native workers and depressing wages. The second is that immigrants burden the public coffers. The labor market complaint is the subject of this chapter, while the next chapter addresses the costs and revenues of immigrants.

The image of immigrants as labor market demons is fueled by comments such as those of Congressman Lamar Smith of Texas, who authored major legislation in the House of Representatives in 1996: "[I]n places where immigrants tend to congregate, particularly in the cities, . . . the direct impact on citizens, particularly low-income, low-skill citizens, is that they lose jobs and their wages are depressed as a result."[1] Consider also the views of Daniel A. Stein, executive director of the Federation for American Immigration Reform: "This is throwing kerosene on the blaze. . . . Immigration is destroying the American middle class. . . . It's one of the key factors degrading labor in this country."[2]

Accompanying these negative images are a host of state and federal policy proposals—some aimed at undocumented aliens, but many directed at lawful immigrants and refugees. These efforts extend far beyond the 1986 law making it illegal for employers to hire undocumented workers or California's Proposition 187 which would preclude undocumented aliens from attending public schools, receiving welfare, and obtaining services from publicly funded health facilities. While the constitutionality of Proposition 187 is being determined by the federal courts, it is emblematic of several legislative actions and proposals. These include cutting back on public benefits and social programs available to legal immigrants (ranging from Supplemental Security Income to school lunch and milk programs for lawful resident schoolchildren), denying driver's licenses to undocumented aliens, making it a felony for an undocumented person to apply to a state university, adding resources to the Border Patrol, calling out the National Guard to help enforce the border, charging a border toll, amending the Fourteenth Amendment so that birth in the United States does not confer citizenship upon a newborn if the parents are undocumented, and cutting back on legal immigration by a third.

The twin economic allegations and the flurry of legislation directed against immigrants demand that we inform ourselves as much as possible before forming judgments (and policies) on proposals that are premised on beliefs about economic impact. A fair reading of available, accurate research suggests that allegations of the negative impact of immigrants on the economy are overblown and largely unsupported. The most reliable studies show that the level of anti-immigrant rhetoric based on economic arguments is simply not justified.

Before considering actual studies that have been conducted on immigrants and the labor market, a theoretical framework—developed from observations of the market—is helpful.

Thinking about Jobs and Wages

Immigrants and Job Creation

One concern about immigrants is that every job that goes to an immigrant is a job that a native worker loses (or fails to gain). The fear that immigrants take away jobs from native workers rests on the theory that the number of jobs is static or fixed. Under this theory, when immigrants get jobs, fewer jobs are left for native workers thereby causing increases in unemployment among native laborers.

The idea of a fixed workforce has a certain commonsense appeal, but is inaccurate. The number of jobs is dynamic rather than fixed. As more persons begin working and spending their earnings, the demand for more goods follows, and generally more labor is needed. Immigrants are not simply workers—they are also consumers. Like everyone else, immigrants need basic goods such as food, shelter, and clothing. Immigrant workers spend their earnings on these goods as well as (to the extent they can afford them) on other nonessential items. Immigrants therefore increase the total demand for goods. In response, businesses increase their production. To do this, they must increase their labor force and hire more workers. Thus, the entry of immigrants into the labor market ultimately creates jobs by pressuring businesses to expand their production. In fact, the mere presence of a new immigrant—even one who is not working—can increase consumption or the demand for goods and services, and cause the same result. Thus, all native workers—including minorities and women—would find better job opportunities due to overall economic growth.[3]

If immigrants actually create jobs for native workers, why do so many people believe that immigrants pose a threat to native workers' jobs? This may be a matter of what we think we see. While the average person may actually see an immigrant working in a job once held by a native worker, the more indirect job-creation process attributable to immigrants (and verified by studies discussed below) is not as easily perceived.[4] This may help account for much of the public suspicion of immigrants and jobs.

IMMIGRANTS ARE COMPLEMENTARY WORKERS

The notion that increases in immigration correspond to losses in native workers' jobs relies not only upon a model of the workforce as static, but also upon the belief that immigrants and native workers are vying for the same types of jobs. However, immigrants and native workers generally do not compete for the same jobs. Immigrants largely fill undesirable, unskilled jobs in which native workers have little interest, thereby serving as complements to, rather than substitutes for, native workers in the labor force.

The labor market is divided into primary "good" jobs and secondary "bad" jobs. The first group is largely populated by native workers, the latter by migrants. Primary sector jobs are situated in so-called "core" industries, where investments and financing of production are relatively high, and mainly large-scale and unionized, and where instability has been minimized by such market features as little effective competition. Workers who fill such jobs must have relatively high skills. They are well paid and work under generally desirable conditions. By contrast, secondary jobs are found in smaller firms where production is not as highly financed and products face highly competitive markets. Positions tend to be unstable, low or unskilled, relatively low paying, and generally marked by undesirable working conditions.[5]

Migrants are more suited for these low-paying, low-skilled jobs due to (1) the flexibility of the migrant workforce; (2) the lasting nature of the migrant labor supply; and (3) their susceptibility to manipulation and control. Migrants thus dominate low-paying, low-skilled jobs. The question then is whether, on account of immigrant domination of secondary jobs, native workers are pushed into primary jobs, or whether they are unemployed. President Ronald Reagan's Council of Economic Advisors, agreeing with the principle that immigrants generally do not displace native workers, emphasized the job and occupational mobility of native workers. Native workers can move from one sector of the labor market to another, while immigrants generally cannot.[6]

Yet this conclusion is not comforting for native workers ill-suited, on account of skills and/or geography, to occupy primary jobs. Further, immigrants get secondary jobs because they are more subject to manipulation and control—in other words, exploitation. Emphasizing the exploitability of immigrants for "good" economic effect is troubling even if such an approach does help us understand that immigrants generally do not take jobs that native workers desire. (These concerns are more fully addressed in chapter 7.)

Immigrants are likely to fill secondary jobs: immigrants commonly inhabit ethnic enclaves and are able to settle into a certain part of the labor market without having to assimilate into the larger society. The social norms of immigrant enclaves differ greatly from those of native workers with regard to the way in which secondary, low-paying, low-skilled jobs are valued. While the native population generally views such jobs as "low status" and therefore undesirable,[7] the jobs often meet the expectations of members of immigrant enclaves. The reference point by which many immigrants measure the desirability of jobs often differs from that of native workers. Many immigrants, after all, come from countries whose jobs are characterized by even lower wages and worse labor conditions than secondary jobs in America.

Given differences in English ability, education, and job experience between the so-called "typical" Mexican undocumented alien and a native worker, the immigrant seems ill-equipped to fill many of the jobs open to native workers. Thus, many low-skilled immigrant workers and more skilled native workers may fulfill mutual needs (complementary rather than competitive), leading to increased productivity. However, things are probably more complicated; various combinations of complementarity and substitutability among many immigrant and native groups are likely. To the extent that some immigrants serve as (real or potential) substitutes for native workers, their presence increases the supply of workers, and at the very least can depress wage rates. And when wages are lowered, some natives may no longer find it worthwhile to remain in the labor force and may therefore drop out.[8]

While many of the low-wage jobs filled by immigrants might otherwise go to teenagers and retirees (e.g., at McDonald's), such a phenomenon should not be considered the same as displacement of a typical native worker. We should look at the long-run positive general effect of immigrants on the job market, even though in the short run some specific groups may be harmed by one group of immigrants. Additionally, absent immigrants, some of the advertised jobs which currently go to immigrants would remain unfilled and therefore be withdrawn after a while because employers may choose to use machines or cut back.[9] Immigrants who fill such positions pose no direct harm to native workers.

THE IMPACT OF IMMIGRANTS ON WAGES

Assuming little substitution of native workers and the stimulation of job growth by the presence of immigrants as consumers, President Reagan's Council explained that immigrants have little negative impact on native wages. The Council acknowledged that wages can drop when the supply of labor increases (either because of immigration or the increased participation of native workers). But the Council urged us to look beyond short-term wage depression or job loss for the following reason: in the sectors where native workers are complementary with immigrant labor, both labor demand and wages will increase. The demand for labor increases because the availability of immigrant workers encourages investment in industries that have become more competitive. This increased demand in labor provides opportunities for new jobs and better wages for many native workers who were displaced in the noncomplementary sector. Therefore, short-term negative effects are outweighed by new opportunities, and the total combined income of the native population is actually increased.[10]

In a sense this position urges us to think of short-term wage depression as an investment of sorts, made for the purpose of attaining a long-term increase in prosperity. But we must recognize that short-term wage depression is a serious problem that should not be casually disregarded or even easily sacrificed for the benefit of long-term gains. However, better methods can be implemented to ameliorate this problem than by restricting immigration, for example, raising the minimum wage and/or expanding the Earned Income Tax Credit. Better job training and investment in our educational institutions are also relevant.

Immigration causes income benefits which are spread throughout the economy in other ways. Beyond the increased job opportunities and higher wages for some native workers, lower product prices and higher business profits also result. The concentration of unskilled immigrants in industries such as agriculture keeps prices down, thereby increasing the real income (or purchasing power) of native consumers.[11]

Higher business profits benefit those with personal investments, savings, and pension holdings. Even if some immigrants have the short-term effect of depressing wages in particular sectors, natives experiencing wage loss may be able to make up for those losses on account of the higher business profits which result. For example, if a native worker sees that her wage is being depressed by immigrant competition, she can contribute a little less to the pension fund to compensate for that lower wage, but still take solace in the fact that her pension fund is paying her a return. Increased business profits also make possible greater amounts of capital investment and innovation to the benefit of all.

The concern is that although the aggregate benefits may outweigh the costs, this scenario raises serious equity problems. The aggregate-benefit-to-all argument may actually be hard to swallow for native workers whose wages are being depressed if they do not have pension plans or personal holdings. Higher-skilled native workers who have such assets are relatively immune from competition. Few lower-skilled workers have pensions or holdings, and are therefore unable to make adjustments or reap benefits from increased profits; the higher-skilled workers (and management) benefit from the higher returns to capital without losing anything at all.

Studying Immigrants and the Labor Market

The array of studies that have examined the labor market effects of immigration can be categorized as regional or sectoral. Regional studies examine the effects of immigrants upon the entire labor market of a particular geographical segment of the country, such as Miami or California. Sectoral studies examine the effects of immigrants upon a single labor market—that related to a particular job sector such as the automobile or restaurant industry. Each perspective has its own advantages and disadvantages, and both are helpful to a better understanding of the way immigrants impact America's labor market.

Looking at job displacement and wage issues from a regional perspective causes us to consider the significance of variations in regional economies and demographic characteristics. Jobs are not distributed equally across the country. Nor are immigrants distributed evenly throughout the United States; different immigrant groups have unique histories in different regions of the country. For example, those who are foreign-born make up approximately 22 percent of the total population in California, about 10 percent in the Northeast (16 percent in New York and 13.5 percent in New Jersey), 13 percent in Florida, and about 9 percent in Illinois and Texas. Most of the foreign-born in Florida are Cuban, in Texas Mexican, in California Mexican and Asian, and in New

York a small percentage of each. The majority of Asian Indians reside in a single state, New Jersey.

Given regional variations in labor markets as well as the uneven geographic and ethnic distributions of immigrants, the impact of immigrants no doubt varies according to the region of the country. Consequently, we should wonder about the impact of Cubans and Haitians in Miami versus that of Mexicans, Central Americans, and certain Asians in Los Angeles. But even considering Cubans in Miami, one might wonder about differences between the effects of Cubans who entered in the 1960s versus those who entered as part of the Mariel boatlift around 1980. And given the long social and economic relationship between the United States and Mexico, one also suspects that there is a unique set of effects in places such as California, New Mexico, Arizona, and Texas.

Some general themes emerge with respect to regional differences. In terms of geographic distribution, Asian and European immigrants tend to be dispersed throughout the general population, in contrast to Mexicans, Cubans, and other Latinos, who tend to be concentrated in particular regions. The legalization (or amnesty) program in the late 1980s revealed that a substantial portion of the undocumented population in the United States enters from Mexico and resides in the West. During a period of significant labor force growth between 1970 and 1980 in the West, foreign-born workers contributed nearly 20 percent of the growth. Differences between jobs held by foreign-born and native workers are greater between Latinos and natives than between Asians and natives, and greater for women than for men. Occupational differences between immigrants and natives are greater in California, Texas, and Illinois than in Florida and New York. And the data suggest that the concentration of Mexican immigrants in the West depresses the average human capital and earnings of the foreign-born population in the region.[12]

A sectoral perspective compels one to consider the different effects that might be found between different industries such as manufacturing versus agriculture, or food processing compared to high-tech industries. Sectoral studies raise the further question of whether the presence of immigrant workers causes a delay in implementing technological advances or prompts reconsideration about the relocation of certain plant facilities to a different country. In the latter situation, the unavailability of immigrant workers would not necessarily open up jobs for native workers.

Regional studies are considered first.

1. REGIONAL AND LOCAL DIFFERENCES

a. Regional Unemployment Statistics

Economist Donald Huddle created a commotion in 1993 when he issued a report that purports to be the "first comprehensive study of the public sector costs of legal and illegal immigration." [13] Huddle argues that part of the cost of immigration is the cost of public assistance to those whose jobs are displaced by immigrant workers. In order to calculate the cost of public assistance to these displaced U.S. workers, Huddle assumes that for every one hundred immigrant workers that enter the labor market, twenty-five low-skilled U.S. workers lose their jobs (a 4:1 ratio).

Huddle provides no basis for this assumption. Presumably relying on INS data (he fails to offer a clear explanation), he determines that the percentage of less skilled immigrant workers who entered in 1992 was 62.2 percent. Extrapolating, he figures that 4.24 million low-skilled immigrants have entered the labor force since 1970. Therefore, applying a displacement coefficient of 25 percent to this number, he estimates that legal immigrants caused more than a million U.S. workers to lose their jobs in 1992. He further hypothesizes that because undocumented and formerly undocumented (amnestied) aliens have

> markedly lower skills than legal immigrants and higher labor force participation, their displacing effect on less skilled native born workers is more severe. The number of less skilled among 3.7 million undocumented labor force members is almost 3.0 million—80 percent. Assuming a displacement rate of 25 percent, 741,000 low-skill U.S. workers are jobless because of [undocumented] immigration. Some 265,000 additional workers are displaced by amnestied alien workers. [14]

The most questionable aspect of this analysis is, of course, the displacement rate of 25 percent. The figure is completely undefended in the paper, other than a brief mention of an unpublished piece by Huddle entitled "Immigration and Jobs: The Process of Displacement." [15] In light of theoretical and empirical works that suggest that immigrants actually create jobs, it seems unsound that such an important figure would go unexplained. In fact, if every four immigrants also created one job opening, there would be no adverse displacement effect from immigration. Another well-publicized 1993 report, by the Los Angeles County Internal Services Department on the public sector costs of immigrants, recognizes that most of the extant empirical studies "have found no evidence to show that immigrants displace native workers." [16] The Urban Institute, responding to both the Huddle and LA reports, points out that labor market empirical work does not support this supposition of job displacement by immigrants.[17] (The public sector cost aspects of these reports are discussed in chapter 5.)

One way to test the economic theory that immigrants create more jobs than they take, thereby facilitating increased job opportunities, is to examine regional unemployment statistics. If, as much political commentary charges, immigration takes more jobs than it creates, one would expect that high immigration leads to high unemployment.[18] If, on the other hand, relatively high levels of immigration are accompanied by average or low levels of unemployment, one may take this as an indication that immigration does, in fact, lead to overall job creation.

A comprehensive study by the Alexis de Tocqueville Institution yields striking results on the relationship between immigration and unemployment. The researchers examined every state comparing unemployment figures and foreign-born populations from 1900 to 1989. Their findings were unequivocal: the median unemployment rate was higher in states with relatively little immigrant presence. If anything, unemployment seemed negatively associated with immigration—the more immigrants, the less unemployment; immigration does not cause unemployment.[19]

The study gave particular attention to the effects of recent immigrants, and concluded that even recent waves of immigration have reduced joblessness. In response to the current debate over immigration, the researchers performed an analysis that looked exclusively at the 1980s. They looked at the ten states with the highest unemployment, compared them with the ten states with the lowest unemployment, and found that the immigrant population (defined as foreign-born) in the high unemployment states was much lower than in the low unemploy-

ment states. Then they looked at the ten states with the largest proportion of immigrants, compared their unemployment rates with the ten
states with the smallest immigrant population, and found that the typical
unemployment rate in the states with low immigration was nearly one-
third higher than in the states with relatively high immigration.[20] Of
course, one might wonder if the causal relationship between high immigration and low unemployment could work in the other direction—
namely, whether high unemployment states simply attract fewer immigrants. But that relationship has been discounted by others.[21]

Anecdotal evidence of individuals who are perceived to have lost
jobs due to immigration is more than offset by the less visible, positive
employment effects that immigration provides. Immigration is not associated with higher unemployment. Instead, immigrants actually create
more jobs than they take, thereby reducing the overall rate of unemployment and producing increased employment opportunities for immigrants
and native workers alike.[22]

b. New York

In its own survey of labor market studies in New York City, the
Department of Labor concluded that immigrants did not have a negative
impact on the employment or wage rates of native workers. For example, African Americans tended to be concentrated in employment areas
with few immigrant workers, thereby decreasing the chance for competition from immigrants. And although wage growth in the industries with
the greatest numbers of immigrants fell behind the national average in
the early 1980s, the rest of the New York City labor market had higher
wage growth than the rest of the nation. Most male immigrants, for
example, were employed in manufacturing jobs—female immigrants
were even more likely to be so employed. Some industries, such as
leather and garment producers, were dominated by low-wage immigrant
workers who had been used by business owners as a means to remain
competitive. Many whites had left the city, allowing for the movement
of African Americans into white-collar and public sector jobs.[23]

The availability and use of low-wage immigrant workers in New
York City raise the question of whether immigrants deserve credit for
the viability of certain industries or whether better alternatives exist.
Immigrants have been credited with the continued viability of the tradi-

tionally labor-intensive garment and printing industries, although capital improvements were possibly avoided, and some piecework projects reinstituted, as small business and production sites increased. Similarly, the Department of Labor credits immigrants with the vitality of full service, fresh food restaurants in New York. Without immigrant workers, the food industry in New York would have followed the trend in other regions toward domination by fast-food outlets.[24]

The New York City data (and that of Los Angeles, below) do raise concerns. First, the Latino concentration in manufacturing raises a question about the perpetuation of Latinos in this low-wage sector. Opportunities in other sectors may be limited if ethnic networks are limited, and few "role models" for other occupations are available. The second concern is over the concentration of African Americans in public sector employment. Reliance on that sector as a means for economic advancement may be shaky given government budgetary problems and consequent limited expansion of the public sector.

c. Los Angeles

Although one-third of its population is foreign-born and accounts for as much as 70 percent of the employment growth, immigration does not have a negative impact on job opportunities for native workers in Los Angeles either. However, new arrivals do have a slight adverse effect on earlier groups of immigrants. The group that may suffer from Mexican migration is the rest of the Latino labor force. Job growth in Mexican-dominated industries, such as manufacturing, was 25 percent less than the national average in the 1970s; Latino wage growth was 40 percent less. Latino immigrants in particular hold jobs in manufacturing (e.g., textile, apparel, and furniture).

At the same time, African American job opportunities seemed to have expanded, particularly in the white-collar sector. As in New York, African Americans in Los Angeles have experienced noticeable employment gains in the public sector. Both African American teenagers and adults experienced a job rate increase larger than the national average through the early 1980s. Their wages increased faster than the state average, even in blue-collar work with large proportions of immigrants. Despite a concern over increased joblessness among young or less educated African Americans, the presence of immigrants increased the earnings and opportunities of African Americans who were employed.[25]

Thus, immigrants may create more jobs than they take in fields such as communications and utilities, but take more jobs than they create in manufacturing, retail trade, and restaurants in places like Los Angeles and New York. The effect is a "redistribution" of jobs for native workers away from manufacturing and lower-skilled services toward the white-collar sector, particularly in management and the professions. By 1993, almost a quarter of African Americans, but only one in ten Latinos working in Los Angeles held professional or managerial positions.[26]

Specific research on less skilled workers in the West provides a better understanding of the effect of less skilled immigrants on wages. By comparing wages among less skilled workers in other parts of the country, one finds that the increase of less skilled Latino and Asian immigrants in the West adversely affects the wages of natives. But through immigration, the West has maintained a steady supply of low-wage workers, which helps to explain why wages will not rise as much. In New England, for example, rising schooling levels has reduced the supply of unskilled workers over the past twenty years, which in turn raises wages among unskilled workers.[27]

d. Miami

For almost four decades Cubans have migrated to Miami, creating what the Department of Labor terms a "premier example of the formation of ethnic enclaves."[28] Cubans, however, are not a stereotypical group of low-wage immigrant workers. Through financial and social assistance from friends and families, about 20 percent of Cubans in Miami prior to 1980 were business managers or professionals. The ethnic enclave facilitated jobs and economic development for new arrivals, while those who ventured out of the enclave experienced lower earnings linked in part to language problems.

In one study of the effect of the "Mariel Boatlift" on Miami (discussed more fully in chapter 7), economist David Card found that the influx of 125,000 new Cubans had no effect on the unemployment rates or wages of low-skilled native workers or earlier Cuban immigrants. He posited several explanations for his findings. The Marielitos may have discouraged other immigrants and natives from coming to Miami. For some twenty years prior to the boatlift, Miami had received thousands of Cuban émigrés, making Miami especially prepared for the influx. Miami's strong textile and clothing industries could absorb additional unskilled labor. And the lack of English-speaking ability did not pose a hindrance to entry into Miami's job market.[29]

e. Chicago

Chicago constantly attracts new immigrants. Immigrants first came from northern Europe, and then later from eastern and southern Europe. In recent years, approximately 60,000 new immigrants—half from Mexico—have settled in this metropolitan area each year. Now the area is quite diverse. In 1990, Chicago was 19 percent African American, 10.9 percent Latino, and 3.1 percent Asian American.[30]

In general, studies of immigrants in Chicago have not found a negative labor market impact on native workers. Even a close look at undocumented workers did not disclose a subclass of exploited, non-union workers.[31] In an important study of the poverty and employment rates of African Americans, Mexicans, and Puerto Ricans in Chicago, Robert Aponte sheds light on the effect of immigrants. Assuming that most of the Mexicans were immigrants, he sought explanations for why they had lower poverty rates than Puerto Ricans and African Americans, and better employment rates than those groups as well as whites. Essentially he found that this success was achieved despite conventional predictors of poverty and unemployment (the fact that Mexicans were the group with the least competitive human capital attributes—i.e., education, English proficiency, skills, work experience—and the most limited access to automobiles for commuting), suggesting that there was little negative immigrant impact on the citizen groups.

In terms of whether groups were mired in what Aponte called "secondary jobs" involving low wages, low skill requirements, and poor working conditions, he found that about half of the African Americans surveyed held secondary "black" jobs, and the same proportion of Mexicans had secondary "Mexican" jobs. This was consistent with one of the theoretical assumptions of segmentation theory, namely, that workers are allocated across relatively homogeneous segments of the labor market based on race, ethnicity, or gender. However, unlike African Americans, Mexicans were not "mired in prototypically 'secondary' jobs" especially when those without high school diplomas were compared. Median wages for Mexicans were about the same as for Puerto

Ricans, but higher than for African Americans, contradicting the theory that Mexicans are favored by employers for their exploitable nature.

In order to get a better sense of his findings, Aponte turned to other research for possible explanations. In a large survey of Chicago employers, "discriminatory predispositions" were examined, and immigrant workers—be they Mexican, Asian, or eastern European—were consistently praised and preferred. Employers' disinclination for African American workers was conspicuous. Employers were looking for employees with a "good work ethic." But consistent with the theoretical understandings of why immigrants are net contributors, Aponte suggests that immigrants will "tolerate harsher conditions, lower pay, [and] few upward trajectories" because opportunities in the United States are better than those in Third World sending countries. In his view (consistent with Piore's), this attitude is even more likely to be held by undocumented aliens and others who view their stay in the United States as short term.[32] These issues are addressed more fully in chapter 7.

f. Texas

Several labor market studies were conducted in Texas in the late 1970s that continue to have relevance today. Those focusing on Mexican migration consistently find new Mexican immigrants in unskilled jobs, and, as in Los Angeles, the group with which they compete most directly is earlier Mexican immigrants.

An examination of a large sampling of native and immigrant workers in San Antonio revealed that undocumented aliens had little impact on native wages. About 70 percent of the undocumented workers were laborers or service workers whose jobs were subject to rapid turnover. While all workers of color in San Antonio generally had low wages, the problem was more the product of a lack of unions and the magnitude of low-skilled work, than the presence of undocumented immigrants.[33]

2. CONSIDERING DIFFERENT INDUSTRIES

Citing a regional study to a native worker who believes that she has been displaced by an immigrant worker does little to relieve her anger or resentment toward immigrants. In a sense, this is the "problem" with simply looking at regional studies: anecdotes get lost as things average out, and the aggregate view distances the observer from an important area of impact.

Of course sectoral or industrial case studies may have an analogous problem. When researchers focus on industries that have a large immigrant workforce their results are likely to be quantitatively less rigorous because of the nonrandom selection process. Long-term nuances are difficult to assess because sectoral studies tend to be short-term in focus. Thus displaced workers are judged to be victims, and any long-term benefit to the same workers, for instance the subsequent acquisition of new, fruitful skills, might get ignored altogether.

The industrial studies do invite us to keep in mind a variety of influencing factors: demographic and human capital traits (such as job skills) of the immigrants, ethnic networks, availability of other workers, segmentation of the workforce, and the existence of foreign competition. Despite these factors, arguably in many industries immigrants are complementary to rather than competitive with native workers, and the presence of immigrants willing to take unstable, low-wage, and low-skilled jobs in particular regions of the country has allowed certain industries to survive, thereby preserving some jobs that otherwise would not exist. Likewise, evidence of the immigrants' delaying effect on mechanization in agriculture suggests that immigration restrictions may not free up jobs for native workers, and would raise consumer prices.

a. Manufacturing

As indicated in the regional studies, particularly in New York and Los Angeles, large numbers of immigrants hold manufacturing jobs. The manufacturing example raises a number of questions: Is the use of low-wage immigrant workers by domestic employers necessary for competitiveness in the global economy? Do immigrants have skills which available native workers do not? Is the prevalence of immigrants in particular jobs due to ethnic ties a significant phenomenon? Does the use of immigrant workers primarily delay or substitute for automation and technology and therefore not cause native worker job displacement?

(i) Textile Industry

Immigrant labor has been fundamental to the success of the textile industry over time.[34] A story about Colombian immigrants in the industry illustrates the complementary and job-creating potential of immigrants.

The textile industry was once a cornerstone of the New England economy, but in the 1930s the largest mills relocated to southern states. The few remaining in New England tried different survival strategies, all of which failed, and in 1952 a major textile training school in Lowell, Massachusetts closed. In 1969, however, a Connecticut company recruited twenty skilled loom fixers from the textile industry of Medellin, Colombia. While that firm failed within a few months, one of the recruits ended up in Lowell where he developed an immigrant network for the dying local industry. Eventually four mills came to rely on immigrants, even though two-thirds of their workers were natives. Colombians were only 11 percent of the workforce, but filled key positions that enabled the mills to survive and successfully preserve jobs for about a thousand workers. This was accomplished without major capital expenditure or a formal program to train new workers.[35]

(ii) Automobile Parts

The use of low-wage immigrant workers as a survival strategy is demonstrated in the automotive parts industry. Rebecca Morales examined the use of undocumented workers at twenty-one Los Angeles area businesses, focusing principally on eight automobile parts companies. She found that undocumented workers were used to facilitate structural transitions in reaction to changing economic circumstances.

The context of this study is important. In 1979, automobile manufacturers employed a million workers in Los Angeles; parts suppliers employed 2 million. As a consequence of the 1979 to 1980 stage of the recession, the automobile industry lost about 5,500 jobs at the same time as a sizable influx of low-skilled immigrants (including many undocumented aliens from El Salvador and Guatemala) began to arrive. The major automakers responded to the economic situation by consolidating some operations, shifting some production to foreign affiliates or to the Midwest, automating, and subcontracting some product lines. The two thousand auto parts suppliers, mostly not unionized, did not have the same capacity to react and were more vulnerable to shifting market forces (e.g., demand for original equipment, product aftermarkets, and local labor markets). Since assembly plants were closing, only suppliers who could shift to the aftermarket survived.

Survival strategies were influenced by several factors. Those companies that were subsidiaries of larger corporations were able to tap into the wealth of the parent for finance capital; many independent firms who were less likely to have reliable resources considered merging. Whether workers were unionized was important; a union meant that employers had to bargain over wages, job classifications, benefits, and the like. In order to survive, suppliers needed a more flexible workforce, and many turned to undocumented workers as one solution.[36]

Morales studied two wheel manufacturers, both subsidiaries of larger corporations, one of which used undocumented immigrants while the other did not. Company A was 60 percent undocumented and unionized; Company B was 60 percent native workers and non-unionized, but paid an average of $2.00 per hour more. As part of its survival strategy, Company B began laying off higher-paid workers, which it could do more easily in the absence of a union.[37] Company A's strategy was to seek out more undocumented workers by favoring job applicants and relatives of workers who spoke only Spanish. The undocumented workers became increasingly dissatisfied with the union apparently because of its reluctance to act aggressively on their behalf. Ironically, this reluctance resulted from the union's perception that the undocumented status of the workers weakened its position.

Morales also looked at three battery-making companies, two of which made a high-quality product and were severely harmed by auto plant closures, and a third that manufactured a product lower in quality, and was able to continue selling to government entities and other resalers requiring low prices. The first two firms' batteries were not only better but more expensive: their plants were automated, and their workers were citizens and lawful permanent residents, who were paid twice the hourly rate of the workers at the third company that was more labor intensive. The wages at the third company were stratified, however; native, nonminority workers were paid the most, and permanent residents were paid more than the undocumented workers. But interestingly, all three firms had contracts with the same labor union.

Several noteworthy findings emerged. Firms that were facing difficult market conditions turned to undocumented workers out of a need for a cheap labor force that could contract and expand easily. While unionization and the size of the enterprise were not significant indicators of likely employment of undocumented workers, subsidiaries were more likely than independent firms to hire undocumented aliens. During expansionary periods, legal immigrants are absorbed into the economy. But during a decline, they become redundant and undocumented workers are ideal since they are easily replaced. Lacking legal protection, the undocumenteds benefit employers seeking a means of lowering wages and avoiding unions.

Morales's study raises the question whether undocumented workers—whose labor allows some manufacturers to delay automation and remain competitive—do cause some union and wage erosion. However, they may also make it possible for some industries to survive in the United States, thereby protecting some jobs for natives. Immigration restrictions would not necessarily make it possible for unions to maintain jobs and wages at high levels as the threat of industry relocation to countries with cheaper labor would remain.

(iii) Electronics

A comprehensive study of electronics companies in Southern California found that more than a third of the jobs involved low-wage assembly, more than a third of the workers were immigrants, about two-thirds were women, and the ratio of African American workers to Latinos was 1 to 14.5. Consistent with findings in Chicago, the demographic makeup of the workforce seemed to reflect employer preferences for Latino workers who were regarded as more "diligent," "hardworking," and "loyal" than native workers (including African Americans), who were more aware of their rights.[38]

The focus on Southern California is important. The Department of Labor notes that in 1980 electronics production constituted 60 percent of all manufacturing jobs in the state. And while Silicon Valley in Northern California is known for its electronics industry, production facilities in the 1980s moved south to counties such as Los Angeles, Orange, and San Diego, which now represent the nation's largest concentration of electronics firms. A third of the small firms and half of the large companies decided to locate in Southern California because of the region's labor supply, which, of course, is noted for its immigrant population.

For reasons of competitiveness, electronics firms resort to subcontracting, which in turn depends on a malleable workforce. Subcontracting allows smaller firms to handle technical functions such as design, and larger ones to complete basic production without having to maintain a large permanent workforce. For small firms, subcontracting helps to keep costs down; for large firms, subcontracting provides flexibility. And the availability of immigrants—documented and undocumented—in the area makes this subcontracting and the competitiveness of this industry possible.[39]

(iv) Furniture

More than two-thirds of furniture production jobs continue to be found in southern states (especially North Carolina), where African Americans comprise much of the workforce. California is home to the other third—mostly in Southern California where most workers are Mexican. Even in San Francisco, immigrants constitute much of the furniture workforce. One-third are Latino and one-sixth Asian.[40]

In a study of California furniture manufacturers, Richard Mines looked for trends related to immigrant workers and unions. He found that as unionized firms in San Francisco closed and relocated to Southern California, the new firms were clearly antiunion. (Some managers even attended training seminars on how to circumvent unionization.) Most firms in Los Angeles were nonunion, and many consciously turned over the workforce regularly in order to control wages. Apparently, new immigrants have come to dominate this low-wage, nonunion workforce because they are willing to tolerate these conditions. But even in the unionized workforce with more settled immigrants, new immigrants pose a displacement threat to the workers because the industry is so labor intensive and competitive.

Low-wage, low-skilled immigrants have enabled many furniture manufacturers in Southern California to survive. The competition in much of the industry is between U.S. firms, and thus between various regions of the country. Low-wage immigrant workers give Southern California firms an advantage because they are able to keep labor costs down. But in the process the firms with settled immigrants get underbid by those using new low-wage workers, and settled immigrants can lose ground.[41]

(v) Garment Industry

Immigrants continue to play a critical role in U.S. garment manufacturing.[42] The industry is highly competitive and divided along the lines of product, quality, and price, and especially between menswear and womenswear, where competition is most keen. Skilled tailors in small shops produce most of the high-end clothing. But most of the industry is in the midrange involving highly capitalized firms owned by descendants of Italian and eastern European industry leaders, and a "section" production system under which less skilled workers assemble various sections of a garment. Finally, the smallest garment firms specialize in low-cost apparel and are often owned by Asian immigrants. Workers in these firms are semiskilled and often not unionized.

The immigrant entrepreneurs who operate the small firms use immigrant workers to reduce the risk of failure in this competitive industry. As in other industries, immigrant workers—particularly women—are used to maintain flexibility. On the one hand, employers in these situations might be viewed as flexible themselves, allowing women to bring their children to work or to work at home, and sometimes helping out with social and legal problems. On the other hand, if firms violate wage or labor standards, the arrangement may discourage immigrant workers from complaining. Larger unionized firms are much more formal.

The apparel industry is quite vulnerable to global competition. U.S. garment workers earn only about 60 percent of what the average manufacturing worker in the country makes—which is not surprising considering that labor costs in Korea and Hong Kong are about 15 percent of labor costs here. The shift in consumer tastes toward casual wear that can be manufactured with low-skilled workers also gives foreign firms an advantage over larger, more heavily capitalized U.S. companies.

The New York experience is illustrative of the importance of immigrants to an industry marked by undesirable jobs. Between 1969 and 1975, over 80,000 garment jobs were lost as rent and wage rates changed, foreign competition increased, and fewer native workers were willing to take the work. The industry in New York has, however, been able to reconstitute itself and survive with the aid of immigrant workers. As a "spot market" able to respond quickly to retailer requests, production is turned over to small immigrant-owned firms. These firms rely on a constant supply of immigrant women whose presence makes the quick turnaround required possible. Given the low wages and relatively poor working conditions, native workers have no interest in this work. In order for garment manufacturers to survive, the continuous availability of new immigrants is likely to be necessary.[43]

b. Service Industries

Service-based industries have a set of characteristics that distinguish them from manufacturing and agriculture. Service industries face less foreign competition, involve lower relative capitalization costs, have highly competitive local markets, and are associated with immigrant entrepreneurs and immigrant labor. As the need for more service-based entities has increased, so has the number of service-related jobs.

(i) Restaurant Work

An example of the complementary nature of sectors in which immigrants mostly work without displacing native workers is restaurants. Broad and diverse, the restaurant industry has parts in which immigrants play an important role, and others in which they play only a minimal role. Two studies, one in New York and the other in San Diego, begin to explain why.

In an analysis of New York, the industry can be divided into four parts: fast-food, intermediate, full-service, and immigrant-owned. While all four employ many unskilled workers, only the full-service and immigrant-owned restaurants recruit immigrant workers. Even within this "secondary" labor market group, the workers were imperfect substitutes for one another.

Although change is underway, fast-food chains have historically relied on teenagers for their low-skilled workers. Since most of the food preparation is done ahead of time, fast-food workers perform simple tasks requiring little training. As English-language proficiency is important along with the willingness to work part-time irregular hours, teenagers who are usually interested in quick earnings and short-term commitments have been hired. Their high turnover allows franchises to expand and contract as necessary. Although minimum wage has been the standard in the fast-food industry, wages and benefits have recently increased to attract new workers as demographic changes have decreased the supply of teenagers.

Intermediate restaurants—coffee shops and steak houses—look for workers who are more dependable than teenagers. In this sector, the jobs are considered more stable, and the wages more in line with supporting a family. Some on-the-job training is necessary, and regular turnover undesirable. In New York, this sector has turned to adult women as the preferred worker.

In contrast, full-service restaurants have turned to immigrants for many of the available positions. Because they offer better food, service, and atmosphere, these restaurants maintain a full complement of workers: highly trained cooks, waiters, waitresses, busboys, food preparation assistants, and dishwashers. Managers choose immigrants for the unskilled jobs, as well as some of the semiskilled kitchen positions. Native women are often hired as waitresses, although European immigrant men are also hired as waiters in some more exclusive restaurants.

Immigrant-owned (often ethnic) restaurants provide few job opportunities for native workers. They may vary in size, but many are structured like full-service restaurants. Family members fill many of the jobs, with the others taken by workers from the same ethnic community. The number of jobs can be substantial; in 1981, about 60 percent of all restaurants in Manhattan, Brooklyn, and Queens were owned by first-generation immigrants.

The elimination of immigrant restaurant workers would produce a curious effect. Since full-service and immigrant restaurants need large numbers of immigrants—including undocumented workers—their elimination might devastate those restaurants to the benefit of intermediate and fast-food operations. But the meaning of that benefit has to be carefully evaluated: Increasing the demand for intermediate and fast-food chains means that more work for the least skilled and least stable workers becomes available, which would reduce the average wage and skill levels in the industry.

A further illustration of the complementary nature of the work performed by immigrants in the restaurant industry is a unique look at full-service and immigrant-owned restaurants in San Diego: American/Seafood places and Mexican food businesses. Both groups used Mexican workers, but to different degrees. In the American/Seafood restaurants, 20 percent of the workers were Mexican, compared to 80 percent in the Mexican food restaurants. In both cases, Mexicans dominated the kitchen help and busboy positions. And to create an ambience of authenticity in the Mexican-theme restaurants, Mexicans held most of the jobs in the "front-of-the-house" in those restaurants. Front-of-the-house positions are important as they comprise 80 percent of restaurant jobs. That these jobs are not so readily accessible to Mexican workers in non-Mexican restaurants was experienced by Rodolfo (recall chapter 3).

While he was able to work his way up from dishwashing to kitchen work, he did not feel that he could reasonably aspire to a front-of-the-house job.

In San Diego the busboy and kitchen help jobs were less attractive to native workers. Family contacts and networks help Mexican immigrants obtain these jobs, and new immigrants are often happy with any steady job. Many will work two part-time jobs to earn more (as did Rodolfo). On the other hand, native workers have more options. Often their language ability provides more opportunities, even part-time, and restaurant hours may be too odd and irregular for their needs. Child care issues may also be more overriding for native workers.[44]

(ii) Janitorial Work

Often cited by anti-immigrant forces as an example of native job displacement by immigrants is a study of janitors in Los Angeles. While troubling questions are raised, the report fails to provide complete information about the situation, and thus is not necessarily a definitive indictment of the role of immigrants in the labor market.

In the late 1970s and early 1980s in Los Angeles, small family-run operations held most of the small building cleaning contracts; midsized nonunion firms controlled the suburban midsized buildings; and large unionized companies dominated large downtown and suburban buildings. With this domination, by 1983 the wage and benefit package for Service Employees International Union (SEIU) janitors working in downtown buildings was worth almost $13 an hour. A large proportion of the workers were African American.

Change occurred in the early 1980s. Realizing that downtown buildings were becoming increasingly cost-conscious, midsized nonunion companies seized the moment, offering much lower contract prices and a free month of service. The nonunion firms were able to undercut prices largely because they employed mostly temporary immigrant workers who were paid only $3.35 per hour. As a result, the nonunion firms took over most of the downtown contracts; even the larger union companies had to hire immigrant workers at lower wages in order to keep their suburban contracts. The number of unionized African American janitors dropped from 2,500 in 1977 to 600 in 1985.[45]

No doubt the nature of the industry drastically changed during this period. Turnover is even higher now, as nonunion firms hire and fire workers depending on building contract needs. And certainly, the faded picture of a unionized worker who had a $13 per hour wage and benefits package working in a downtown building is disheartening. But the average janitor in Los Angeles at the time was not making that amount. The Department of Labor reports that average hourly janitorial wage in current dollars was $4.38 for 1978; $6.15 for 1982; $6.58 for 1983, and $5.63 for 1985.[46] Also, no one tracked the former unionized African American janitors in order to determine the economic impact on them after the disappearance of unionized janitorial work.

The nature of janitorial contracts is also relevant. The adage that "all you need is a mop and a bucket" to be a janitor is still true. The business is fiercely competitive, and typically janitorial contracts have a one month cancellation policy. Every day, building managers receive calls from start-up companies. Once the unionized price in Los Angeles reached a certain level, building managers more readily looked for cheaper contracts. But it turns out that in the 1980s, the building service industry was ripe for competition regardless of the presence of new immigrants. In fact, in 1988 a union organizing campaign called "Justice for Janitors" was initiated because the trend of buildings turning to low-wage nonunion contractors had caught hold throughout the country in cities such as Chicago and Washington, D.C., as well as places like Detroit, Pittsburgh, and Atlanta that had few immigrants. Furthermore, SEIU now represents about nine of ten building service workers in Los Angeles, up from 30 percent in 1988.[47]

c. Construction Industry

Yet another example of the potentially complementary nature of immigrants' participation in the labor market is their role in the construction industry as contractors and workers. While major builders continue to dominate the large construction project market, immigrant entrepreneurs in New York, for example, have become strong competitors with nonunion shops and African American-owned construction firms in the nonstandardized residential market and to a degree as subcontractors for major builders. These smaller firms have become more important as the construction industry has changed during its economic swings. But as most African American and immigrant-owned companies have had capitalization problems, African American companies often rely on government (minority) contract work, while immigrant-owned companies specialize in residential additions and rehabilitation work.

Because of historical exclusionary policies of many building trades' unions, African Americans and other minorities have been slow to enter the field as workers, particularly with major builders on large construction projects. Although the change has been gradual, some evidence has surfaced, at least in Los Angeles, that African Americans continue to be discriminated against by some major builders who show a preference for Latinos if minorities are added to crews. On the other hand, native workers (including many African Americans) seem to be hired with regularity in the construction business in Washington, D.C., along with many undocumented Salvadoran laborers.

Finally, the phenomenon of the "drive-by labor markets" involving day laborers who stand at well-known street corners looking for any kind of work has become more common. The Department of Labor recognizes that this available pool of workers may be important, given the ups and downs of the industry, because builders need more flexibility in their labor supply. As in other cases, immigrants may provide that flexibility in terms of ease of hiring and dismissal.[48]

d. Food Processing

Food processing industries are constantly transforming as technology advances, tastes change, and increasingly both parents in traditional households are working, all of which require different approaches to food preparation. More demand for preprocessed foods and fast-food restaurants has increased the amount of food processed in packing plants and restaurants. Increased awareness of health considerations has affected consumer tastes which in turn impacts which foods are demanded, and how those foods should be processed. Technology has also led to new products and a continually expanding array of merchandise in supermarkets.

(i) Beef Packing

Southeast Asian refugees have become a major workforce for the meatpacking industry which once provided work for unskilled European immigrants, urban African Americans, and winter work for Midwest farmers.

At the turn of the century, refrigerated freight trains facilitated centralization of beef packing in large Midwest cities (e.g., Chicago) where low-wage workers were available. But after World War II, companies sought to reduce production costs by locating plants in rural areas of the Corn Belt (especially Iowa and Illinois); new interstate highways made this feasible. Along with automation, this geographic shift resulted in job losses for African Americans who would or could not relocate. As poultry gained increased popularity in the 1970s, beef plants were forced to restructure so that jobs were made simpler, and production more efficient and repetitive. Foreign-born nonunion packers took over many of the functions which had once been performed by unionized grocery store butchers.[49] In recent years plants have moved closer to feedlots in High Plains states with weaker union traditions. For example, IBP, the nation's largest beef packer, set up a nonunion plant paying wages at half the industry average. Today, three companies pack 90 percent of all U.S. beef.

To fill the workforce needs of plants now relocated in lightly populated areas, the companies had to recruit vigorously. While some migrant and unemployed workers were attracted, the companies were most successful in using the Refugee Resettlement Program to recruit Southeast Asian refugees, who had no significant established communities in the United States to draw them, and limited employment options. Clearly, recruitment and relocation of refugees and immigrants were a beef packing industry durability strategy. In the process urban and unionized workers, including many African Americans, were phased out of the industry.[50]

(ii) Poultry Processing

Immigrants have become a major part of the workforce in California's poultry processing industry, and are becoming increasingly important in other regions. As in the beef industry, there was a time when chickens were slaughtered by unionized butchers in the city. But today, farmers contract with processing plants in order to prepare chickens for sale. Mechanization, technology resulting in faster growing chickens, and product diversification such as delivery of some chickens cut up or in lunch meat form have radically changed the processing function.

In California, Mexicans hold a good proportion of poultry jobs. On ranches, where chickens and turkeys are raised and eggs collected, except for management positions, the workforce is almost all Mexican. Processing plants also hire many Mexicans. The two dominant poultry producers in the state have a unionized native workforce, with the best wage and benefits package in the country. They do not employ undocumented workers. Smaller producers use a greater immigrant workforce, but are also unionized and pay well.

Poultry producers in the southeastern part of the country employ mostly rural native workers, but are gradually hiring more and more Southeast Asian and Latino immigrants. Farms in this region continue to be small and more family-run than those in California. The demand for workers is cyclical, so jobs are hard to fill and turnover is high; managers must constantly focus on recruitment. In North Carolina the plants have a good market. More than half the workforce is African American, 40 percent is white, and 4 percent immigrant, but additional workers are hard to find. As a result recruitment efforts directed at immigrants have been stepped up. Employers in Delaware, Maryland, Virginia, and Georgia run union firms and pay good wages, but are also short of workers. They too have looked to immigrants, including Haitians, Asians, and Latinos.[51]

e. Agriculture

Agriculture is perhaps the industry which the public associates most with immigrants. Of course the history of this relationship is long— growers even sought repeal of Chinese exclusion laws soon after their enactment in the late 1800s because of their impact on the pool of available laborers. Today, Mexican migrant workers play a critical role in the agricultural industry, particularly in California where half the nation's fresh produce is grown. Many of the native workers are Mexican Americans whose parents were Mexican immigrants.[52]

A mass hiring approach has emerged from the availability of migrant workers. Since the work is seasonal and unpredictable, the vast majority of farm workers are temporary. So even though the number of workers outnumbers available jobs, farmers hire many more times the number of workers needed in order to yield a good harvesting crew. Some workers do not like the work, and others are temporary workers who want to earn extra money. The workers have little control over the length of work, as crews of workers are hired and dismissed to suit the growers' needs. In order to work year-round, a worker might have to commit to eighteen separate jobs during the year. Individuals come to rely on crew leaders or contractors for regular employment because the latter maintain relationships and contacts with growers.

Bilingual foremen are used by farm labor contractors as well as grower corporations. They help to recruit, assign work, supervise, distribute pay, and on occasion arrange for transportation and housing. Since 90 percent of the foremen are Mexican-born, the continued hiring and use of Mexican workers is facilitated.

The work of agricultural economist Philip Martin suggests that the availability of immigrant labor has retarded mechanization in California agriculture. The use of unskilled workers is less expensive and less risky than some available labor-saving technology. Furthermore, many growers planted orchards of standard sized trees (which last for generations and require pickers on ladders), when dwarf varieties were available, and failed to prune in a manner which would have made orchards accessible to mechanical harvesters.

The availability of Mexican migrant workers has contributed to the decline of unionization among California's agricultural workers. In the Central Valley, unions are uncommon and ineffective; some workers are charged for the use of tools, transportation, or housing that was once provided by the growers. North of the Valley, unions are more effective in influencing employment strategies and working conditions. In its heyday in the 1970s, the Caesar Chavez-led United Farm Workers (UFW) boasted a membership of a hundred thousand. By the early 1990s, the UFW had fewer than twenty thousand members. But after securing a historic lettuce contract with Bruce Church Inc. in 1996 following a seventeen-year battle, the union gained confidence and expected its twenty-five thousand membership to keep climbing.[53]

f. A New American Labor Movement?

The intersection between immigrants and unions is apparent in a number of sectoral studies such as those of the garment, janitorial, meat processing, agriculture, and construction industries. But this relationship has to be viewed in the context of changes occurring within the labor movement. Foremost among these changes is the steady decline in union membership, as low-paying, nonunion service sector jobs replace high-paying unionized industrialized ones.[54] Unions often find these jobs in the hands of the undocumented. Rather than point to these newcomers as the problem, a number of unions instituted radically new organizational strategies focusing on bringing them into their unions. The belief is that as courageous risk takers with strong political views, the newcomers may be more open to being organized than the native-born.[55]

A good example is the Service Employees' International Union's (SEIU) Justice for Janitors approach. Initiated in 1988 in fifteen cities, the campaign employs a variety of new tactics including direct action and civil disobedience. As a result of its aggressive focus on immigrant workers, the union has registered substantial membership gains across the country, including Milwaukee, Washington, D.C., Hartford, Northern New Jersey, and California's Silicon Valley. SEIU now represents about nine of ten building service workers in Los Angeles, up from 30 percent in 1988.[56]

Some unions, including the Union of Needletrades Industrial and Textile Employees, allow unorganized immigrant workers to become "associate members." Associate members are eligible for a variety of benefits, including health insurance. The union also helps associate members with sexual harassment, discrimination, unemployment, and unpaid wage claims, as well as immigration law matters.[57]

The powerful AFL-CIO has begun to see the possibilities. In 1991, Lane Kirkland, then president of the AFL-CIO, responded to claims that the labor movement fails to address the needs of low-wage immigrant workers by pointing to the organization's Labor Immigrant Assistant Project and its creation of the California Immigrant Workers' Association that provides a wide range of social services to nonunion immigrants, including legal help to fight workplace abuses. The AFL-CIO recognizes that immigrants are a major source for new members who want to organize. The new AFL-CIO Organizing Institute trains organizers—many of them women and minorities—in new techniques.[58]

g. Sectoral Studies and Native Wages

Where immigrants are clustered in sectors that are complementary to and not competitive with native worker-dominated ones, the latter will be shielded from any wage depression in the immigrant-dominated sectors (i.e., parts of the restaurant industry, the construction industry, and the garment industry).

In other industries, immigrants—particularly undocumented ones—may be used to reduce costs and wages, and undercut unions (i.e., the automobile parts industry, electronics, the furniture industry, and janitorial work). For example, one manufacturer of automobile headers increasingly used machines for production and hired computer programmers who were undocumented. This reduced the need for and skill level of assembly workers. But the union was able to keep wages up and fight attempts to eliminate jobs. Eventually, the company merged with another company and moved production to Mexico where wages were $1.60 per hour compared to $6.50 in Los Angeles.[59] This example raises the question of whether the elimination of immigrants—documented and undocumented—willing to take low-wage, low-skilled, and unstable employment would necessarily open up jobs for natives.

In addition, some industries (i.e., the textile and garment industries) owed their very survival to immigrants, thereby possibly preserving some employment opportunities for native workers. If wages were depressed in some sectors that immigrants came to dominate, the possibility that native workers found better-paying opportunities in other sectors cannot be discounted.

Given recent debates over trade agreements, questions related to the impact of such agreements on jobs and immigration and conversely the impact of immigration on industries affected by trade agreements are appropriate. Without looking at the actual effect of immigrants, one study has concluded that increased immigration of either skilled or unskilled workers will in the long run cause a reduction in wages of U.S. workers.[60] In examining manufacturing industries, the researchers reasoned that since skilled labor is used intensively in exports while unskilled labor is intensive in import-competing industries, increased immigration of any sort would result in an increase in the price of nontraded goods, which causes a reduction in wages. But the inquiry should not end there. The fact that owners of capital benefit from this scenario is important (this could mean more investment). What this might mean to the overall benefit of the economy should not be ignored, especially as the base of the economy continues to shift from manufacturing to services.

These regional and sectoral studies demonstrate the complexity of the issues involved in the job displacement and wage effects of immigrants. They do provide evidence that immigrants do not cause massive job displacement, and perhaps even create jobs by providing unique skills (i.e., the textile industry); allowing industries to remain competitive and survive (i.e., the automobile parts, electronics, furniture, and garment industries); working in sectors complementary to and not competitive with ones dominated by native workers (i.e., restaurant work and construction in New York and Los Angeles); and taking low-wage, low-skilled, and unstable jobs unwanted by natives (i.e., the garment and beef-packing industries). There is also evidence that the presence of immigrants delays mechanization or plant relocation to other countries in some industries (i.e., agriculture and electronics); this suggests, however, that immigration restrictions would not necessarily yield more job opportunities for native workers.

Of course other factors are involved, such as employer discrimination against African American workers in favor of Latino, Asian, and immigrant workers. On the one hand, employer disinclination for African American workers might suggest that in the absence of immigrants, employers might be forced to hire African Americans. However, such discrimination might be more effectively attacked through employment discrimination claims rather than through immigration restrictions. Likewise, employers' desire to undercut unionization, and the impact of new immigration on the employment and wages of earlier groups of immigrants are also relevant.

Lastly, these studies did not take into account some job-creation effects—that is, the demand for goods and services caused by immigrants as consumers that in turn leads to investment in various sectors and more jobs—which are arguably difficult to measure. Not counted in these studies as well are the effects of such factors as higher returns to capital and lower consumer prices which reap large benefits for workers and the economy and occur because of the presence of immigrants.

chapter 5

How Much Do Immigrants Cost?
The Methodology Wars

COMMON SENSE OR POPULAR IMAGE

Two competing ways of looking at the question of immigrants and the public fisc are apparent. One is the popular image of immigrants as culprits, fueled by a handful of studies and advanced by those calling for restrictions on immigration. The other is a common-sense perception of immigrants as net contributors, promoted by many economists and espoused by pro-immigrant forces. Those calling for immigration restrictions claim that immigrants impose net costs on taxpayers. This argument focuses on the fiscal impact of immigrants on the public sector, and suggests that immigrants consume more in public services such as education, public assistance, health care, and infrastructure than they contribute in taxes. California Governor Pete Wilson champions this complaint in forceful terms:

> What are the results of this irrational and self-contradictory federal immigration policy which rewards illegal immigrants for violating U.S. law? We don't have to speculate about this. The results are painfully clear . . .

- Because federal law requires it, California state and federal taxpayers pay over a billion dollars per year to educate illegal immigrants.
- Because federal law requires it, California state and federal taxpayers pay well over 3/4 of a billion dollars per year for emergency health care of illegal immigrants.
- Because safety requires it, California taxpayers pay half a billion dollars per year to imprison or jail illegal immigrants who by themselves could fill 8 state prisons to design capacity. . . . We can no longer allow compassion to overrule reason.[1]

Even then-Governor Mario M. Cuomo of New York, a second-generation American known for praising immigrants, sounded a similar note in a 1994 radio interview, saying: "They are part of our strength. They will be a nourishment for our future. . . . They are also expensive."[2] Other critics of immigration are more apocalyptic. Glenn Spencer, a cofounder of Citizens Together, an anti-immigrant group in Southern California, warns: "What we're faced with here is an out-and-out invasion of the United States of America. . . . We've got to stop it . . . People don't want to admit it, but the numbers are there. We're essentially importing poverty."[3]

One manifestation of the popular image that immigrants are costly are the lawsuits recently filed on behalf of some states against the federal government for the "costs" of immigrants. Under the direction of Governor Pete Wilson, California has filed a number of lawsuits against the federal government seeking reimbursement for the costs of imprisoning undocumented felons and for providing emergency health care to undocumented residents. Governor Lawton Chiles of Florida has also ordered his state attorney general to sue the federal government to "recoup the money Florida is forced to spend on social services" for undocumented immigrants. Before she was defeated, then-Texas Governor Ann Richards, decided to join in the suit.[4] While some of the complaints are lodged specifically to recover the costs of undocumented aliens, others are aimed at legal immigrants and refugees as well.

These governors can point to several reports that purport to demonstrate just how costly immigrants—documented and undocumented—are. Two of the most publicized are a report prepared by the Internal Services Department of Los Angeles County and Donald Huddle's paper.[5] But the research of others, including that of the Urban Institute, questions the methodology and findings of these reports.

The popular image of immigrants as a drain on our public coffers does not agree with the way many economists have come to think about the role of immigrants. Immigrants are generally understood to contribute more in taxes than they consume in public services. In order to properly explain the effect of immigrants on the public sector, one must account for all taxes paid and services received over their life spans; on the average immigrants more than pay their way. According to President Reagan's Council of Economic Advisors, one has to consider not only the tax contributions of immigrant workers, but also the fact that the improved income of native workers who have benefited from immigrants means a reduction in benefit payments and an increase in tax payments. The "net fiscal spillover" is greater in the presence of immigrants than without immigration.[6]

Much of this is premised on the assumption that most immigrants are young, of working age, energetic, and motivated to succeed. They are a self-selected group imbued with the work ethic, arriving without aged dependents and with few children, and producing more than they consume. Of course one might not buy the assumption that all immigrants are highly motivated workers. Persons with drive and motivation might well seek their success at home. And many migrants without economic drive and motivation may simply be following a spouse or relative. But regardless of these concerns, the fact is that most immigrants are young and of working age, although we probably do need to know much more about different groups at different times to judge their motivations.

Using Social Security as an example, the benefits of young, hardworking immigrants are apparent. Since immigrants begin working soon after arrival, they begin adding to the Social Security fund immediately. Their own eventual receipt of benefits dozens of years later does not negate the immediate benefit to native workers. By the time the immigrant retires, her children are contributing to Social Security, and a dollar paid out in the distant future is worth less now.[7] So native workers receive a "one-time benefit" from immigrants who become instant workers and contributors.[8] Thus, a recent analysis of the Social Security system reveals that largely immigrant Asian Pacific American and Latino populations contribute more and receive far less in transfers from the Social Security system than their white counterparts; indeed, without Latino and Asian Pacific American contributions, the precarious Social Security system would be even more shaky.[9]

Immigrants: The Nation's Benefactors

Before launching into a description of recent methodology wars, consider a review of public sector costs conducted through 1991. Generally speaking, national studies which took into account all levels of government reveal that immigrants are not a financial burden on the native population. They put in more than they take out. As with their native counterparts, most of the taxes paid by immigrants go to the federal government. The understanding is that many of these federal tax dollars are returned to the states in the form of bloc grants for various programs. State studies were mixed, because some states take on more responsibilities than others. Analyses at the local level found that all residents—citizens and immigrants alike—were a net fiscal burden.[10]

Consider also a commonsense framework espoused by economists concerning the efficiency, human potential, and economic stimulation provided by immigrants.

IMMIGRATION AS WELFARE-ENHANCING

Immigration is almost always beneficial if one looks at the big picture. The reasons are standard (i.e., the efficient flow of labor allows countries to specialize in comparative advantage production, as individuals with those specialized skills emigrate to take advantage of different countries' areas of specialization). Pursuant to market principles, output increases and productivity improves with immigration in a competitive economy. Restrictions on immigration might be inefficient overall, even though they might benefit certain low-wage native workers, or for that matter, more skilled workers.[11] Beyond efficiency, the increased business profits from immigration can foster further investment which leads to even more growth.

IMMIGRANTS, THE STOCK OF USEFUL KNOWLEDGE, AND HUMAN POTENTIAL

Perhaps the most important quality that immigrants provide is their varied "contribution to our stock of useful knowledge." The more minds available, the greater the sources of information, the greater the possibility for innovation and technology, and thus the greater the potential for increased productivity. Recent studies of Silicon Valley show that our nation's leadership in the high-tech industry is directly related to the creativity and ingenuity of immigrant engineers and entrepreneurs.[12] Variety is a key to invention, and immigrants bring a variety of perspectives.[13] The fact that immigrants come as young adults with several productive years ahead of them, and from different countries, means that their contributions will likely be immediate (i.e., the first generation's one-shot contributions to Social Security) and varied. This distinguishes immigration's contribution to the stock of knowledge and human potential from that resulting from mere population increases among natives.

Bigger and more variety are better where population is concerned. This notion—that the bigger and more varied the population, the greater the scientific knowledge and output—could explain why the United States produces more scientific knowledge than, for instance, smaller and more homogeneous Sweden. Likewise, highly populated India, despite its poverty, has one of the largest scientific communities.[14]

INCREASED CONSUMPTION AND STIMULATION OF INVESTMENT AND TECHNOLOGY

In contrast with the Malthusian presumption that increasing numbers of people impose a negative effect on the income of all others, immigrants are better viewed as additional consumers who increase the market size for consumption goods, thus leading to greater production efficiency and investment. Increased numbers of consumers result in more research and development, new technology, a more specialized division of labor, and eventually an increase in output.

Although one must recognize the potential for diseconomies of scale due to congestion, in general population growth results in the development and adoption of better technology and innovation to overcome or avoid congestion. In fact some technology for avoiding those problems probably already exists, but society has to be pushed (e.g., with the threat of congestion) before adopting the new technology.[15]

1. THE LOS ANGELES STUDY

Pursuant to a 1993 resolution by the Los Angeles County Board of Supervisors, the Internal Services Department was asked to study the effects of four groups: recent legal immigrants, amnesty immigrants, undocumented workers, and the citizen children of the undocumented. The purpose of the study was to determine the costs and overall impact of these groups on county services and school districts, while also providing estimates as to government revenues, taxes, and fees attributable to the groups. But the study group acknowledged a major limitation imposed by the parameters set forth by the Board of Supervisors: research was limited to estimating costs and revenues in fiscal year 1991–92. Thus, the study represented a "snapshot analysis" of the fiscal impact of immigrants rather than a long-term picture.[16]

The researchers found that although the four groups comprised 25 percent of Los Angeles County's total population,[17] they accounted for 30.9 percent of the county's total costs (for the Department of Health Services, justice-related departments, Department of Public Social Services, and Department of Mental Health).[18] But these immigrants paid only $139 million in tax revenue to Los Angeles County, which meant, according to the researchers, that immigrants represent a net cost of about $808 million per year to the county. The report acknowledges that the groups accounted for $4.3 billion in aggregate taxes, for a net benefit, but that most of the revenue went to federal coffers. But by their calculation that figure is only 8.7 percent of the total revenues generated for all levels of government (county, state, federal) by the entire county population. Even considered separately, each group constituted a net cost at the county level. See table 1.

Although the LA Study has a number of problems, the report is forthright and readers can understand the basis and method of research. However, the bottom line is that its headline-inspiring conclusions as to costs are only based on estimates of *local* costs and revenues associated with immigrants. Thus, the only conclusion that the report is capable of arriving at is that immigrants, like the rest of the population, take more locally than they contribute locally. The costs and revenues analysis is likely to be different when total contributions—including those at the federal level—are considered. But this study did not measure total costs and benefits.

2. THE URBAN INSTITUTE: A DIFFERENT LOOK AT COSTS AND REVENUES

In response to the LA Study, researchers from the Urban Institute issued a separate report on Los Angeles County.[19] In calculating tax contribu-

TABLE 1. LOS ANGELES STUDY

Los Angeles County Population (1992)

Recent Legal Immigrants	630,000 (6.9%)
Amnesty Immigrants	720,000 (7.8%)
Undocumenteds	700,000 (7.6%)
Citizen Children of Undocumenteds	250,000 (2.7%)

Net County Costs (30.9% of total county costs)

Recent Legal Immigrants	$352 million
Amnesty Immigrants	$194 million
Undocumenteds	$308 million
Citizen Children of Undocumenteds	$ 92 million

Estimated Costs to School Districts (23% of total school costs)

Recent Legal Immigrant Children	$331 million
Amnesty Children	$123 million
Undocumented Children	$368 million
Citizen Children of Undocumenteds	$662 million

Total Revenues (8.7% of total revenues to all levels of government)

Recent Legal Immigrants	$1.9 billion
Amnesty Immigrants	$1.5 billion
Undocumenteds	$0.9 billion

Revenues Generated to Each Level of Government

County	$139 million
State	$1.2 billion
Federal	$2.6 billion
Other Local	$356 million

Revenues Generated to Los Angeles County (10% of total)

Recent Legal Immigrants	$ 56 million
Amnesty Immigrants	$ 47 million
Undocumenteds	$ 36 million

tions,[20] long-term immigrants (who came before 1980) and recent immigrants (who entered between 1980 and 1990) were separated. Recent immigrants accounted for 1.53 million residents, while long-term immigrants numbered 1.34 million, and natives 5.94 million. See table 3. Data were broken down (microdata) rather than combined (aggregate).

First, the Urban Institute researchers found that immigrants within LA County pay a total of $10.6 billion on the five taxes examined, compared to the LA Study's total tax contribution of $139 million. Recent immigrants account for $3.7 billion, representing 10 percent of the taxes for a group comprising 17 percent of the population, and long-term immigrants pay the remaining $6.9 billion, representing 18.1 percent of the taxes for a group comprising 15.2 percent of the population.[21]

Estimated revenues from recent immigrants exceed the LA Study estimates by $848 million (or 30 percent). This is particularly significant because the Urban Institute's recent immigrant group is really a subgroup of the LA Study's immigrant population. We would therefore have expected that the Urban Institute's estimates of total tax contributions of immigrants would be smaller than those of the LA Study. Instead, the Urban Institute calculation for this figure was one-third larger! This translates into $3,066 per person, as opposed to the LA Study's estimate of $1,637. This is because in some cases immigrants make dramatically higher tax payments per person than the LA Study assumed.

As to costs, Urban Institute researchers found that the costs to the county of recent legal immigrants are between $80 million and $137 million *less than* the LA Study estimate. In a procedural leap of faith, the LA Study attributed to *recent* legal immigrants the costs of county health and public social services used by *all* legal immigrants. That is, in these two categories, the data include costs incurred by both pre- and post-1980 immigrants. Apparently the Department of Health Services was not able to separate cost estimates for legal immigrants by date of entry. Now, if it were the case that these two types of services are consumed heavily by *long-term immigrants* (which seems reasonable, as the two categories are basically health and schooling), then clearly these estimates overstate the costs of immigrants as defined by the study. Not only is this procedure biased, but it is also inconsistent with the LA Study's exclusion of the tax contributions made by long-term immigrants from the contributions attributed by the study to recent immigrants.

Even using three alternative assumptions, the Urban Institute researchers disagree with the LA Study findings of costs. First, assuming that the per person cost for recent immigrants is the same as for long-term immigrants, the cost for recent immigrants turns out to be roughly the same as their population share. Second, assuming that the average cost of health and public social services for recent immigrants is twice as high as that for long-term immigrants, the cost due to recent immigration accounts for more than their population contributes, but is still 28.6 percent less than the LA Study estimate. Finally, using the (unlikely) assumption that the average cost of health and public social services is three times as high for recent immigrants as for long-term immigrants, the Urban Institute calculation of the costs of recent immigrants still comes out almost 23 percent lower than that of the LA Study.

The Urban Institute report points out several weaknesses in the methodology of the LA Study: (1) Studying only county-level costs and revenues neglects the fact that the federal and state governments frequently give transfer payments to the county governments. (2) The LA Study procedure or methodology invariably predicts that *every* group, not only recent immigrants, will use more in county services than they contribute to county revenues. This contradicts Los Angeles County's legal obligation to balance its budget and occurred because the LA Study omitted major revenue sources, including commercial property taxes.[22] (3) The LA Study incorrectly allocates the benefits of public goods evenly to all individuals. The benefits likely go disproportionately to businesses, which are predominantly owned by nonimmigrants. (4) Further, even if public goods are evenly distributed, calculating their costs per family rather than per person would be more accurate. Since immigrants tend to live in larger families, this would again bring the "cost" of immigrants down.

In addition to these criticisms, a number of other problems can be seen in the LA Study. First, the contributions of immigrants may be significantly underestimated by the study's failure to take into consideration: (1) any of the revenue (and the tax therefrom) generated by immigrant-owned businesses; (2) any "multiplier effect" from state revenues of immigrant-owned businesses that create jobs for residents; (3) estimated remittances to home countries;[23] (4) the extent to which certain immigrants (especially undocumented ones) pay their taxes and then do not file for their refunds; (5) any of the revenues paid while amnesty recipients were undocumented; and (6) the indirect benefits of immigration through economic growth (i.e., the effect on county revenue of immigrant consumer dollars circulating in the economy was not calculated). Likewise, the study's treatment of "long-term" immigrants as simply members of the overall population underestimates immigrants' tax contributions.

The exclusion of some of these factors is perhaps understandable, since some may be difficult to measure. However, it suggests that the findings have to be taken with an additional grain of salt. Just as the Urban Institute came up with a range of results given various assumptions about health and social service costs, one could come up with a measure of indirect benefits by deriving some type of "multiplier" on the taxes paid by immigrants to estimate their total contribution to the economy.

Second, the LA Study's number of immigrants suffers from two shortcomings. First, the study is not dynamic in nature. By lumping pre-1980 immigrants into the general nonimmigrant population, the study undercuts the long-term benefits that immigration might have. It only represents a "one-year snapshot" of the impact of a small proportion of immigrants on some county revenues and services. Indeed, the actual net benefit of an immigrant is the present value of her contributions less the present value of her costs. If the latter exceeds the former in early years, but the former exceeds the latter in later years, immigration might represent a net benefit to society—but this study would assess it as a net cost. The second numbers problem is the use of exact estimates for inexact numbers of immigrants. The study would have been fairer if ranges of numbers of immigrants had been used to present different possibilities rather than a specific number. Consequently estimate figures inspire little statistical confidence.[24]

Overall, the methodology of the Urban Institute report inspires more confidence, and demonstrates that the "net cost" of immigrants at the local level is not nearly as large as the LA Study suggests. Certainly, the federal government is the primary recipient of tax benefits from immigrants.[25]

3. THE HUDDLE REPORT AND RESPONSES

Donald Huddle's 1993 report and his op-ed pieces based on the report have received extensive national attention. With a good deal of fanfare, the report has been touted as the "first comprehensive study of the public sector costs of legal and illegal immigration."[26] He claims: "This report examines comprehensively the current yearly net public assistance costs of immigrants who have settled in the country since 1970 and, prospectively, the net costs of all post-1970 immigrants who are expected to be settled in the United States by the year 2002. Included in the estimates are the costs of public assistance to U.S. residents who are displaced from their jobs by immigrant workers."[27]

As the LA Study did, Huddle purports to examine both the costs and contributions of immigrants. He examined twenty-two federal, state, and local government assistance programs, including a package of ten county welfare and health services open to legal immigrants, refugees, asylees, and amnestied aliens, and fourteen programs open to undocumented aliens. He (1) calculated the annual nationwide cost per beneficiary—citizen and immigrant—for each program, using 1991 government data, or the most recent available, adjusted for inflation; and (2) determined the probability of immigrant assistance in each program.[28] He also looked at five federal and state assistance programs available to U.S. residents who might be displaced from jobs by immigrants. (However, the method of this adjustment was not made clear.) Data on poverty and public assistance use were taken from samples of the 1990 census and from other researchers.

To calculate revenues from immigrants, Huddle considered federal, state, and local income, sales, excise, and property tax contributions for legal, undocumented, and amnestied aliens. Tax payments of the various immigrant subpopulations were estimated by using individual and household income and tax data in the 1992 Statistical Abstract and the LA Study. By Huddle's calculation, immigrants pay 53.4 percent of their taxes to the federal government; 38.3 percent to the states; and 8.2 percent to local governments.[29] Huddle also believes that legal immigrants pay a considerably greater share of their taxes as income taxes than do undocumented ones, whose major revenue contributions are through sales and excise taxes.

As discussed earlier, Huddle tries to calculate the cost of public assistance to displaced U.S. workers in a questionable fashion, by assuming that for every hundred immigrant workers that enter the labor market, twenty-five low-skilled U.S. workers lose their jobs; and by estimating the average cost of assistance programs for a displaced worker. He claims that 741,000 low-skilled U.S. workers were displaced by undocumented immigrants, and another 265,000 by amnestied alien workers,[30] and that the one-year public assistance cost is $6.1 billion for the 1.06 million U.S. workers displaced by legal immigrants, and $5.8 billion for those displaced by undocumented and amnestied aliens. Finally, Huddle makes a number of growth projections.[31]

Huddle's main conclusions are: (1) the poverty rate of immigrants is 42.8 percent higher than for natives; (2) immigrants as a group are 13.5 percent more likely to receive public assistance, and their households receive 44.2 percent more public assistance dollars than do native households; (3) net immigrant costs in 1992 at the county, state, and national levels were $42.5 billion for the 19.3 million legal and illegal immigrants who have settled in the United States since 1970, compared to $20.20

billion in taxes contributed. See table 2. The biggest expense was for primary and secondary public education, followed by Medicaid and county social and health services.[32] Concluding that taxes contributed by immigrants were small (with his findings relying greatly on the LA Study conclusion), he claims that both legal and undocumented immigrants cost Texans more than $4 billion in 1992 for education, health care, and other services beyond what they paid in Texas.[33] See table 2.

In comparison to immigrants, the total cost of native-born consumption of the same federal, state, and local programs in 1992 was $595.7 billion, while their contribution to the same tax categories was $637.3 billion. The excess of taxes paid over cost yields a per capita surplus of $120 for the native-born population.

As to undocumented immigrants, Huddle found that in 1992 the 4.8 million undocumented consumed $10.1 billion in assistance and services, while they paid an estimated $2.5 billion in taxes. More than 70 percent of the $10.1 billion was for public education, county health and welfare services, and criminal justice. The average individual cost of public assistance for undocumented persons was $2,103, while per capita tax payments were only $519. Huddle attributed this deficit to "dramatically higher poverty rates (151 percent higher than native born rates), lower tax compliance, and [a] relatively high propensity to use public assistance programs and services not barred to them."[34] As to amnestied aliens, Huddle felt that they resembled the undocumented in terms of low skills and weak earning power, but are "no longer barred from public assistance."[35] Thus, he calculated their public assistance cost at $5.51 billion for 1992.

As in the case with the LA Study, the Urban Institute has issued a separate report responding to Huddle's findings.[36] This report (1) uses more widely accepted numbers of immigrants (e.g., the INS estimate of the undocumented population), (2) finds that Huddle grossly understates the taxes paid by immigrants, (3) argues that Huddle overstates the government benefits received by immigrants, and (4) disagrees with Huddle's hypothesis that immigrants displace native workers. As a result, the Urban Institute finds that immigrants are net contributors to public coffers. See table 3.

The Urban Institute points out four major flaws in Huddle's estimates of immigrant tax contributions. First, Huddle relies on the LA Study's per capita taxes for Los Angeles County though the earlier Urban Institute report had disclosed that that study understated tax collections

TABLE 2. HUDDLE REPORT

1. *Legal immigrants who have settled since 1970, including refugees, asylees, and other humanitarian entrants.*
   Estimated population size in 1992   11.97 million
   Net cost for 1992 $ 25.60 billion
   Net cost for 1993–2002 decade
   (in 1993 dollars) $482.10 billion

2. *Undocumented alien residents as of 1992.*
   Estimated population size in 1992   4.80 million
   Net cost for 1992 $ 11.90 billion
   Net cost for 1993–2002 decade $186.40 billion

3. *Amnestied aliens, formerly undocumented aliens legalized under the general and farm workers' amnesties of 1986.*
   Estimated population size in 1992   2.52 million
   Net cost for 1992 $ 5.00 billion

4. *Overall assistance and displacement costs. (Taxes Paid have been subtracted in totals 1–4.)*
   Net cost for 1992 $ 42.50 billion
   Net cost for 1993–2002 decade $668.40 billion

5. *U.S. workers displaced from jobs by immigrants. (The following costs are included in totals 1–4.)*
   Displaced workers in 1992   2.07 million
   Cost for 1992 $ 11.90 billion
   Cost for 1993–2002 decade $171.50 billion

6. *Total revenues from immigrants*
   1992 contributions $ 20.20 billion
   Contributions, 1993–2002 $283.20 billion

for immigrants by 30 percent. Huddle further used the contributions of 1980–90 legal immigrants to estimate taxes paid by 1970–92 immigrants, even though those who entered in the 1970s are known to have higher incomes than those who entered a decade later.[37] Second, Huddle estimates national immigrant income by erroneously assuming that since natives in Los Angeles earn more than average natives nationally, immigrants in Los Angeles must do the same.[38] Third, Huddle tries to adjust for the different levels of taxation in Los Angeles than found in the rest of the country by taking the ratio of national per capita taxes to per capita taxes paid in the county by natives and immigrants combined, but fails to recognize that per capita taxes paid depends on income levels as well as taxation levels, further underestimating taxes paid by immi-

TABLE 3. URBAN INSTITUTE STUDY

Response to Huddle
  [INS Estimate of Undocumented Population 3.2 million]
  Benefits from Immigrants
    Taxes paid $ 70.3 billion
  Costs for Immigrants
    Government services $ 41.6 billion
    Displacement $ 0.00
  Net Effect   + $ 28.7 billion

Response to LA Study
  Los Angeles County Population (1990)
    Recent Immigrants   1.53 million (17.4%)
    Long-term Immigrants   1.34 million (15.2%)
    Natives   5.94 million (67.4%)

  Federal and State Income Taxes for 1989
    Federal Income Taxes
      United States $432.9 billion
      Los Angeles County $ 16.4 billion
    California State Income Taxes
      California $ 15.8 billion

  Estimated Taxes Paid by Residents of Los Angeles County
    Natives $ 27.7 billion
    Long-term immigrants $ 6.9 billion
    Recent immigrants $ 3.7 billion
      (immigrants paid 27.7% of total taxes of LA County)

  Each adult paid in taxes
    Natives $6,902
    Long-term immigrants $5,386
    Recent immigrants $3,066

---

grants. Finally, in calculating revenue, Huddle leaves out five of the thirteen taxes included in the LA Study—FICA (Social Security and Medicare taxes), unemployment insurance, vehicle license and registration fees, and federal and state gasoline taxes—which account for 44 percent of the revenues from immigrants in Los Angeles. Both the Huddle and LA Study also omit corporate income tax, local income tax, commercial property tax, and utility taxes. Thus, using a corrected version of Huddle's revenue framework, the Urban Institute finds that immigrants contribute an additional $50 billion.

The Urban Institute finds that Huddle overstates immigrant costs by relying on the LA Study's overestimate of per capita service costs for recent legal immigrants (making his cost estimate higher by $2.5 billion); using inflated participation rates in such programs as Headstart (his costs for programs such as Headstart is thus overstated by $1 billion); applying a school attendance rate based on five- to seventeen-year-olds for immigrants aged five to nineteen (his estimate for schooling costs is thus wrong by over $2 billion); and using the national average for Medicaid payments as a measure for immigrants who tend to be younger than the average population (making his estimated costs off by $5 billion). While acknowledging that Huddle may have understated some costs by omitting Social Security payments to immigrants who entered after 1970, the Urban Institute argues that Huddle's displacement costs for native workers should be completely disregarded because every other credible study concludes that no such displacement occurs. Indeed, the Urban Institute submits that immigrants "actually create jobs through entrepreneurship and consumer spending."[39]

Huddle's report has some other serious problems. Perhaps most noteworthy is its failure to provide information on the bases of his calculations that may be duplicated or followed by other researchers interested in the subject. Second, many of Huddle's announced figures are statistically misleading. Estimating both the current and future tax contributions from immigrants on the basis of figures from 1992, a recessionary year, systematically underpredicts expected future tax contributions. The use of Los Angeles County data to analogize to the rest of the country is undoubtedly misleading, since the immigration population there has unique characteristics. Then again, the LA Study's estimate of per capita school spending ($4,672) is somewhat lower than Huddle's estimate ($5,603), even though Huddle uses categories of the LA Study to come up with his estimates.

Finally, the Huddle Report's announcement of the overall public costs of immigration—for example, $7.614 billion in 1992 since undocumented immigrants consumed $10.1 billion of public services at both the state and federal levels while paying a total of only $2.5 billion in taxes—is misleading. Ignoring for the moment the error of using a single-year snapshot analysis of the costs of immigrants and accepting the figures as accurate, there are strong reasons to question whether this comparison is even meaningful. First, since the U.S. economy has been plagued with a growing debt the past twenty years or so, a similar deficit between consumption and taxes would be found for *any* group. Thus, if we take any group, for example middle-class white Americans, and do a similar comparison as Huddle did, we would expect such a gap. In fact according to the estimates from the January 1993 Economic Report to the President, total government expenditures at the state and federal levels exceeded total receipts by $295 billion.

Moreover, Huddle's analysis ignores any future benefits from immigration. For example, it is almost certainly true that during any given year the consumption of public services outweighs the taxes paid by the children of U.S. natives. But it would be very misleading to derisively call this deficit "the cost of children." Also, Huddle's cost of immigration ignores the source of the deficit. While the concept of excluding immigrants to lower the "cost of immigrants" sounds logical, the costs can be reduced by raising taxes or reforming social programs as well. Huddle provides no guidance as to why either of these policies (or others) are inferior to restrictions on immigration.

Huddle's growth rate calculations and general thrust are reached by assuming that everything stays the same over time except for some exponential growth in the population of migrants. This exponential growth will obviously exponentially increase a present problem when projected into the future. This analysis overlooks immigrants' own incentives to move off public assistance, and the fact that immigrants tend to be younger than the average population and will improve their skill level and job prospects as they age. In other words, in a report such as Huddle's, what might be accurate for a short time horizon is not necessarily true in a longer time frame over which immigrants age, gain skills, and potentially become more productive. Broadening the time horizon and focusing on the particular (microeconomic) details opens up a range of alternative policy responses such as improved schooling, improved access to capital, and/or a jobs program.

Overall, large-scale, broad-brush (macroeconomic) analyses such as those by LA County and Huddle are arguably too general and lacking in an appreciation of the institutional context within which immigration occurs. For example, immigrants often have stronger social networks and family ties than other groups. These "family values" should affect how we view immigrants in comparison to other groups. They should also affect immigrants' ability to adapt and potentially improve their productivity. Once institutional details are introduced into the analysis, some of the generalizations in these reports may be put into proper perspective.

By way of comparison, the U.S. Department of Justice specifically asked researchers at the Urban Institute to examine the costs attributable to undocumented aliens for incarceration, public education, and emergency medical care in seven states—Arizona, California, Florida, Illinois, New Jersey, New York, and Texas.[40] Their estimates were carefully based on the same methodology and sources of governmental data for all states, to ensure that differences across the states reflected true differences in costs and revenues. They found that the incarceration cost of undocumented aliens in the seven states was $471 million in 1994, that $3.1 billion was spent on public education for undocumented children in 1993, and that $445 million was expended on Medicaid costs for undocumenteds in 1993. Yet the seven states only collected $1.9 billion from undocumented aliens in sales taxes, property taxes, and state income taxes. With 1.4 million of the estimated 3.4 million undocumented in the United States, California bears the brunt of the costs. But the researchers were quick to point out that they had not been asked to calculate federal tax contributions nor to measure the positive impact that such aliens might have on the states' economies as workers, business owners, or consumers.

Questioning Educational Costs

The Los Angeles Study also included public schooling in its complaints about the costs of immigrants. See table 1. But its calculation of schooling costs is also suspect. The researchers derived these figures by using 1990 census data to calculate the ratio of school-age population to population under age eighteen for people identified as either "Asian/ Pacific Islander or Hispanic." The ratio (0.68) was multiplied by the under age eighteen population of each of three immigrant groups to get estimates of school-age population. They then used another estimate (weighted mean) of school participation rates to estimate the participation rate (0.86). They subtracted the number of students in the three immigrant groups (331,000)[41] from 1,441,000, the total number of students in Los Angeles County public schools to get the number of other students. Then they multiplied the number of students in each group by $4,480 (the estimated cost per pupil in 1991–92) to get an estimate of total educational costs.[42]

Several problems can be raised with respect to the LA Study's schooling costs. (1) The study's estimates of schooling costs (public facilities costs) does not take into account the difference between fixed costs that have to be spent regardless of the size of the student body and costs that can vary with the size of the student body. Assuming substantial fixed costs associated with public schooling, then attributing a pro-rated amount to the new immigrant population and claiming that it represents "added" costs of education imposed by immigrants is inappropriate. To what extent fixed costs are fixed costs as opposed to variable costs, however, remains a question mark. This is an economies of scales notion. The cost of building a school is fixed irrespective of the number of immigrants; indeed, in a sense the costs per pupil is reduced with the addition of immigrant students. (2) The costs of educating U.S. citizen children are being added to the costs of educating undocumented children and the entire population is being labeled "illegal" for the purposes of cost calculations. (3) It is misleading to characterize education costs as accruing to LA County—they accrue to the school districts and are paid mostly by the state. (4) Also, the number of immigrant students and the cost per immigrant student have been overestimated. Since, as the study acknowledges, schools do not record the immigration status of students, the figures used by the LA Study are estimates based on questionable assumptions.[43] (5) The study infers an 86 percent public school participation rate among immigrants, based on an assumption about Asian and Latino students. But the dropout rate for Latinos and Asians is understated, thus inflating the number of students. (6) Multiplying the resulting numbers by the average cost per pupil is also misleading since LA Unified School District spends more per student in predominantly white neighborhoods.

Perhaps the biggest problem with the LA Study's characterization of schooling costs is its static nature. By taking a snapshot of a single year of costs, we lose sight of the purposes of education and of the need to view these costs as an investment in human capital that pays long-term benefits. By immigrating, an individual may earn free education in the United States, but at the same time she will be increasing her future earnings potential. As a result, the expected amount of *future* tax revenues contributed by the educated immigrant is likely to increase.[44] The short-run cost of educating immigrant children produces taxpayers tomorrow. The Supreme Court took this perspective in *Plyler v. Doe*,[45] by holding that undocumented children have a right to public education. The Court found it "difficult to understand what would be accomplished by creating and perpetuating a subclass of illiterates within our borders, adding to problems and costs of unemployment, welfare, and crime. Whatever savings are wholly insubstantial in light of the costs involved to these children, the state and the nation." Native students also benefit from the opportunity to interact with individuals from other countries.[46]

In their consideration of this human capital approach to education, Paul Ong and Linda Wing remind us of the multiple purposes behind our society's social contract to educate our children: to transmit knowledge, culture, and skills from one generation to the next, to enable children to care for the future. Only a foolish country would not do its best to educate all its children. Even the most cynical should realize that the payoff comes in terms of productivity and tax contributions. The fair way to view the so-called "cost of education" is as an investment in human capital. Only after considering the person's entire life—including the working years when the education pays off—is it fair to judge whether the educational expense was too costly. In order to begin an inquiry into the payoff, Ong and Wing cite the higher than average earnings and property tax payments of Asian Pacific Americans (which is tied to educational attainment). The implications are clear: educating the children of immigrants and immigrant children pays off in the long run.[47] In short, children should be viewed as investment opportunities.

IMMIGRANTS AND THE WELFARE DISTORTION

1. THE HUDDLE REPORT

Huddle's sensational findings—that the poverty rate of immigrants is 42.8 percent higher than for natives, and that immigrant households receive 44.2 percent more public assistance dollars than do native households—are also misleading and likely inaccurate.

First, by claiming that since 18 percent of immigrants and 12.6 percent of natives are below the poverty line, the poverty rate of immigrants is 42.8 percent higher than for natives, Huddle is statistically misleading. This percentage is not an absolute percentage of immigrants but the incremental percentage over natives; in other words, even using Huddle's figures, the difference is really only 5.4 percent. Likewise, Huddle uses a misleading and unclear calculation in his conclusion that immigrants as a group are 13.5 percent more likely to receive public assistance, and after adjusting for the amount received, are 44.2 percent more likely. He finds that *heads of households* in immigrant families are more likely to receive public assistance than are natives (5.9 percent instead of 5.2 percent)—which gives him his 13.5 percent figure. In reality, the difference is only 0.7 percent and the probability of an immigrant receiving public assistance is nearly identical.

Huddle's estimation of the probability of immigrant public assistance is particularly troubling. According to his report, the probability of immigrant public assistance was based on a national rate adjusted by an "estimation of the extent of variation in immigration rates from the overall rate."[48] If that estimation was taken from other studies, they are not identified by Huddle. Thus the figure is more likely Huddle's own calculation. While sometimes one has no alternative but to make such calculations, the margin of error is quite high, and should be acknowledged. In fact, because these estimates are what economists would call "point" estimates, little statistical significance is attached to them, and one should hesitate to make policy based on them.

The undocumented population is for the most part not eligible for the fourteen programs (i.e., Aid to Families with Dependent Children, or AFDC) cited in Huddle's calculation for assistance received by undocumented aliens. He also incorrectly assumes that amnestied aliens, unlike the undocumented, are no longer barred from public assistance, and thus includes all the federal, state, and local programs in calculating the costs of these immigrants. But amnestied aliens are not eligible for all these programs.

2. THE JENSEN STUDY

Other studies give a more in-depth, nuanced, and accurate sense of the public assistance usage of immigrants. Leif Jensen, a sociologist and anthropologist, analyzed immigrants' poverty levels and public assistance utilization by looking at Public Use Sample (PUS) Data from the 1960, 1970, and 1980 censuses.[49] Public assistance utilization was defined as income derived from AFDC, general assistance, and Supplemental Security Income (SSI).[50] For the definition and measurement of poverty Jensen used both an absolute and a relative measure.[51] He identified an immigrant family as one in which the head of the household was foreign-born.

On balance, Jensen concluded that immigrant families are not disproportionate users of welfare benefits, either with respect to their propensity to receive them or the amount of benefits received among welfare families. If anything, the evidence suggests that immigrants represent less of a drain on public assistance resources than do natives. Some of Jensen's most noteworthy findings were:

1. Absolute poverty among U.S. families declined sharply during the 1960s, but this decline was far less impressive among immigrant families. In fact, poverty increased among immigrant families between 1969 and 1979, probably because of an increase among post-1965 immigrants. That this was primarily driven by an increase among recent white immigrant families rebuts the assertion that the declining economic status of succeeding waves of immigrants is largely due to the changing racial composition of immigrants. Breaking down the data by race, significant increase in absolute poverty was indicated for white and black recent immigrant families, but not Latino and Asian recent immigrant families. Jensen's analysis shows that white and black recent immigrant families had the sharpest increase in poverty.[52]

2. Although the findings indicate that poverty among recent immigrants has increased, this does not mean that turning to public assistance and social services has increased. For the population as a whole, immigrant families (except recent immigrants) were significantly *less* likely to receive welfare benefits than otherwise comparable natives. And disregarding race, long-term immigrants are significantly less likely to receive assistance, while recent immigrants were *not* more likely than natives to use welfare. Recent black immigrants were significantly less likely and recent Asian immigrants (combined) were significantly more likely than their respective native counterparts to receive welfare, while recent white and Latino immigrants differed little from natives. Thus, new immigrants appear to be no more likely to receive public assistance than anyone else, even after accounting for racial differences.

3. Descriptive tables reveal that taken as a group, immigrant families (including refugees) had only minimally higher public assistance recipiency rates compared to native families. Looking at these immigrant-native comparisons by race revealed that immigrants had greater welfare receipt among Latino and Asian families, while natives had higher receipt among white and black families.

4. A comparison between 1969 and 1979 groups who had been in the country the same amount of time provided little support for the contention that recent immigrants in 1979 were disproportionately more

likely than their counterparts in 1969 to receive assistance. There were a few exceptions to this generalization. Recent Asian immigrants in 1979 were much more likely than recent Asian immigrants in 1969 to receive assistance, due in part to the influx of Southeast Asian refugees in the post-1975 period. Recent black immigrants were also disproportionately more likely to receive welfare than their 1969 counterparts.[53] Finally, the descriptive tables documented a *decline* in the receipt of welfare by the most recent group of Latino immigrants. A preference for friendship and kinship networks over government transfers would explain this negative effect of immigrant status on welfare receipt for Mexicans.

5. For the population as a whole as well as with race groups (except Asians) the greater total use of benefits by immigrants was explained by their tendency to live in states with higher welfare benefits. Some argue that immigrants prefer to live in states with higher welfare benefits in part to take advantage of these greater benefits. But various models revealed no significant effect of state benefit levels on the probability of welfare receipt.[54]

Jensen's work represents relatively rigorous research techniques to determine the incidence of both absolute and relative poverty among immigrants. One problem is that his data would now be regarded as fairly old (i.e., they do not really measure the "new" immigration subsequent to the 1980 census), and there is evidence of an increase in public assistance utilization over the years.[55] Also, his combining of much of the data—especially mixing refugees together with immigrants— produces some misleading findings, as refugees are the only major non-native population eligible to participate broadly in the nation's welfare state from the date of entry.

3. URBAN INSTITUTE AND WELFARE

Researchers at the Urban Institute have also looked at poverty and public assistance usage among immigrants. In addressing poverty, they demonstrate the differences among the immigrant communities. While 46 percent of recent immigrants (post-1980) from refugee-sending countries have less than a high school diploma, as do 75 percent of immigrants from the major source countries for undocumented immigrants, only 26 percent of legal immigrants fall into the low educational group, which is close to 23 percent for natives of the United States. Households headed by immigrants entering before 1980 have average incomes of

about $40,900, which is about 10 percent greater than native house-
holds. Recent immigrant households average only $31,100 ($23,900 for
undocumented and $34,800 for documented immigrant households).[56]

As to welfare, the Urban Institute researchers conclude that participation by immigrants arriving in the past ten years is lower than is
commonly believed. The 1990 census indicates that the share of recent
immigrants (i.e., those arriving between 1980 and 1990) using public
assistance (defined here as AFDC, SSI, and General Assistance) is 4.7
percent, slightly higher than the 4.2 percent rate for natives. But they
separated the foreign-born into those from "refugee countries,"[57] and
all others, and found that 15.6 percent of those from refugee countries
were receiving welfare. On the other hand, only 2.8 percent of immigrants from nonrefugee sending countries during the 1980s were reported to be using public benefits in 1989—much lower than the welfare
participation rate of natives (4.2 percent).

In further analysis, Urban Institute researchers have found that while
immigrants use welfare at slightly higher rates than natives, non-native
use is concentrated among two groups: elderly immigrants and refugees.
The higher rate among refugees is understandable since they are fleeing
persecution and have fewer economic or family ties in the United States
than other immigrants. There is also substantial overlap between elderly
and refugee benefit use, as refugees account for 27 percent of immigrants
over 65 who receive public benefits. Welfare use among working-age
immigrants (18–64) who did not enter as refugees is about the same as
for natives.[58] While elderly Asian Pacific immigrants maintain a higher-
than-average welfare use, they have an extremely lower-than-average
rate of Social Security use, suggesting that many were unable to enter at
an age that enabled them to earn Social Security credits as workers.[59]

In sum, welfare use among recent arrivals is largely concentrated
among refugees, who have strong equitable claims to its receipt. Furthermore, welfare use among the overall foreign-born population is margin-
ally higher than the native population, but when we account for social
and economic characteristics, immigrant households are no more likely
to receive public assistance than native households.

4. GEORGE BORJAS

With this understanding, recent findings by George Borjas of higher-
than-average welfare use among immigrants can be placed into context.

When his data were broken down by country of origin, those from Vietnam had a high rate, but the rates for immigrants from the Philippines, China, and India were about the same as that for natives. The welfare rate for Korean immigrants was only half that of natives.[60] Furthermore, there may be some concern with his data source: the Survey of Income and Program Participation (SIPP). The SIPP surveys only 50,000 persons in 20,000 households, with an emphasis on program participation. The sample size is relatively small and its Southeast Asian category includes only Vietnamese. In fairness, another data source such as the Current Population Survey (CPS) ought to be reviewed as well. The CPS survey includes Cambodians, Laotians, Thais, and Vietnamese in its Southeast Asian category and contains a question about parents' country of birth, which would allow an examination of the second generation as well. From the Borjas and Urban Institute findings, one can also infer that second-generation Americans use welfare at a rate much lower than the general population. This suggests that their parents used welfare only as a means of transition; therefore, high use among parents might be less of a policy concern since it did not become a way of life for the next generation of citizens.

5. GAO

In response to inquiries from members of Congress contemplating welfare reform in early 1995, the General Accounting Office reported figures that at first blush contravene those of Jensen and the Urban Institute. Since Jensen's data only went through the 1980 census, the GAO revelation that between "1983 and 1993, the number of immigrants receiving SSI more than quadrupled" was stunning.[61] And it reported that 6 percent of "all immigrants," compared to 3.4 percent of citizens, were receiving SSI or AFDC in 1993.

The GAO report received immediate attention from the media and was cited by policymakers looking for ammunition to support welfare reform intended at least in part to disqualify legal immigrants from welfare. Yet the GAO's reporting method was quite misleading. For example, while the GAO reported that 6 percent of "all immigrants" were receiving welfare, readers concerned with distinguishing refugees from lawful permanent residents had to look at the data carefully and make their own computations. Indeed, to the casual reader or listener, the GAO's use of the term "all immigrants" might be synonymous with "lawful permanent residents," but the GAO was using the term to include refugees, lawful permanent residents, and those permanently residing "under color of law" (deportable aliens whose departure is of low priority to the INS). The GAO's terminology was misleading because many people distinguish immigrants from refugees. Using figures available in different parts of the GAO report, when one separates lawful permanent residents for independent calculation, as the Urban Institute researchers attempted in their report, probably fewer than 5 percent of lawful permanent residents receive welfare compared with 3.4 percent of citizens.[62] But the 5 percent figure is probably still too high, because GAO researchers acknowledge that the lawful permanent resident numbers likely include individuals who first entered the country as refugees and who subsequently applied for and received lawful permanent resident status. Furthermore, the number of lawful permanent resident recipients was also based in part on estimates made by the Congressional Budget Office of which current citizen recipients had once been immigrants.[63]

These studies underscore the fact that the use of public programs (e.g., low-income assistance, social insurance, education, and health services) or public services (e.g., fire and police protection) by immigrants does not impose any unusual fiscal burden on society. Although individuals vary, while an immigrant's demands (and that of her family) for public education and other services may grow over time, so will the immigrant's ability to pay for those services. In fact, the presence of immigrants may actually lighten the burden on natives of financing public programs and services, given the productivity, age, and family composition of immigrants.[64]

The Reagan Council recognized that international migrants pay their own way from a public finance standpoint. Most come to the United States to work; government benefits do not serve as a major attraction. Their initial dependence on welfare benefits is usually limited, and they finance their receipt of Social Security retirement benefits with years of contributions.[65]

These empirical wars demonstrate the complexity of determining the exact contributions and costs of immigrants. However, they strongly demonstrate that, in the aggregate, immigrants are net contributors in the public sector. And as with comparable native groups, they consume more than they contribute at the *local* level, but do so at a much lower rate than headlines trumpeting the LA Study or Huddle Report findings would have us believe. Likewise, the weight of the evidence demonstrates that immigrants are no more likely to receive public assistance than natives, yet another contradiction of the popular media image. The fact that the bulk of immigrant taxes go to federal coffers must be considered in evaluating the true "cost" of immigrants, but does not lend support to restrictions on immigrant access to public services or to the United States itself. Instead, that is an issue that state governments must work out with the federal government.

UNDOCUMENTED IMMIGRANTS: THE GREATEST NET CONTRIBUTORS

The concern that the undocumented population will swallow up the social service system may be totally erroneous. Undocumented immigrants may contribute more than documented immigrants because the participation of undocumenteds in social services such as old-age entitlement is insignificant.[66] Since many undocumented workers enter without their families, they are much more economical than low-wage workers with families.

As President Reagan's Council of Economic Advisors noted, undocumented immigrants "may find it possible to evade some taxes, but they use fewer public services."[67] This is not surprising since undocumented immigrants are ineligible for most public benefits. Among the few programs for which they are eligible are emergency medical care under Medicaid (if they are otherwise eligible) and the Women Infant and Child nutrition program.

Likewise, immigrants who were given amnesty under the 1986 legalization law (IRCA) and those granted Temporary Protected Status under the Immigration Act of 1990 (temporary refuge from countries in the midst of civil strife) are barred from most federal benefit programs. Those who were legalized under IRCA's five-year-prior-residence provision may not receive most federally funded public assistance programs, including AFDC, Medicaid, and Food Stamps for a period of five years. Those who were legalized under IRCA's Special Agricultural Worker program face the same restrictions, but may receive Food Stamps.[68]

In addition, even before the recent changes in welfare, legal permanent residents were effectively barred from most cash assistance programs during their first five years in the United States because during this period their sponsor's income was "deemed" to be theirs when determining eligibility for public benefits.[69] Under certain circumstances, they can also be deported if they use public benefits during their first five years in the country. And their use of public welfare can hinder their efforts to bring their relatives into the United States.

The only major non-native population eligible to participate broadly in the nation's welfare state from the date of entry is refugees. However, refugees only represent roughly 10 percent of newcomers entering each year. Because they are fleeing persecution, their departure is usually unplanned; and because they often arrive traumatized by war, providing them with support upon arrival makes sense.

Undocumented aliens contribute in another way. Undocumented farm workers enable many U.S. crops to remain competitive with those of other countries. Even though restricting such labor might encourage mechanization, the result could be increased farm production costs. Since capital-intensive production is not necessarily more cost effective, competitiveness could suffer, thereby endangering more jobs and raising consumer prices.[70]

Of course the line between appreciating and exploiting undocumented workers may be murky. This issue is addressed more fully in chapter 7.

IMMIGRANTS AND CAPITAL

Implicit in the LA Study's complaint about educational costs is the general concern that immigrants benefit from public capital and assets provided by native workers. Before viewing immigrants as opportunists, one might distinguish "production" capital used by immigrants on the job from "demographic" capital, or governmental expenditures on public services such as schooling or health care for which increased use by immigrants would impose additional costs. As for production capital, immigrants actually boost capital investment rather than dilute it. Some immigrants may also bring production capital with them for investment. The results would be different if immigrants worked mostly in the government sector because in that case immigrants would benefit as much as natives.[71] However, citizenship restrictions on all federal jobs and on many state jobs preclude this possibility.

In terms of demographic capital associated with the public sector, much of public capital's costs have already been expended or "sunk." Therefore immigrants' use of this capital will not affect natives unless a "congestion" or overcrowding effect exists. This effect, however, will not occur with all forms of expenditures on public services. For example, most federal capital (e.g., intercity highways, space exploration, and the Statue of Liberty) are public goods rather than demographic capital. The use of these examples of public capital by natives is not affected by immigrants. But most state and local capital (e.g., schools and hospitals) are demographic and subject to congestion. More immigrants may cause more need for such capital if "service standards are not to fall." It does "cost" natives to equip immigrants with demographic capital, but this cost is smaller than the benefit natives get from immigrants whose use of welfare services is low and contribution of taxes high.[72]

Whether the presence of an immigrant has a favorable or unfavorable effect on natives with respect to a particular public asset is of little relative concern. Although public assets can be valuable, the value of the attached public debt can be significant as well. The immigrant not only shares the public asset, but also shares the obligation to repay the public debt.[73]

The Contributions of Immigrant Entrepreneurs

A glaring oversight in the highly publicized studies that purport to calculate the costs and revenues of immigrants is the lack of information on the economic contributions of immigrant entrepreneurs. However, a series of recent studies have initiated an attempt to quantify this important part of the economy. Recent immigrant entrepreneurs from the Middle East, Latin America, and the Asia Pacific region have continued the pattern established by earlier immigrants and refugees from Europe. In fact, although the 1992 uprising in South Central Los Angeles often highlighted the impact on Korean American businesses, at least a third of the businesses affected were Latino-owned. Total sales and receipts of Asian Pacific American-owned businesses alone in the late 1980s were over $33 billion annually, with a payroll of $3 billion and over 350,000 employees. And while many Asian Americans may be best known for their "mom and pop" stores and while recent refugees from Cambodia and Vietnam have come to dominate doughnut stores and manicure shops, Asian Pacific American entrepreneurs have played an instrumental role in the success of Silicon Valley's high-tech industry. Their background has also helped to attract about $300 million a year in venture capital investment from abroad.[74]

The contributions that immigrant entrepreneurs make to local taxes by creating businesses that generate sales taxes, improving property values—thus raising property taxes, and creating employment—thereby increasing income taxes are no doubt significant. And the psychic values that these businesses bring to sections of inner cities that they have helped to rejuvenate are likely incalculable.

IMMIGRANTS, TRADE, AND A GLOBAL PERSPECTIVE

1. IMMIGRANTS AS A FORM OF TRADE BETWEEN NATIONS

As with the international trade in goods, services, and financial claims, international migration connects domestic and international markets. The free flow of resources in response to market signals leads to specialization by countries in their areas of comparative advantage production, and thus produces efficiency and economic gains for both producers and consumers. Both parties to an exchange of people, goods, and capital gain from trade and, in the absence of restrictions, the exchange will continue until the potential benefits are exhausted. The movement of labor across borders can be a partial substitute for the movement of goods and capital. When international trade in goods or capital flows is hindered, pressures are heightened for people to migrate instead.[75]

Consider an example offered by Alan Sykes in which one country is endowed with more capital relative to another. If trade were allowed, comparative advantage would predict that capital-intensive goods would be produced in the capital-rich country and labor-intensive goods in the labor-intensive country, leaving no incentive for immigration. However, if trade between the countries were constrained or completely absent but migration were allowed, laborers from the labor-wealthy country could exploit the high returns to labor in the capital-intensive country for producing the labor-intensive good that is not available on the international market. As such the immigrants represent an opening of trade between the immigrant group and the capital-intensive country—a type of international trade between countries that subverts tariffs. This clearly benefits the host country, benefits the immigrants, and probably hurts the labor-abundant country until it overcomes some of the original constraints to trade between the two.

In the presence of trade, however, the situation may change. In general, the influx of immigration could help or hurt the host country. Though no general conclusion is possible, the models with trade included arguably tend to reinforce the conclusions of the models without it. The former certainly do not provide any reason to suppose that the residents of the country of immigration would systematically lose as a consequence of the influx. On a more concrete level, however, two caveats must be considered. First, immigration is likely to benefit the owners of capital in the host country, since it creates the ability to compete in the labor-intensive good, thereby giving the host country a better "threat" point in trade. If the owners of capital are foreign, immigration can then turn things around on the host country, giving most of the benefits to the foreign owners. Second, if capital is more mobile than labor, then host country owners of capital would likely move their plants elsewhere even though keeping the plant in the host country and importing laborers is globally efficient. The loss borne by the host country is likely to surpass the gain in the country to which the capital was transferred. Thus, Sykes argues that whenever a factory that would have been best located domestically with foreign workers moves abroad due to immigration restrictions, a net loss occurs. If the factory were built domestically, the taxes that would be paid on the returns to investors in the factory would exceed the incremental costs of government services necessitated by its presence.[76]

2. THE IMPACT OF IMMIGRATION RESTRICTIONS ON COMPETITIVENESS

Concern for global economic competitiveness leads to little support for immigration restrictions. Arguments supporting immigration restrictions to protect jobs are no different from those in favor of protectionist trade barriers. The results are similar as well—costs imposed on consumers, investors, and other workers—even though the demand for some native workers may increase.[77]

In the presence of unfair trade practices, U.S. firms are often pressured to employ low-wage immigrant workers in order to remain competitive. Price competition in the international economy makes the use of low-wage workers attractive to those industries that must respond to such market conditions.[78]

3. EVALUATING IMMIGRATION AND ECONOMIC ISSUES GLOBALLY

Economists remind us that immigration may be viewed from a global as well as a national perspective. In considering economic policy, the "global" and the "national" perspectives may actually be in conflict. So even in the face of significant national unemployment in a host country, immigration to that country is not necessarily undesirable from a global welfare perspective, unless the immigrants are close substitutes for the chronically unemployed.

The national welfare benefits immediately from the immigrant who is excluded from welfare payments until some time after she pays taxes. A large country such as the United States that is attractive to immigrants enjoys a competitive advantage in the international labor market that can be exploited in the form of immigrant admissions.[79]

The Department of Labor reminds us that immigration has always been a vital part of the "internationalization of the U.S. economy:"

> The timing, direction, volume, and composition of international migration, therefore, are fundamentally rooted in the structure and growth of the regional economy in which the United States is most actively involved. Flows of labor occur within an international division of labor with increasingly integrated production, exchange, and consumption processes that extend beyond national boundaries. Within this international division of labor, sectors of national economies become integrated into international production processes and specialize in particular tasks. At different historical moments, a country may be an exporter of labor and/or capital, or a net importer of such resources and a leader in the export of manufactured commodities.[80]

Unquestionably, the volume and nature of immigration to the United States have been largely influenced by the role of the U.S. market in the regional and global domains.

chapter 6

Contextualizing Immigration

Whether intentionally or not, many who subscribe to restrictionist views today ignore the largely positive economic data about immigrants. Laying the blame for unemployment levels and the fiscal crises in our local governments and schools on immigrants is hard to resist. To restrictionists, the source of these problems is easily identified: too many immigrants cross our borders, take our jobs, and sap our coffers. And the solution seems easy: enact restrictive laws that increase border patrols, that complicate the lives of the undocumented who are already here, that reduce or halt legal immigration, and that block legal immigrants from receiving public benefits. Seems simple enough. After all, fewer undocumenteds mean less job competition, less strain on local economies, and relief for our budgetary crises.

Unfortunately, things just aren't that simple. Certainly, we hear anecdotes of immigrants displacing natives from jobs, depressing wages, and increasing the need for public welfare-related services. But beyond the fact that the evidence with which to accuse immigrants of hurting the economy is simply not there, we really should ask ourselves whether restrictive immigration policies mask the actual, more complex questions about how labor markets and fiscal policies stimulate the movement of people. In fact, the story of immigrants' impact on our economy is much brighter than proponents of restrictive immigration policies advance, and, as we have seen in the previous chapters, a strong case can be made that immigrants, documented and undocumented, improve the economy. In short, we should analyze and understand why people relocate and how jobs are created and lost before we start pointing fingers.

Until we can understand the *real* causes of our fears about job loss and public bankruptcy, we cannot evaluate immigrants' actual collective role in our economy. In this chapter I raise some preliminary points on economic issues in the hope of placing the immigration debate in proper perspective. Since California seems to be the hotbed for most of the anti-immigrant fervor today, I begin by examining the genesis of such hostility: its shaken economy and strained budget. I examine the loss of jobs that the country experienced in recent years and the globalization of the economy as the probable cause. Finally, I counter arguments from immigration opponents who say that like Japan, we can operate our economy quite well without immigrant workers.

The California Economy

The economic situation in California has been used to foment anti-immigrant hysteria. During the first half of the 1990s, the state endured a monumental fiscal crisis and its worst recession since the Great Depression. Throughout this period a state budget deficit persisted, and from 1990 to 1993, California lost more than half a million jobs.[1] Anti-immigrant sentiment was bolstered by these economic woes. Many restrictionists, including Governor Pete Wilson who was facing an uphill battle for re-election in 1994, blamed immigrants for much of the crisis. His views on the costs of immigrants and his advocacy for the overwhelmingly popular Proposition 187 propelled Wilson into the governor's house for a second term.

While the California economy is changing, the anti-immigrant rhetoric is not. Opponents of immigrants continue to blame immigrants for job losses and budget problems in spite of reports that jobs lost during the recession will soon be recovered, the unemployment rate is falling, state revenues are expected to produce a $1 billion surplus in 1996, sales of homes are on the rise, and Wall Street rating agencies have raised the state's bond rating for the first time since the 1990 recession began.[2] For some, the economic argument is simply an excuse for social and racial complaints that they have about immigrants, invoking whatever plausible argument they can against immigrants. Others who have relied upon economic concerns in good faith might begin to rethink their position in light of the more positive economic picture. But they may continue to cling to the economic complaint because what may be rosy to economists has not translated into better schools, job security, better wages, and better city services in their day-to-day lives.

However, even the casual, thoughtful observer might have some questions about the relevance of blaming immigrants. After all, with the effects of the Proposition 13 taxpayer revolt still lingering, the highly publicized cutbacks in defense industry contracts still stinging, and the sluggish economy across the nation—even in places that have few immigrants—one might wonder whether the accusatory rhetoric leveled at immigrants for California's economic difficulties is a bit overblown.

THE EFFECTS OF PUBLIC DISINVESTMENT

An analysis of the state's economy by the Center on Budget and Policy Priorities provides us with a better understanding of the true origins of the state's current fiscal crisis.[3] In the 1950s and 1960s, the state of California and its local governments made substantial investments in public services by creating an outstanding elementary and secondary school system and developing other infrastructure projects. These actions provided a solid foundation for economic growth, a good quality of life, and a wonderful image as a state in which to live or operate a business. But since 1970, when the state began to scale back on public spending, many of these advantages have been squandered.

The depth of California's investments in the 1950s and 1960s may have temporarily hidden the results of the public disinvestment after 1970, but now the adverse effects of disinvestment are becoming increasingly apparent. In 1992, the California Business Roundtable pointed out that low public sector investment in general impedes private sector productivity growth.

More specifically, California has failed to make adequate infrastructural investments over the past thirty years. Today, Californians must make do with an infrastructure—roads, bridges, sewers, other utilities, and schools—that ranks in the bottom third of the states. The recent fiscal crisis has derailed plans (such as the State Transportation Improvement Project) to rebuild portions of the infrastructure pursuant to 1990 voter initiatives.

Plumbing the origins of the state's fiscal crisis may present a chicken-or-egg problem: which came first, a depressed economy or the decrease in public spending? Regardless of the answer, economists and business leaders agree that the impact of Proposition 13 on local government revenue has affected the overall quality of life in California, which in turn has damaged economic growth. Local governments play an important function in affecting people's quality of life—for example, with regard to public safety, roads and parks, libraries, cultural facilities, and health care to the indigent. Because of Proposition 13, county property tax and general purpose revenues were lower in fiscal year 1988–89 than in fiscal year 1977–78, even though the state's population rose 27 percent during that period. City revenues per person were 17.5 percent lower in 1987–88 than in 1977–78. Although most of the reduction in city revenues resulted from a decline in federal aid, California cities could not readily replace lost federal funds because of Propositions 13's restrictions on their revenue-raising ability.

At the same time, local governments have become overburdened. In 1983, the state transferred the responsibility for serving medically indigent adults to the counties. In 1989–90, state funds to counties for defraying these costs covered less than 60 percent of the total. Actions to close state budget deficits during the recent fiscal crisis also shifted the burden of funding education to local governments. From 1992 to 1994, about $4 billion in property tax revenues was shifted permanently from counties and cities to school and community college districts. But new local government revenue sources replaced less than half the property tax revenues lost in those two years.

TAXING AND SPENDING POLICIES THAT CRIPPLE

Botched tax policies and uncontrolled hidden spending create a major hurdle to the state's ability to return to adequate levels of investment and social support. These problems include poorly controlled spending buried in the tax code, which has lowered the revenues available for other priorities; a sales tax limited to tangible goods that covers a shrinking proportion of consumption; and a property tax, hampered by Proposition 13, that will not allow counties and cities to compensate for cuts in federal and state funding.

First, the state assembly has increasingly relied on spending programs that operate through the tax code, often referred to as "tax expenditures." They are the least scrutinized portion of the state's budget, even though their effects on both the state budget and the recipients of the expenditures are equivalent to other spending programs. For example, when the state provides a subsidy in the form of a tax credit to parents who pay for child care, it has the same effect as giving parents a check for that amount of money. These tax expenditures are a significant share of state spending. In 1992, when general fund expenditures were more than $43 billion, another $20 billion was spent through tax expenditures—more than the combined general fund spending on the Department of Education ($16.4 billion) and the Department of Corrections ($2.4 billion).

Yet tax expenditures are rarely viewed by policymakers as spending programs that merely substitute for on-budget programs provided for in the state's budget. In fact, attempts to reduce spending through the tax code are considered tax increases, while proposals to increase spending through tax expenditures are presented as tax cuts. This is particularly important considering California's supermajority requirement for raising taxes. While a simple majority is needed to institute a tax expenditure, reducing or eliminating an inefficient or ineffective tax expenditure is considered a tax increase and requires a two-thirds vote. Thus, initiating these spending programs is far easier than limiting them. Further, unlike direct spending programs, tax expenditures are not scrutinized annually or compared with on-budget spending to determine whether they are an efficient use of scarce resources. A tax expenditure that begins to fail the test of good policy is far less likely to be changed than a similar on-budget spending item.

Partly for these reasons, California's tax expenditures have grown rapidly, even during the recent fiscal crisis when policymakers held overall spending to a low rate of growth. While on-budget general fund spending grew at an average annual rate of 4.1 percent between fiscal years 1985–86 and 1993–94, spending through personal and corporate income tax codes grew at an estimated annual rate of 7.8 percent. Had tax expenditures been held to the rate of growth of on-budget spending since 1986, California would have had an additional $4.2 billion to spend in 1993–94.

As a result, California maintains a number of tax expenditures that assist, directly and indirectly, middle-class and wealthy taxpayers. For example, the deduction for mortgage interest is widely viewed as an appropriate way to help families improve their living conditions through home ownership. Four million state tax filers benefit from this deduction. But in 1990, more than one-third of the $2.5 billion annual subsidy—or about $850 million—went to the 4 percent of California taxpayers with incomes above $100,000. Also, California completely excludes Social Security payments from taxation, regardless of the recipient's income. The state loses approximately $200 million annually by not following the federal rule requiring higher-income recipients to pay tax on some of their benefits. Yet another example: although California effectively imposes no taxes on inheritance, it forgoes $200 million annually in taxes by allowing heirs permanently to avoid capital gains taxes on the increase in the value of assets before they were inherited, no matter how large the estate.[4]

A second overarching problem is that state taxes are unresponsive to economic growth, changes in population, and federal policy. Two problems are particularly serious. One is the shift from a production to a service economy, which has resulted in weak sales tax growth in states such as California that tax primarily tangible goods. The other is the decline in the role of the property tax, which has forced state and local governments to rely on less stable and more regressive taxes as well as other revenue sources, such as user fees. Californians have lost billions of dollars in revenue because of the dual weaknesses in the sales and property tax, coupled with the high rate of growth in spending through the tax code. In fiscal year 1993–94, the revenue loss totaled roughly $10 billion.

In a healthy tax system, sales tax revenues should grow with the consumption of retail goods and services, without changes in the sales tax rate. But in California, the growth of sales tax revenue has lagged significantly behind the growth in personal income; during the 1980s, personal income in the state grew at 8.6 percent per year, but sales tax revenue grew 7.4 percent per year—a full percentage point behind personal income growth. This significant gap is largely because the sales tax applies only to a narrow—and declining—segment of total consumption, namely, tangible goods, to the exclusion of most services. Between 1960 and 1990, the share of national consumption devoted to durable and nondurable goods other than food dropped from 34 percent to 29 percent, while the share of consumption devoted to services rose from 26 percent to 40 percent. California applies the sales tax to just nineteen services, placing it forty-third among states in this regard.

In 1978, when California residents enacted Proposition 13, they reduced the state's reliance on the property tax for financing local government services and schools; property tax revenues were cut in half. In the late 1970s, California raised $55 in property tax for every $1,000 in personal income. By 1990, the figure was $30. During the same period, the share of state and local taxes represented by property taxes fell from 40 percent to 27 percent. In a study of the effective 1992 residential tax rate—average property tax liability as a percentage of the full market value of property—in the largest city in each state, California was last in the nation. The state will not be able to rely on new construction to bolster property taxes because real estate activity has dropped significantly, and a solid rebound is not expected for some time.[5]

Much is made of the so-called economic impact that immigrant children have on the education budget in places such as California. But as noted in chapter 5, the fairer way of looking at these costs is as an investment in human capital that is repaid over the lifetime of the individual who actually becomes a net, working contributor to society. The calculation of schooling costs has been misleading in terms of public capital expenditures as well. The more accurate way of explaining the state's education budget woes is by revisiting matters such as Proposition 13. Although the decline of the educational budget in California was prompted by a variety of factors, the passage of Proposition 13 marked an even sharper decline. California, which was once one of the five highest states in spending per pupil, with high student performance, now ranks fortieth in spending per pupil, and student performance has dropped. California taxpayers pay only half the amount that New York and New Jersey pay per pupil.[6]

Thus, California's systemic fiscal problems have little to do with the influx of immigrants. Indeed, given the results of the various labor market and cost studies highlighted in chapters 4 and 5, a strong case can be made that immigrants have helped to ease the state's fiscal problems by contributing taxes, stimulating the economy, and providing a cheap, largely complementary workforce.

UNDERSTANDING THE LOSS OF JOBS

Meet Craig Miller. He was a sheet-metal worker for TWA making $15.65 an hour. Financially troubled, the airline laid Mr. Miller off in the summer of 1992. When he began to search for another job, he quickly learned the market value of a blue-collar worker with a strong back and a good work ethic but few special skills: about $5 an hour. Now this thirty-seven-year-old works behind the counter at McDonald's and drives a school bus part-time.

Craig Miller is not alone. For whatever reason—global competition, mechanization, specialization, consumer attitudes, marketing techniques, military spending, or inventive management styles—the U.S. workforce has undergone substantial change even in the last two decades. Although the economy is growing and American companies are prospering, job cuts are more numerous than ever. Competition between one another, rather than with immigrants is the real difficulty. Many American companies have become as efficient and modern as those in Japan and Germany, but several forces have emerged that continue to push corporations to shed workers. Advances in technology enable companies to produce much more with fewer employees. Price increases are hard to secure, and corporate America increasingly maintains profits by slicing labor costs. Finally, workforce reduction has become fashionable—the mark of a good manager. A typical headline reads, "Sara Lee to trim work force by 6%," in a story highlighting the layoffs of some eight to nine thousand employees in the corporation's worldwide workforce. The layoffs for this food and personal products conglomerate occurred in spite of "record annual sales and earnings." The Wall Street response? Sara Lee's stock went up.[7] Downsizing is not viewed as an economic problem by the powers-that-be, but rather as "part of an ongoing restructuring that is in some senses healthy for the economy."[8]

A number of factors account for the job loss. For the aerospace industry, the dual impetus for layoffs was continuing military cutbacks and reductions in orders from troubled commercial airlines. In the telecommunications field, sharper competition for market share caused significant discounting; labor cuts have helped the companies maintain profits. And overall, endless modernization helped corporate America produce substantially more than people can buy.

In the 1980s, the last era of job shedding, Rust Belt factories closed or modernized so companies could make the same number of cars, steel, appliances, machinery, and other products with a fraction of the old workforce. Over 6 million jobs were lost in 1994 and 1995, and the number of manufacturing jobs alone fell 8.3 percent from 1989 through February 1994. The reason: manufacturing jobs are influenced by technology, and every six years the number of product assembly workers needed is cut in half thanks to new technology. As advances in technology have reduced jobs, tens of thousands of others have moved abroad.[9]

At the same time, more jobs are actually being added; recent headlines even cheer the increase in jobs. Until about 1950, the migration was from the farms to the new "job multiplier" industries: railroads, automobiles, highway construction, aircraft manufacturing, and airlines. Now, the migration is to the service sector—retailing, health care, restaurants, finance, security, and similar jobs. These are the job-multiplier industries in late-twentieth-century America and they have, in fact, created enough jobs during the last decade or so to more than offset the cutbacks. In 1993, despite the cutbacks, 2 million people were added to the nation's total workforce. So to some, the layoffs and downsizing are not job cutbacks, but job "dislocation"—the dislocation being the time it takes a worker laid off from AT&T, for example, to find a new job, quite likely at lower pay. Over 200,000 jobs a month were being added in 1996.[10]

But the increases in job opportunities are deceptive. Despite lower unemployment—the Labor Department said that the jobless rate dropped to 5.3 percent by mid-1996—the dramatic restructuring of U.S. business has made for major changes in the job market. Work is more specialized, information is harder to come by, employers are smaller and exceedingly cautious about hiring. In most places, home builders cannot find carpenters, trucking lines scramble for drivers, mortgage bankers scrape to hire loan processors, but this is misleading. Although total employment might increase by 230,000 in a single month, many of these new jobs are temporary; moreover, eight million people are out of work, and many more can expect pink slips in the near future. Specialized training requirements and hard-to-find occupational niches complicate the job search. For example, three-quarters of new jobs in the late 1980s were at plants with fewer than five hundred workers. New service jobs are widely dispersed as well. Those midsized employers are more likely to occupy obscure suburban business parks than to blaze their names atop skyscrapers. Divining exactly what niche a company fills means looking at trade magazines, reading the business section of the local paper and, most of all, asking around.[11]

Thus, the economy's response to employment data can be puzzling and counterintuitive. As the Sara Lee example illustrates, in today's highly integrated global marketplace, economies can grow in size, company profits can soar, a stock market can rise, and yet many people can be unemployed or underemployed. Capital and technology are so mobile that they do not always create good jobs in their own backyard. In the middle of 1996, the nation's unemployment rate fell to 5.3 percent, the lowest level in six years. But this meant that the Federal Reserve would likely start raising interest rates to ward off inflationary pressures; economists believed that the Fed would worry that tight labor markets would trigger rising wage demands and higher prices. In response, the Dow Jones Industrial Average was down 113 points on the day the low unemployment rate was announced.[12]

The United States' unemployment and wage figures illustrate that we have made different choices than our industrialized peers. Broadly speaking, Europe and Canada have managed to keep wages and benefits rising for their workers, but at the price of relatively high unemployment for many who are sustained with generous unemployment insurance. The United States, which has been out of recession the longest, created many more jobs than Europe, but only by getting workers to take more low-paying jobs, thereby widening the gap between highest-paid and lowest-paid workers.

In the United States the unemployment rate currently holds at under 6 percent, during a booming economic recovery, while in Canada and Western Europe, it averages around 11 percent, with Spain topping the list at 23 percent, and Japan at a comfortable unemployment level of 2.9 percent. But that does not include many workers who are kept in make-work jobs as part of Japan's lifetime employment policies. Meanwhile, total compensation—wages, health benefits, vacations—for the typical American manufacturing worker has declined slightly or remained flat since the mid-1970s, while in Europe and Japan it has increased by 40 percent. In general, countries with higher unemployment sustain higher wages. Minimum wage levels tend to be higher in Europe, with cost of living increases and at least four-week annual vacations virtually guaranteed. Average manufacturing compensation in Germany is $26 an hour, while in the United States it is $16. Europe has comfortable social safety nets, which have left many workers preferring to stay on welfare rather than take the sort of low-paying jobs accepted by many workers in the United States. In most of the European Union, an unemployed worker can receive close to $1,000 a month indefinitely. But the Europeans and Japanese have done a much better job of developing apprenticeship and training programs for those between the ages of thirteen and seventeen who are not going to college. To former Secretary of Labor Robert Reich, the issue is whether "we [are] condemned to choose between more jobs but greater inequality and insecurity, as we have in this country, or better jobs, but higher unemployment and a thicker social safety net, as in Europe."[13]

The stratification of jobs in the United States means that those with a high school diploma are still stuck with low-end jobs. In Memphis, Tennessee, for example, at one time a high school graduate could secure a job with a $12– or $13–hourly wage at International Harvester or Firestone Tire and Rubber. But those companies have departed, leaving behind fast growing, lower-wage industries. Federal Express is now the biggest employer in town, and offers high school graduates twenty-hour-a-week jobs for $8 an hour. As a result of these types of changes, most high school graduates who plan to go straight to work are offered the same low wages, the same part-time hours and the same assignments in the restaurants, supermarkets, motels, and gasoline stations where they worked in after-school jobs as students. Nationwide in 1993, a quarter of high school graduates who did not go on to college and wanted to work were still unemployed in October, compared with 21 percent in the 1980s and 16 percent in the 1970s. Adjusted for inflation, the starting pay for people with degrees from four-year colleges has slipped a bit in two decades, but wages have plunged 25 to 30 percent for men with only high school diplomas and 15 to 18 percent for women in that category.

In sum, the nation's economy is producing 2 million new jobs a year, but they come with wages typically below $8 an hour, or about $16,000 a year, and without health benefits, opportunity for promotion, or promises that the jobs will last.[14]

Students have increasingly responded by going to college and vocational schools, although the current economy does not assure them job security. In 1993, almost two-thirds of high school graduates entered two- or four-year colleges, compared with only half in 1980. But the growth of low-paid, low-skilled jobs outpaces the growth of higher-skilled jobs in fields like health care and data processing. At the same time, industry is eliminating middle-management jobs held by college graduates, and those laid-off college graduates compete for blue-collar jobs, in turn displacing high school graduates.[15]

In short, U.S. industry shows systemic weaknesses, rooted in outdated, short-sighted modes of managing human resources that hamper the ability of many firms to adapt to a changing international business environment. In particular, the MIT Commission on Industrial Productivity has observed six weaknesses: outdated strategies; neglect of human resources; failure of cooperation; technological weaknesses in development and production; government and industry working at cross-purposes; and short time horizons.[16]

Today's skewed and inflexible job market grew out of forty years of industry practice. In the 1950s and 1960s American industry pursued flexibility by hiring and firing workers who had limited skills rather than by relying on multiskilled workers. Worker responsibility and input progressively narrowed, and management tended to treat workers as a cost to be controlled, not as an asset to be developed. Likewise with training: workers often receive limited training while on the job, typically amounting to watching a colleague at work. Even in firms offering organized training programs, in-plant training is usually short and highly focused on transmitting specific, narrow skills for immediate application. In other countries one finds a greater inclination to regard firms as learning institutions, where, through education and training, employees can develop breadth and flexibility in their skills, and acquire a willingness to learn new skills over the long term. In a system once based on the mass production of standard goods where cost mattered more than quality, the neglect of human resources by companies may have been compatible with good economic performance; today, this strategy plays a major part in the United States' productivity and concomitant employment problem.

Fortunately, not all industries in all locations create low-wage jobs. Although Jackson, Tennessee struggled through the 1980s with factory closures, its job market is now so tight that when a new faucet plant was proposed, the company extracted a promise from the chamber of commerce not to solicit new companies for half a year. A local factory-equipment company increased salaries for machinists 15 percent in 1994 to $15.62 an hour. The local bank created additional full-time teller positions paying $8 or more an hour; part-timers had been receiving $6. Across the nation, service sector wages may be a low $315 per week, but companies in Jackson are hiring heavily in the $575–a-week range, especially the computer literate.[17]

The neglect of human resources in the United States actually begins long before young Americans enter the workforce and has little to do with immigrants. In primary and secondary school they learn the fundamental skills they will apply throughout life: reading, writing, and problem solving. Yet cross-national research on educational achievement shows American children falling further and further behind children in other societies in mathematics, science, and language attainment as they progress through school. The school system, from kindergarten through high school, is leaving large numbers of its graduates without basic skills. Unless the nation begins to remedy these inadequacies in education, real progress in improving the country's productive performance will remain elusive.[18]

GLOBAL EFFECT OF INTERNATIONALIZATION OF THE ECONOMY

In defending his daring package of almost $50 billion in U.S. and international loan guarantees to rescue the Mexican economy in 1995, President Clinton explained what was at stake: "thousands of [U.S.] jobs," "billions of dollars of American exports," and "the potential of an even more serious illegal immigration problem."[19] His reasoning was based on what economists have come to understand—that an evolving global economy and trade and monetary policies may affect the movement of people far beyond the control of immigration policy.

Viewing the flow of immigrants and immigration restrictions in terms of trade and trade theory has many implications. Appreciating the emerging world economy assists us in understanding the flow of immigrants, as well as their role in the labor market. Circumstances and events in other parts of the world and the United States' role on the world stage are also relevant to understanding why people move to the United States. Shifts in the volume and direction of labor flows result more from the restructuring of international markets than from changes in domestic unemployment or production demands, or changes in immigration legislation. The structure of the U.S. economy and labor market also influences the demand for labor and the characteristics of workers who are attracted at different times.

The postwar history of the Del Monte fruit and vegetable processing company illustrates the wide-ranging effects of internationalization and its impact on local labor markets. Once a California-based business, by the early 1950s Del Monte had established major processing plants in fourteen states. Over the next decade, in anticipation of growing world demand, plants were also established in Canada, Italy, Brazil, Mexico, Costa Rica, Ecuador, Venezuela, Kenya, and South Africa. Changes in taste at home and uncertainties abroad prompted the company to develop new product lines and branch out into transportation services. By 1973, fewer than half the company's total sales came from domestically canned output, and the company was divesting itself of its unprofitable plants in this country. Correspondingly, domestic workers lost their jobs.[20]

The trends in the fruit and vegetable industry also illustrate how international competition influences jobs. Over the years, consumer tastes have changed in favor of fresh produce and frozen vegetables (rather than cannery-produced goods), and U.S.-owned operations in Mexico have taken over much of that market. Under present farm-labor practices, the cost of growing broccoli in California squares poorly against that in Mexico and Guatemala (15 cents per pound, compared with 5 to 6 cents). Local California canneries' profits have disappeared.[21] This has led to concessionary cuts in wages and benefits, eroding work conditions, and many closings. Between 1977 and 1986, 32 plants employing 23,000 workers closed. Ultimately, the price of produce in the field, rather than cannery labor, will decide the fate of the industry in California.

Agriculture is relevant to migration in a number of ways. In places such as California the industry continues to depend heavily on immigrant workers. But what happens in places like Mexico is important as well. In most Third World countries, peasants produce food for the nation, and rich farmers produce exports. In Mexico, the most fertile land is being used to produce exports. If agriculture were to collapse in Mexico, for example because of new competition from the United States, this could lead to a push for migration out of Mexico. This would lead to a workforce problem in Mexico and only exacerbate the local Mexican agricultural problem.[22]

Global competition and trade policies also have implications for the movement of peoples across borders and to other jobs. The go-go 1980s once masked unease over America's changed economic position. Now, in a time of massive layoffs that threaten to continue even as the overall economy improves, trade has become the focus of a debate on whether the United States is turning into a society of economic haves and have-nots. For example, the completion of the Uruguay round of the General Agreement on Tariffs and Trade (GATT) in December 1993 extended free trade principles to services, meaning more access to foreign markets for U.S. banks and telecommunications companies. But the changes may come at a price. Just as NAFTA is likely to chip away at low-paying U.S. manufacturing jobs, so too GATT is expected to hurt industries like apparel, where U.S. goods will be forced to compete with a growing flood of cheap imports. Thus, the AFL-CIO has concerns about GATT that parallel its concerns about NAFTA.[23] But GATT may result in more jobs in the exporting countries, easing emigration pressures.

International copyright agreements are another example. In return for agreeing to tough copyright protection and a more open climate for services, Asian countries have successfully pushed for concessions in another agreement, the multifiber agreement, which restricts U.S. imports of textiles and clothing from developing countries. Labor believes that the phaseout of these restrictions is also likely to cost American jobs.[24]

The first quarter report after NAFTA became effective began to shed some light on how trade policies influence jobs, and in turn immigration patterns. To the surprise of many economists and trade experts, imports from Mexico grew more rapidly than U.S. exports, cutting the U.S. trade surplus with Mexico for this period in half. U.S. labor leaders viewed this development as a threat to U.S. jobs, but the then U.S. trade representative, Mickey Kantor, believed the increase in trade would mean that jobs would be created. Many economists think that both nations are likely to gain jobs from increased trade. The clear message to emerge is that while some jobs are lost, others are helped or created. For example, Allied Signal (Autolite spark plugs), Texas Instruments, and General Motors have already demonstrated substantial gains and plan to increase their U.S. workforce.[25]

NAFTA has revealed other complexities of job creation. Within two years after NAFTA was put in place, Key Tronic Corporation, a manufacturer of computer keyboards in Spokane, Washington, laid off

277 workers and moved the jobs to a plant in Mexico, where wages were a fourth less. But the decreased manufacturing costs enabled the company to lower prices and win new orders; since keyboard component parts came from plants near Spokane, overall employment in the area actually increased. Exports to Mexico of many agricultural products, like lettuce and peaches, have risen since NAFTA lowered tariffs on many of those commodities. Lettuce was cheaper to produce in California using Mexican labor than in Mexico. But reservations about NAFTA persist, as the agreement places downward pressure on American wages and reduces jobs without providing sufficient help for displaced workers. According to the U.S. Department of Labor, by the beginning of 1996 about 60,000 were lost due to NAFTA, but 140,000 new jobs were created.[26]

Much is made of jobs being lost because of plant relocations abroad. These moves are commonly attributed to the supply of exploitable, low-wage workers abroad. But the National Research Council reports that increasingly U.S. manufacturers move abroad primarily to gain access to new markets, manufacturing processes, technologies, and components. Yes, in the 1970s and 1980s, many U.S. companies moved facilities overseas to take advantage of low wages, but these were mainly simple assembly operations. Today's high-tech, automatic manufacturing depends much less on human labor. AT&T has been producing consumer telephones in Singapore since 1984, but a recent study attributed the operation's success more to lower material costs than to cheaper wages. Moreover, foreign companies have been relocating here, thus belying the argument that U.S. labor costs are prohibitively high: examining automobile, consumer electronics, and semiconductor industries, researchers found that Japanese automakers have actually *moved to* North America and Europe in order to respond more quickly to market changes and consumer demand. For example, Toshiba began producing color picture tubes in New York in 1985 mainly to gain closer access to the U.S. market, and structured the plant to be its least costly operation.

The United States is not too expensive for manufacturing. Higher wages may be a factor, but our country offers features that companies most desire, including a large market of affluent consumers, skilled workers, a strong technological base, and a tradition of innovation. Unfortunately, not all U.S. manufacturers have learned to take advantage of these assets. Many have not adapted to a world in which quality, flexibility, and speed are essential. These failures put American jobs at risk. With broader vision, the United States can attract industry here, and our available workers can be an asset.[27]

The Johnston Tombigbee Furniture Manufacturing Company in Columbus, Mississippi serves as an example of globalization harnessed to help U.S. workers. The company entered into an agreement with a Chinese factory which quoted prices for chairs that were two-thirds lower than what it was paying in countries like Brazil. For Johnston Tombigbee, the cheap labor and materials in China are the backbone of an expansion strategy. Its furniture is made mostly of foreign parts. Seven years ago, the company faced collapse because of family warfare and weak management. But it has turned itself around through foreign manufacturing agreements, and many production jobs in its Mississippi operations have been saved.[28]

Just as many American industries and jobs may hinge on the globalization of the economy, the United States can influence economic conditions abroad through import restrictions, foreign aid, and debt repayment subsidies, as well as by supporting reforms in the policies of the World Bank and the International Monetary Fund. For example, the World Bank and the IMF contend that structural adjustment policies—including trade liberalization, devaluation, removal of government subsidies and price controls, "cost recovery" in health and education, privatization, credit squeezes, and increased interest rates—will reduce poverty by restoring economic growth. Critics argue, however, that the programs are in fact designed to meet the needs of industrialized countries by ensuring debt repayment and encouraging Third World countries to export cheap raw materials. Many nongovernmental organizations charge that structural adjustment programs imposed by the World Bank and the IMF have brought disaster to the working poor of perhaps a hundred countries.[29] These economic policies, which are often ignored in discussions of immigration policy, partly determine America's allure in the immigration market and influence the movement of migrants.

WE ARE NOT JAPAN

In response to pro-immigrant arguments that immigrants—especially low-wage, low-skilled workers—are necessary to our economy, restrictionists such as Peter Brimelow offer Japan as the counterexample of a country that has achieved economic viability without immigrant workers.

> The {???} factor is the explanation for the great counter-factual episode hanging like the sword of Damocles over contemporary pro-immigration polemics: the success of Japan since WWII. Despite its population of only 125 million and virtually no immigration at all, Japan has grown into the second largest economy on earth. The Japanese seem to have been able to substitute capital for labor, in the shape of factory robots. And they have apparently steadily reconfigured their economy, concentrating on high value added production, exporting low skilled jobs to factories in nearby cheap-labor countries rather than importing the low-skilled labor to Japan.[30]

In other words, we do not need immigrants because Japan does not need immigrants.

Brimelow correctly points out that labor and capital are often substitutable. However, he fails to appreciate the consequences of this relationship. Any increase in labor can be offset by a change in technological progress that makes the current labor force more productive. But innovation is simply one factor of production. Firms presumably find the correct mix of inputs to maximize profits and minimize costs. Thus, suppose an employer were to become disenchanted with the labor intensity of her apple growing business, and she wanted to "innovate" in a way that would allow her to reduce her total labor bill. She might invent a robot that could replicate the functions of a worker, or she might invent a device that one worker could use which would make him as productive as two.

The first thing to consider is what happens to her demand for labor. The result is not clear. Indeed, if the apple grower chooses the second option, the addition of the device is *complementary* to the use of labor, and it increases each employee's marginal product. Since it is profit maximizing for the firm to hire labor up to the point where the real wage just equals the marginal product of the last employee-hour, this may result in an *increase* rather than a decrease in labor demand.[31] Second, although substituting other factors for labor is *possible,* this does not mean that doing so is optimal. In any given case, the cost of capital innovations may exceed the labor savings that result.

In this respect, Japan may be quite different from the United States. The prevailing view among economists is that capital innovations are more likely to be optimal in Japan because it has historically had lower capital costs than the United States (as manifested in the prevailing interest rate). As such, investing may be optimal for Japanese business in industries where it may be suboptimal for the United States to do so. Furthermore, the cost of capital in Japan may in fact not be lower in the long term.[32]

Certainly, the cost of capital is important, but other factors are also of consequence to the long-term capital investment decisions of firms in Japan or the United States. The nature of the institutions that influence the supply of capital may affect investment decisions at least as much as the cost of capital.

A large and growing share of the capital of U.S. firms is owned by mutual funds and pension funds, which hold assets in the form of a market basket of securities. The actual equity holders, the clients of the funds, are far removed from managerial decision making. The fund managers also have no long-term loyalty to the corporations in which they invest and have no representation on their boards. (Indeed, legislation prohibits their participation in corporate planning.) Although some fund managers do invest for the long term, most turn over their stock holdings rapidly in an effort to maximize the current value of their investment portfolio, since this is the main criterion against which their own performance is judged. Firms respond to this financial environment by maximizing their short-term profit, in the belief that investment policies oriented toward the long term will be undervalued by the market and thus render them vulnerable to a takeover. At the same time, senior executives are motivated to maintain a steady growth in earnings by their own profit-related bonus plans and stock options. A chief executive whose compensation is a strong function of her company's financial performance in the current year will naturally stress short-term results. Explanations that cite the cost of capital and the sources of financing all tend to depict corporate managers as victims of circumstances, forced by external conditions into a short-term mind-set. Yet one can argue that executive ranks have come to be dominated by individuals who know too little about their firm's products, markets, and production processes, and who rely instead on quantifiable short-term financial criteria. These modern executives are more likely to engage in restructuring to bolster profits than to take risks on technological innovation.[33]

Beyond cost-of-capital issues, Japan has traditionally not faced many export barriers in sending intermediate goods to be assembled abroad (despite Japan's significant import barriers). Thus, in this sense, offshore assembly substitutes for immigrant labor. High export barriers (e.g., into Mexico) have partially kept the United States from being able to utilize the same potential advantages of specializing domestically in capital/skill intensive production. GATT and NAFTA become relevant in this regard.

The problem with discussing these issues as though Japan does not use immigrant workers is that the assumption is not true. Foreign workers started to flood into Japan in the mid-1980s, when Japan suffered serious labor shortages. Immigrants, eager to earn salaries that were "astronomical" compared to what they were earning back home, availed themselves of thousands of jobs in bars, restaurants, small factories, and construction. In spite of a recession, the demand for foreign labor in Japan has not eased. Employers have difficulty finding native workers to take low-paying and physically taxing work at construction sites and in factories. Many foreign workers do not have proper visas, and the Japanese labor ministry estimated the presence of 280,000 undocumented workers in 1993, mostly from the Philippines, Thailand, Pakistan, Sri Lanka, Bangladesh, and the Middle East.[34]

Japan has finally recognized its need for immigrant workers. Like South Korea, Hong Kong, Taiwan, Singapore, and Malaysia, Japan is a country short of labor which has experienced a steady and perceptible flow of unskilled foreign workers. Interestingly, the flow of undocumented workers into Japan continues to grow in spite of stringent amendments to Japanese immigration laws in 1990. Legal immigration of 114,000 foreign workers occurred in the first year after the changes, while another 150,000 second- or third-generation Japanese arrived from South America. Recognizing the need for these workers, the Japanese government proposed a technical job training program for foreign workers, permitting unskilled foreign workers to reside in Japan for up to two years. Today, foreign workers are viewed by some Japanese opinion leaders as a "labor-saving investment" that would complement native workers and make it easier for women and older people to enter and stay in the Japanese workforce.[35]

Comparing the world-renowned Japanese automobile industry with that in the United States and Europe is also instructive on the question of whether the Japanese have it right and we are wrong. The Japanese "lean" production system is highly extolled. Among the key elements are "continual improvement, teamwork, elimination of waste, and efficient use of resources, all bound together by a communication system that extends from the design center, research lab, factory and suppliers to the dealer and customer."[36] But the system has very real technical, organizational, political, economic, environmental, and social constraints. In the North American and European plants where the system has been transplanted, direct conflicts with political forces and social values in many Western countries have surfaced. Predictably, personnel and legal problems have increased.

For example, Detroit is learning what Japan learned early on from its American transplant experience: the lean system is a linear, mass production system designed for long continuous production runs, and does not perform well in such highly cyclical economies as North America. And Japan itself is experiencing a backlash from its lean system: a serious labor shortage has fomented labor unrest and demands for improved working conditions on assembly lines. Moreover, the labor shortage is allowing Japanese youth to be more selective in their job search. Assembly-line jobs in the automobile industries are particularly shunned as "3K" workplaces: *Kitanai* (dirty), *Kiken* (dangerous), and *Kitsui* (difficult). The Japanese auto industry, faced with this growing national resistance to 3K assembly-line jobs, is increasingly resorting to hiring foreign workers. Sociopolitical and environmental resistance to the lean system's drain on human and natural resources has also emerged. The Japanese are bemoaning the lean system's stressful and wasteful short model cycle and its street-congesting and polluting "just-in-time" distribution system. As a result, great changes are needed in the lean system in order to survive in the highly competitive global automobile industry.[37]

The Japanese economic system has other characteristics that the United States may not wish to emulate. For example, Japan's retail system is decidedly proproducer at the expense of consumers. Japanese-made goods are expensive, even domestically. Clothes cost twice as much in Tokyo as in New York, food about three times as much, and gasoline about two and a half times more. In essence, Japanese policies protect producers in a way that penalizes consumers. When competition in Europe or the United States pushes down the price of VCRs, cars, and semiconductor chips, Japanese producers still maintain high prices within Japan. In effect, producers wring monopoly profits out of their own people in order to build a war chest for competition overseas. When the yen doubled in value against the dollar from 1985 to 1988, retail prices in Japan should have fallen significantly—but they barely budged. Japanese corporations were taxing their own people with artificially high prices so that they could maintain artificially low prices in export markets in Europe and North America. In return for this tax, the Japanese people receive strong organizations and full employment. This may not be an attractive bargain from the Western viewpoint, and no individual Japanese likes paying higher prices. But the public supports this social bargain in order to keep the nation's producers strong and the nation prosperous.[38]

Unlike the U.S. and European models, Japanese workers have for several decades traded artificially low wages for the promise of full employment. The wages are artificially low because throughout much of the postwar era, earnings have lagged behind the increase in corporate productivity. By Western economic logic, wages should have risen much more rapidly. Similarly, Japanese corporations have traded artificially low profits for their equivalent of full employment, which is an ever growing market share. In 1991, a business survey listed the thirty most profitable large companies in the world. Twenty-three of them were American, four were British, and none were Japanese. The belief is that inconvenience to consumers is less damaging in the long run than the weakness of a nation's productive base.[39]

In short, we are not Japan. And we may not want to be.

chapter 7

Low-Wage Immigrants and African Americans

During the fall of 1994, I opposed Proposition 187 and participated in many 187 debates on radio, television, and public forums. Time and time again, one of the bases for passage urged by proponents of the initiative was that excluding immigrants—in this case the undocumented—would be beneficial to African Americans. Of course in most debates where this issue came up, the proponent generally was not African American, and was certainly not sympathetic to civil rights issues supported by most African Americans. As far as the drafters and primary organizers of Proposition 187 were concerned, the for-the-benefit-of-the-African-American-community argument was insincere, designed to pit one subordinated group against another. For many proponents, the dispute was about freeing up low-wage jobs for African Americans who ought to be happy with those opportunities rather than living on welfare or crime. Invariably, however, although most African Americans I met were opposed, occasionally an African American in a public or talk show audience would voice support for Proposition 187.

In spite of the fact that exit polls revealed that most African Americans opposed Proposition 187 and that the Congressional Black Caucus has a long record of support for immigration, an image persists among many African Americans that immigrants are competing for their jobs, depressing their wages, or taking away business opportunities in their own communities. Consider the comments of Joyce Punch, a retired Houston public schoolteacher:

> In the hotel industry and in some of the other industries where you used to see predominantly blacks, you don't see blacks now; . . . [for example] waiting tables; [and] many of the construction jobs have been taken by the Hispanics and the Asians who have come into the area.

Or the views of Steve Holt, the owner of an auto repair business in Chicago:

> The immigrants over here . . . work at a very low scale. So that's what's hurting different businesses [that are black-owned]. . . . Where I'm making a labor scale of twenty-two dollars an hour and an immigrant would take on a job for maybe five or six dollars an hour. . . . That kind of cuts my throat.[1]

In the aftermath of the South Central Los Angeles uprising, African Americans who burned and looted Korean businesses said they had not been respected when they shopped, and complained that Koreans would not hire African Americans to work in their businesses. In the words of one resident, "They raped us. They come in here and open up a liquor store on every corner."[2] These are words reminiscent of the views of Nation of Islam leader Reverend Louis Farrakhan:

> When we use the term bloodsucker, it doesn't just apply to some members of the Jewish community. That could apply to any human being who does nothing for another but lays on that human being to suck the value of its life without returning anything. . . . And when the Jews left, the Palestinian Arabs came, Koreans came, Vietnamese and other ethnic and racial groups came. And so this is a type and we call them bloodsuckers.[3]

Without a doubt, African Americans face severe underemployment and unemployment problems in the United States. But pointing to immigrants as a major source of the problems is an error and runs the serious risk of diverting attention away from the real causes and from the work to be done. Whatever negative impact immigrants do have on the African American community must also be placed in a larger context.

DISASTROUS AFRICAN AMERICAN UNEMPLOYMENT AND UNDEREMPLOYMENT

More than three decades after the beginning of civil rights era advances, the position of African Americans is still woefully behind white Americans by virtually all measures of economic and educational success. The percentage of African American families earning an average income has steadily decreased.[4] African Americans are disproportionately poverty-stricken. Furthermore, African Americans are represented in disproportionate numbers among the prison population, high school dropouts, and teen homicides.[5]

Many of these problems are due to unemployment among African Americans, which is reaching epidemic proportions. In 1989, the unemployment rate for African American men over the age of twenty was almost 10 percent compared with about 4 percent for white men. One in three African American youth (16–19) was unemployed compared to only one in eight white youth. These figures do not include the people who have dropped out of the labor market altogether by ceasing to look for employment.[6]

Underemployment is a problem as well. When African American workers are employed, especially in white-collar positions, they are clustered in the lower echelon, lower-paying occupations. When they do reach management level positions, African Americans are often found in departments from which much less upward mobility is available, such as personnel and public relations departments.[7]

Much of this underemployment is attributable to racial discrimination and racist assumptions by employers. Many employers will discount an African American's qualifications, even if they are equivalent to a competing white applicant's qualifications. Even with affirmative action programs, the current social disapproval of overt racism, and the prevalent ideal of an interviewing and selection process based solely on merit, employers continue to wield vast discretion in hiring decisions. This militates against African American job applicants even when their qualifications are superior to those of white applicants.

The experiences of African American workers are debilitating and humiliating. They endure the daily frustration of being underutilized at work and are often overlooked for promotions. However, these African Americans are the lucky ones. Many do not even get a foot in the door of a company.[8]

Employment problems faced by African Americans in places like Los Angeles, which attracts thousands of low-wage immigrants annually, provide the impetus for charges of job competition between immigrants and African Americans. Analyzing Los Angeles thus confronts the issue of job security directly and forces one to wonder about the relevance of the immigrant-worker-competition argument.

Consider the examples of the construction and manufacturing industries in Southern California. First, construction, an industry that has traditionally employed many African Americans, suffered severe cutbacks during the recent recession, largely because the Savings and Loan (S&L)-inspired "building boom of the late '80s" resulted in many nice, new, and now-abandoned buildings, thus deterring new construction today. As an example of this phenomenon, the six-county Southern California region accounted for just 40 percent of the state's new housing in 1993, versus 63 percent five years earlier.[9] This decrease in construction accounts for substantial African American job loss.

A second labor sector with large concentrations of African American employees is manufacturing. Thousands of manufacturing jobs in Southern California were lost in the 1970s and continued to bleed out in the early 1980s with the closure of Ford Motor Company in Pico Rivera and the GM plant in South Gate. The last auto plant in Southern California, the GM plant in Van Nuys, closed down in 1992, causing a loss of 2,600 jobs in an area where thousands of aerospace and defense jobs had already been taken away. From 1978 to 1982 South Central Los Angeles lost 70,000 high-paying manufacturing jobs. More recently, 100,000 manufacturing jobs evaporated in Los Angeles County between 1989 and 1992, and the aerospace industry—the region's industrial backbone—will continue to suffer from a diminished national defense budget. The GM, Bethlehem, Goodyear, and Firestone plants—steel, rubber, and auto—that used to be the core of South Central Los Angeles's economy are now gone. The effect of defense and construction-related job losses rippled into retail where African Americans lost jobs at a rate 50 percent higher than the rest of the retail workforce.[10]

Other policies and phenomena at work beyond Los Angeles and its specific industries reveal much of the problem African Americans face. Corporate downsizing—which, as we have seen, can be caused by global competition, technology, deregulation, and rising employment costs relative to capital costs—is perhaps as big a problem as defense cutbacks. At times this has been manifested in the flight of businesses out of the country or out of an urban area, often attributed to the business climate, strategic business reasons, and quality of life issues. These job losses seem to have affected African Americans more than other ethnic groups. During the 1990–91 economic downturn, African Americans were the only racial group to suffer a net job loss. This phenomenon can be partially explained by their relatively low seniority in companies and heavy concentration in the types of jobs eliminated.[11] But as we saw in chapter 4, given the fact that some employers "prefer" immigrant workers over African American ones, one suspects that discrimination may be at play as well.

Corporate decisions to abandon inner-city offices, factories, and franchise outlets further contribute to African American job loss because new suburban locations are not easily accessible to inner-city African American residents. For example, the retail giant Sears has lost many African American employees in recent years, simply by eliminating expensive distribution centers in the inner cities and closing two major urban distribution centers in 1991. The operations were relocated to suburbs largely inaccessible to inner-city residents without cars, who are primarily African Americans.[12] Other entities have relocated far beyond the suburbs to parts of the Midwest, where many African Americans find it difficult to cope socially. Even if social inhospitability were less of a problem, many people do not have the option of moving across the country to follow job openings.

A related problem is that when jobs are not easily accessible, information about available jobs is inadequate for inner-city residents. The urban poor tend to find out about job opportunities through informal rather than formal contacts. Typically, inner-city residents learn about employment opportunities through relatives or friends. Only a small percentage of jobs are actually discovered through agencies and newspaper ads.[13] It follows that inner-city residents seeking jobs find it difficult to locate the relatively few, and inaccessible, job openings.

The result of companies leaving the inner cities and moving to the suburbs is a severe labor shortage in the suburban areas where low-skilled, entry-level jobs are plentiful, while inner-city jobless rates remain alarmingly high—up to 30 percent or worse for African American teenagers. Eighty-seven percent of the nearly half a million new jobs created around Washington, D.C. during the 1980s were in the suburbs. The vast majority of new low-skilled jobs were in the suburbs. When new city-based jobs appear, they usually require higher skills which most inner-city poor workers lack.[14]

The inner city disadvantages the employment-seeking abilities and job performance of young, inner-city African Americans in other ways. Lack of access to jobs is primarily due to sustained segregation and inadequate education. Extreme segregation flowing from racial antipathy contributes to the high unemployment level among African Americans. Desegregation, on the other hand, is favorably linked to occupational advancement among African Americans. More than forty years after *Brown v. Board of Education*[15] outlawed de jure segregation, many African Americans still experience almost complete residential and educational segregation. The link between segregation and unemployment has become more evident over the past years, as many jobs have moved out of urban areas to the suburbs. Because so many members of the African American community are isolated in urban areas, and therefore do not live near many desirable jobs they often do not have the social contacts that would enable them to hear of job vacancies. In addition, they find it difficult to get to jobs when they do hear of them. For example, in Chicago, the "el," the most extensive public transportation network in the city, bypasses almost all of the African American neighborhoods which are most in need of public transportation. In Washington, D.C., the Metro system almost completely bypasses most predominantly poor or working-class African American neighborhoods.[16]

The inner city also often has an appalling educational system. It remains an inescapable truth that the dearth of skills in the African American community is greater than that among almost any other racial group. Growing numbers of African American youth are not acquiring the skills needed to enter the job market and compete for high-paying, prestigious positions. This problem begins and ends with education. In the United States, the education of many African American children, especially poor African American children, is almost completely neglected. This neglect is traceable to racism and this society's almost mystical ability to avoid making the endemic problems of the country's citizens of color a priority. Thus from East Los Angeles to East St. Louis, from Chicago to New York, the stories of outdated books, teacher shortages, unhealthy conditions, little modern technology, miserable student-teacher ratios, and insufficient per pupil educational spending in inner-city schools are shocking.[17]

But the inner city means more than second-class schools. It means second-class homes, menial jobs, or long-term unemployment. It also means the lure of gangs and criminal activity—which often provide the sole vision of a future, in a city core lacking educational and legitimate employment opportunities.[18]

African American leaders contend that another cause of African American unemployment is government apathy. Elaine Jones, director-counsel of the NAACP Legal Defense and Education Fund, agrees that if the country is in the midst of an economic downturn, "African Americans, like everybody else, are going to lose jobs." But she faults the administrative policies of former Presidents Reagan and Bush for sending a "national message" that diversity—meaning, in part, inclusion of African Americans in the workplace—was no longer a national priority.[19] The message meant that at places like Sears, the "old-boy network" influenced layoff decisions, and African American workers—discouraged by the atmosphere—were eager to take early retirement buyouts.[20]

Another problem is that years of discrimination and frustration in finding employment affect the emotional state of many under- and unemployed men, particularly African Americans. Some approach job-seeking or work with a long history characterized by not being able to support themselves or their families. Individuals born of this experience come to the job flat, lacking confidence, and terrified of being tested and having their shortcomings exposed. This emotional framework only perpetuates the cycle of failure and leads to the workers' inability and lack of eagerness even to seek employment.

Yet another problem is the lack of African American-owned business. Of the few that exist, African American-owned and ghetto-based business and industry provide job training and job opportunities, contribute to the inner-city tax base, help to improve the inner-city economy, and stand as proof of personal achievement resulting from study and industry.

Finally, many African Americans are employed in service industries that do not offer full-time, year-round work. For example, restaurants and hotels that cater to tourists are normally seasonal employers, and educational institutions often have reduced needs for service workers in the summertime. This means that periods of unemployment and nonparticipation in the labor force are common for these African American workers.[21]

COMPETITION BETWEEN AFRICAN AMERICANS AND IMMIGRANTS

Anecdotes of African American job displacement are difficult to grapple with, especially when you stand face-to-face with an African American whose old job is now filled by an immigrant who is working for lower pay. Arguing that we should be interested only in net outcomes for the entire African American community is plainly an inadequate response. Pointing to an African American who is working because of new immigrant consumerism might register. But doing so ignores certain individuals at the bottom or at the margin, the ones most vulnerable to hard times, the likely victims in each anecdote. Keeping the real causes of African American job loss in perspective is critical, but may prove unsatisfying—especially to those who, like janitors or construction workers in Los Angeles, appear anecdotally to be victims of displacement. In the aggregate, the entire economic system may benefit from the presence of immigrants, but does one segment, such as low-income African Americans, get hurt?

While it may be too simplistic for anti-immigrant groups to make broad, sweeping claims that immigrants take jobs away from native workers, equally simplistic are the claims of pro-immigrant groups that immigrants take only those jobs that native workers do not want. The pro-immigrant claim may be *generally* true, but willingness to take a job also depends on a person's age, stage in life, attitude, opinion of the job, the wage, work conditions, and the like. Moreover, native workers' willingness to take certain jobs could change drastically if job conditions changed even minimally, say by raising the pay or improving work conditions. Differences of opinion exist within the African American community over whether or not African Americans should or would take low-paying jobs,[22] and commentators and policymakers should not overgeneralize about who would or would not take a low-paying job.

Native workers who have been displaced because of the economic recession or structural adjustments in major industries are generally not in competition with immigrants. So the low-wage, unstable, menial jobs held by most immigrants are not long-term solutions for the natives who have lost jobs. Certainly, some displaced workers might be willing to take such jobs for a while, but few would take the humiliation of the small income and drop in social status permanently. What they need is retraining and relocation assistance in order to regain their dignity.

In Michael Piore's opinion, the "social status" argument is relevant to understanding African American youth:

> Employers perceived a change in black attitudes toward the work which made them difficult to manage, and recruited migrants to replace them. Black attitudes changed because an older generation, raised in the rural south with a background and motivations similar to the immigrants of today, was replaced by a new generation who grew up in northern urban areas. These younger workers associated the jobs with the inferior social status to which their race had been condemned in the United States and feared that they would be confined in them permanently through prejudice and discrimination.[23]

From this perspective, the conventional view that immigration restrictions serve to help disadvantaged native workers by freeing up low-wage, low-skilled (dead-end) jobs for African Americans has an aura of offensiveness. Anti-immigrant forces that toe this line "on behalf of" African Americans appear to be unconcerned with broader social goals, such as achieving equal opportunity for socioeconomic advancement for African Americans. Certainly some African Americans might (and do) take these jobs, but many would decline these "opportunities," and that refusal should be understandable. Since immigrants are concentrated in the secondary sector, restricting immigrants might increase these native workers in the secondary sector. But while access to secondary sector jobs may arguably provide a basis for social mobility among the disadvantaged, social pressures to isolate the secondary sector from primary sector jobs persist. Therefore, the limits on social mobility currently borne by migrants would be transferred to native workers.

When we view immigrants' impact on African American unemployment in the aggregate, there is little evidence of a cause and effect. African Americans face severe rates of unemployment and poverty in many parts of the country, but this is not restricted to places with large numbers of immigrants. And as we saw in chapter 4, in places with large numbers of immigrants such as New York and Los Angeles, African Americans have not lost jobs but have moved into the public sector. One study of Miami is particularly interesting.

Between May and September of 1980, some 125,000 Cubans arrived as part of the "Mariel Boatlift," an event which followed Fidel Castro's late April declaration that any Cuban wanting to leave was free to do so. About half of these "Marielitos" settled in Miami, representing an overnight increase of 7 percent in the city's labor force. In a close examination of this event, economist David Card found that the influx had no effect on the wages or unemployment rates of low-skilled native workers or earlier Cuban immigrants. Taking data for 1979 to 1985 for Miami and other metropolitan areas throughout the country, Card found that although the unemployment rate in Miami increased from 5 percent in April 1980 to 7.1 percent in July, state and national unemployment rates followed the same trend.[24]

In the longer run, the flood did not create more joblessness or lower wages for African Americans or whites. Although unemployment rates fluctuated between 1982 and 1984, by 1985 the rate returned to pre-1980 lows; the Cuban unemployment rate followed the same pattern. Real wages for whites between 1979 and 1985 remained constant in Miami and the comparison cities. Wages for African Americans in Miami were constant from 1979 to 1981, dropped in 1982–83, then increased to previous levels by 1984; in the comparison cities, African American wages steadily declined during this period.[25] Thus, the influx of low-wage workers may actually have helped African Americans in Miami in the long run.

Other researchers suspect some relationship between immigrants and African American joblessness. In an analysis of two Los Angeles groups—young African Americans and those with limited education—Paul Ong and Abel Valenzuela found a small increase in joblessness resulting from the increased presence of Latino immigrants with limited education. They noticed, however, that the findings resulted from employer racism. When a pool of low-skilled Latino workers was available, employers were able to reject African Americans. Interestingly, the relationship between low-skilled immigrants and African American joblessness only applied to Latino immigrants.[26]

Consider also an important study of the poverty and employment rates of African Americans, Mexicans, and Puerto Ricans in Chicago. Assuming that most of the Mexicans were immigrants, economist Robert

Aponte sought an explanation for why they had lower poverty rates than Puerto Ricans and African Americans, and better employment rates than those groups as well as whites. He found that this success was achieved despite conventional predictors of poverty and unemployment (the fact that Mexicans were the group with the least competitive human capital attributes—i.e., education, English proficiency, skills, work experience—and the most limited access to automobiles for commuting). About half of the African Americans surveyed held secondary "black" jobs (low wage, low skilled, and poor working conditions) and the same proportion of Mexicans had secondary "Mexican" jobs. However, unlike African Americans, Mexicans were not "mired in prototypically 'secondary' jobs" especially when those without high school diplomas were compared. Median wages for Mexicans were about the same as for Puerto Ricans, but higher than for African Americans, contradicting the theory that Mexicans are favored by employers for their exploitable nature.[27]

In order to get a better sense of these findings, other research provides possible explanations. The "discriminatory predispositions" of Chicago employers were examined, and as with Ong and Valenzuela's Los Angeles results, immigrant workers—be they Mexican, Asian, or eastern European—were consistently praised and preferred. Employers' prejudice against African American workers was conspicuous.[28]

These labor economic surveys confirm a serious societal evil—employers continue to discriminate against African Americans. Thus, in areas of the country such as Los Angeles and Chicago where a ready supply of low-wage immigrant workers exists, employers with discriminatory instincts against African Americans choose immigrants over low-skilled, less educated African Americans. Solving this problem is a matter of eradicating prejudice, and the degree to which keeping aliens out would contribute to changing racist attitudes about African Americans is questionable. At the very least, we should think carefully about whether attempting to change attitudes at the expense of others who are also generally disadvantaged is the strategy we really want to pursue.

Anecdotes of job loss must, however, be considered in light of other findings that support the hypothesis that immigrants are not taking jobs that are either available to or desired by African Americans. An analysis of the hotel and restaurant sectors suggests that African Americans have opted out of these sectors in response to rising expectations. For example, some employers perceive that African American employees "just expected more." In more pejorative terms, one employer noted, "They either have an attitude you owe them a job because they're black male, or they kick back and say if you fire them they'll sue for discrimination and you can't do anything about it."[29] But does all this only mean that employers think immigrants are more "flexible" and have a better attitude, while African Americans have become too "uppity"? Undoubtedly, employers who look at African Americans this way have exacerbated African American unemployment.

In Chicago and Los Angeles, employers have used network (word of mouth) hiring, which reproduces the characteristics of the existing workforce and systematically narrows opportunities for less educated African Americans. Employers operate with a hierarchy of ethnic preferences, with native whites at the top, followed by immigrant whites, immigrant Latinos, and native African Americans at the bottom.[30] Yet in contrast to Chicago, African Americans in Boston have done well relative to Latinos. Apparently the nature of the economy in Boston provides far more opportunities for English-speaking African Americans than for limited English-speaking Latino workers. Employers have relatively few opportunities for substituting immigrant labor for that of native minorities. In addition, the tightness of the labor market can impose severe costs on employers who discriminate, thereby further benefiting African Americans. Finally, the fact that the Boston economy is apparently inhospitable to the wholesale importation of immigrants may explain why the Boston area is not known as a major receiving area for recent immigrants, despite its phenomenal growth and substantial size.[31]

The fact that African Americans and immigrants are concentrated in different industries and job sectors reduces the likelihood of direct competition between the groups. In the food industry, for example, African Americans generally work in fast-food outlets and intermediate sector chains, while immigrants work in ethnic restaurants. Likewise, African Americans are concentrated in unionized construction, whereas immigrants often work for nonunion contractors or subcontractors. Of course the occupational division is far from complete, and competition far from separate. For example, with fewer immigrants and ethnic restaurants, other restaurants would presumably pick up most (though certainly not all) of this business. Similarly, were it not for nonunion immigrant construction, union firms that employ African Americans would have more opportunities. Although immigrant workers often do not compete with African Americans in a direct sense, if even a significant minority do, African American workers will feel the effects. Also relatively heavy immigrant employment in hotel cleaning and landscaping could represent jobs that would be filled at higher wages were immigrants not available.

On the other hand, many businesses would simply dissolve, move abroad, or automate if they were unable to use immigrant labor. In these cases, immigrants do not directly displace native workers. As we have already seen, research on Los Angeles automotive parts firms supports this argument, and the garment industry, other light manufacturing, and assembly jobs serve as further examples. So immigrants who are used as transitional workers or who comprise certain industries' flexible workforces in order to survive or compete are probably not hurting African Americans.

Such an argument raises two questions, however. First, what is the extent of this threat of capital flight? Fifty percent? Eighty percent? If less than 100 percent, at least one could argue that substitution is taking place, and that wages are being pushed downward. Second, where do these businesses get their capital? If banks and other investors would have placed part of their capital in other investments that paid higher wages and employed native African Americans, then a marginal, but tangible, effect on the economic life of African Americans could be felt. If we look primarily at the effect that immigration has on African Americans, and only secondarily at the total economic activity which is in some way traceable to immigration, the argument that "most" or "many" or even "nearly all" immigrant employment replaces native workers might have less persuasive power.

In order to get a better idea of the nuances involved, we need to know about other options available to the directly affected African American workers. We also need to know the other ramifications of the higher wages that are assumed on their behalf if they remained or became the workers. In downtown Los Angeles buildings, higher maintenance fees would result in higher rents. If so, would that not cause some business tenants at the margin to move or go out of business? And in turn is that not likely to affect the finances of some building owners, and also affect future construction? A similar set of possibilities could be played out with hotels or even landscaping. The point is that we cannot assume that the decision on the part of a manager to hire low-wage immigrant workers is not healthy for the overall economy, or that firm survival was not at stake.

In essence, the tension over current immigration policy and the impact on African Americans yields a combination of questions: Do we have faith in some of the economic theories developed about immigrants in the economy (e.g., that their presence and participation create jobs, stimulate the economy, and serve to complement natives in the workforce)? What confidence do we have in generalizing from the anecdotes about African American job loss after immigrants have moved in? Do the empirical studies showing that immigrants have not hurt the labor market status of African Americans reveal enough to justify holding that belief across the board—in other words, do we know enough to believe that immigrants stimulate the economy and create jobs? If so, what kinds of jobs are created? Are the jobs that are created (or maintained or complemented) the types of jobs that African Americans benefit from, or are they the types of primary sector jobs that benefit mostly non-African Americans (due to structural discrimination, outright discrimination, or preference)? Could African Americans actually be worse off without low-wage immigrant workers and mired in low-end jobs, placing little pressure on primary sectors to open up? Or would African Americans be better off without low-wage immigrant workers because employers would have to "deal" with their own discrimination given fewer options?

Many issues are involved: discrimination against African Americans; employer "preference" for immigrants; the so-called "immigrant work ethic" and willingness to take jobs under bad work conditions; whether or not the higher job expectations of all natives, including African Americans, are justifiable or reasonable; the exclusion of African Americans from primary sector jobs; the constantly changing nature of the economy and labor market.

Those who conclude that African Americans suffer relatively little, if at all, as a result of immigrants are mistaken in disregarding the concerns of those who disagree. But if one's goal is full and fair employment for African American workers while respecting the reasonableness of their attitudes and expectations, then given our contextual understanding of the challenges, we must demand more African American hiring at all levels of the labor market—particularly in the primary sector. Better public schools and job training for all workers must be a top priority. And to guard against managerial decisions to simply exploit low-wage workers, insisting on better wages and work conditions in the secondary sector and organizing immigrant workers (as illustrated in the Justice for Janitors campaign) must be high on the agenda as well.

THE TENSION BETWEEN ENCOURAGING IMMIGRATION AND EXPLOITING POOR WORKERS

The standard pro-immigrant defense of immigrant workers is familiar: they are mostly situated in complementary, secondary jobs; they take jobs others do not want; they serve as transitional and flexible workers that enable businesses to survive; they have a hard work ethic; they stimulate the economy. Immigrant-rights groups as well as free-market economists support these immigrant workers—many of whom are un-documented—and their right to remain in the country. But their condition makes them vulnerable to exploitation, and that vulnerability is reason to give further consideration to what happens to immigrants once they have arrived, and how support of immigration without more monitoring can increase the risk of exploitation. (Recall, however, the findings of Robert Aponte in Chicago that contradict the notion that Mexicans are favored for their exploitable nature.)

For instance, should we condone the use of such workers on the grounds that we need to allow industries the flexibility that such workers afford? At the very least, should wage, health, and safety workplace protections be sought on behalf of these workers? What impact do employer sanctions have on these conditions? Could employer sanctions under the Immigration Reform and Control Act of 1986 negatively affect some native workers whose jobs depend on low-wage undocu-menteds?[32] And if the presence of such workers delays or substitutes for mechanization, how can we determine whether that is good or bad?[33]

In the aggregate, the argument that immigrants help the economy is straightforward and credible. They contribute more to the national economy than they withdraw through social services and government outlays. They usually fill low-wage jobs for which native workers tend not to be hired, spend consumer dollars, pay taxes, and thus stimulate the national economy by lowering costs and creating more jobs. This immigrants-help-the-economy argument is thus available to those who tout a conservative worldview (i.e., "immigrants make this country the strongest country in the world") as well as those who hold a liberal worldview (i.e., "immigrants have a right to come to this country, and they contribute as much as current U.S. citizens").

The fact that the immigrants-help-the-economy argument is so ideologically mobile is problematic. Pro-immigrant groups quickly and uncritically embrace this perspective often without addressing the relationship between poor native workers, poor immigrants, and poor workers around the world.

At least two dangers grow out of the standard economic defense of immigrants. First, we turn a blind eye to the fact that immigrants provide this country with a highly exploited labor pool. In labor market empirical work, the "use of immigrants in order to remain flexible" or to have a "malleable" workforce is frequently promoted. This keeps us from viewing the U.S. economy as a system within a larger and more complex global economic system. We should also explore the impact that U.S. economic, political, and military strategies may have on Third World poverty and First World economic practices (such as debt policy, economic development policy, and multinational expansion). Do any of these effects encourage impoverished workers to come here? Should we analyze the effects of the competition between less skilled U.S. workers and lower-wage labor in other countries? What progressive policies can be generated to respond to this competition?

Second, while the low-wage immigrant labor pool props up the organization of our national economy, the potential for developing sharp divisions within the U.S. economy is facilitated. While studies show that immigrants tend to stimulate the economy viewed nationally, the existence of a highly exploitable labor pool might in fact be hurting some local economies. Beyond the complex relationship with low-wage, low-skilled native workers, the benefits of immigration may accrue disproportionately to the national government rather than to local economies; that is, states and towns shoulder much of the cost of immigration, while the national government gets most of the income. The economic boon from immigrants accrues to some people in some localities, although perhaps not the same people bearing the costs associated with immigration.

In sum, progressive discussion about the economic impact of immigration is absent, even within the immigrant-rights community. As one activist has confided, we often find ourselves in the position of promoting immigration as "the best thing since child labor." [34] The challenge is to generate lucid and nuanced arguments about the economic impact of immigration that do not trade an intelligent, broadly conceived progressive agenda for narrow, short-sighted agendas. Such arguments would need to respond to questions like, "Do immigrants help the economy?" with different questions that would stimulate more progressive answers. These questions would explore the role immigration plays in a U.S. economy that is sharply divided between extreme inner-city and rural poverty on the one hand, and suburban and cosmopolitan wealth on the other. Similarly justified is consideration of the roles immigration plays in a U.S. economy that is just one system within a larger global economic system that is itself sharply divided between First World wealth and economic power on the one hand, and Third World poverty, debt, and socioeconomic exploitation on the other.

Indeed, acknowledging that some sectors have made some choices that have negatively affected native workers may be necessary. Many of the labor market studies reviewed have examined the different ways that certain sectors of manufacturing and agriculture have used immigrant labor to respond to market disruption, foreign and domestic competition, changes in product demand, and demographic and related workforce issues. The choices these industries made to deal with these challenges have had distinct—and often negative—effects on domestic workers.[35]

In short, our inquiry should not end with the acknowledgment that immigrants on balance or in the aggregate benefit the economy. We need to know how this conclusion is reached, and whether elements of its side effects need more attention.

chapter 8

Beyond the Economic Debate:
The Cultural Complaint

I think God made all people good, but if we had to take a million immigrants in, say, Zulus, next year or Englishmen and put them in Virginia, what group would be easier to assimilate and would cause less problems for the people of Virginia? There is nothing wrong with us sitting down and arguing that issue, that we are a European country. . . .

. . . [E]very immigration policy is going to let somebody in and keep somebody out. It's going to have different criteria. What I am saying is culture, language, background are not illegitimate criteria for us to discuss when we discuss legal immigration.

— PATRICK BUCHANAN, December 8, 1991

[M]any modern American intellectuals [are] just unable to handle a plain historical fact: that the American nation has always had a specific ethnic core. And that core has been white. . . .

The American nation of 1965, nearly 90 percent white, was explicitly promised that the new immigration policy would not shift the country's racial balance. But it did. . . .

. . . It is simply common sense that Americans have a legitimate interest in their country's racial balance. It is common sense that they have a right to insist that their government stop shifting it. Indeed, it seems to me that they have a right to insist that it be shifted back.

— PETER BRIMELOW, *Alien Nation*

Advocates calling for greater restrictions on immigration in this country do not limit their arguments to economic themes. For some, the millions of newcomers to this country in recent decades represent a challenge to their conception of America itself. For these

146

critics, such as Republican presidential candidate Patrick Buchanan and journalist Peter Brimelow, cultural and racial issues may be more important.

In this chapter, we will look at the flaws of the Euro-immigrationist and cultural assimilationist positions. These flaws can be merged into two general propositions. The first is the normative premise that America has a strictly white, Christian, European heritage. The second is the Euro-immigrationists' and cultural assimilationists' misguided claim that immigrants of color fail to acculturate.

In his last two campaigns for the Republican presidential nomination, Buchanan has made criticizing current immigration policies an integral part of his political platform. Buchanan attempts to couch his attacks in cultural assimilationist terms, but the core of his claims is race-related. To Buchanan, the notion of immigrants retaining their native cultures is ruining America. "[P]ut[ting] America first . . . mean[s] our Western heritage is going to be handed down to future generations, not dumped onto some landfill called multi-culturalism."[1] Given the demographic composition of today's immigrants, the thrust of Buchanan's assimilation claim collapses into a racial claim because Asian and Latino immigrants, who constitute the majority of today's immigrants, do not come from a Western European racial or cultural heritage. To Buchanan, retaining this heritage is the adulteration and degradation of American culture. Likewise, former Ku Klux Klan leader and 1992 Republican presidential candidate David Duke claimed that immigrants "mongrelize" our culture and dilute our values.[2] And to journalist Peter Brimelow, "immigration is a potential ally" to those who would attack and "further deconstruct the American nation [as do] multiculturalism [and] bilingualism."[3]

Buchanan, Brimelow, and Duke are not the only champions of a failure-to-assimilate attack on immigration. According to the former Senator Alan Simpson, a major architect of U.S. immigration policy, "[i]mmigration to the United States is out of control." "[A]ssimilation to fundamental American public values and institutions may be of far more importance to the future of the United States." "Is it in the national interest to bring in people through chain migration with no skills, who do not learn English, who join their extended family but don't join our society?" In Simpson's view, immigrants must accept the "public culture of the country—as opposed to private ethnic culture."[4]

Similarly, consider the Federation for American Immigration Reform

(FAIR), touted as the nation's "main restrictionist lobbying group."[5] The organization is calling for a moratorium on legal immigration (a position adopted by Buchanan) so that Americans may give themselves some "breathing space" to perform the "task of assimilation."[6] Reform Party presidential candidate Richard Lamm, a former Colorado governor and chair of FAIR's advisory board, adds, "[America] can accept additional immigrants, but we must make sure they become Americans. We can be a Joseph's coat of many nations, but we must be unified."[7] Even some self-described liberals insist that immigrants demonstrate their desire to join other Americans and become "one of us."[8]

While the "mainstream" views of Simpson and FAIR resemble the arguments of extremists such as Buchanan and Brimelow, important conceptual differences exist within the rhetoric of failure-to-assimilate advocates. The language of those who rely on assimilation arguments to oppose the immigration policies of the last three decades can be placed into two sometimes overlapping categories: race-based objections, and culture-based (i.e., nonrace-based) objections. Conventionally, commentators labeled these two categories "Anglo-conformity" assimilation, but given the blending of European immigrants over the years, the term "Euro-American conformity" seems more appropriate.[9]

RACE-BASED OBJECTIONS

Buchanan, Brimelow, and restrictionist immigration groups such as the Americans for Immigration Control (AIC) advocate a Euro-immigrationist philosophy that favors white, European immigrants in the belief that the country can assimilate more easily. Buchanan and Duke's statements reveal the racist nature of their approach to immigration. Their vision for America is white and Christian.[10] Duke submits, "We've got to begin to protect our values. We've got to begin to realize that we're a Christian society. We're part of Western Christian civilization." He says that because of "illegal immigration, . . . [o]ur traditions are being torn away. Our values are being torn away." He also promised that if elected, there would not "be any Haitians setting foot on American soil."[11] Similarly, Buchanan argues that our heritage is white. "Why are we more shocked when a dozen people are killed in Vilnius than [by] a massacre in Burundi? Because they are white people. That's who we are. That's where America comes from."[12]

Central to Buchanan and Duke's assertions is the premise that white Christians alone founded and built this nation. Therefore, only white Christians merit entry; only they can be "American." Buchanan and those like him ignore the enormous contributions people of color have made to this country, notwithstanding the suffering and oppression they have endured.[13] For Buchanan, Duke, and Brimelow, new immigrants of color entering the country threaten the nation's racial and religious "purity."[14] Thus, to race assimilationists such as Buchanan and Duke, the obvious solution is to enact race-based exclusionary immigration laws.

In the same vein, the right-wing AIC supports the notion that the United States should "consider calling a halt to the mass influx of even more millions of hungry, ignorant, unskilled, and culturally-morally-genetically impoverished people." Its spokespersons argue that while "America's apparent decline obviously has multiple causation, a factor of overriding importance is that its ethnically mixed population no longer rallies around common values to the extent necessary for successful attacks on internal and external problems."[15] The AIC correlates race with adhesion to common values. For it, the failure of certain segments of the American population to rally round a core is a function of race and ethnicity. To preserve cultural cohesion, immigration laws must control the race and ethnicity of entering immigrants.

CULTURE-BASED OBJECTIONS

The assimilationist position that raises cultural objections may not be couched in racial language. These assimilationists often express their alarm over the recent increase in non-English speaking immigrants in nonracial tones. Governor Lamm of FAIR, which has had a significant leadership overlap with the English Only movement, says, "We must have English as one of the common threads that hold us together. We should be color blind, but we can't be linguistically deaf. . . ."[16] Senator Simpson feels that "if linguistic and cultural separatism rise above a certain level, the unity and political stability of the nation will in time be seriously eroded."[17] The cultural assimilationist rhetoric of FAIR complains that "large-scale" immigration lowers American living standards and dilutes American culture.[18]

Even the presidential candidate and former Senate majority leader

Bob Dole, often identified as a moderate Republican, indicated his support for English as the dominant language. Although Dole supports limited instruction in schools in the immigrants' native language, he does so only if the school's purpose is "the teaching of English. . . . [W]e must stop the practice of multilingual education as a means of instilling ethnic pride, or as therapy for low self-esteem or out of elitist guilt over a culture built on traditions of the West."[19] For some, a feeling of cultural "superiority" underlies many of their attitudes about how immigrant children should be taught in schools. One public schoolteacher from the group "Save Our State," which pushed for the anti-illegal immigrant ballot effort Proposition 187 in California, felt that Americans

> should not have to apologize for the superiority of our culture. . . .
> That does not say that we are calling other countries inferior, but let's
> face it . . . . it is our Constitution, it is our capitalist free enterprise
> system, it is our good-heartedness that makes us superior. And I don't
> think we should apologize for saying this to our children.[20]

While this culture-based argument studiously avoids race and ethnicity, the argument's implications are distinctly race-based. Given the huge numbers of immigrants who enter this country from Asian and Latin American countries whose citizens are not white and (in most cases) do not speak English, criticism of the inability to speak English coincides neatly with race.

Moreover, the presence of nonwhite immigrants in the United States threatens cultural uniformity because the immigrants bring with them their own languages and cultural practices. Many cultural immigrationists believe that large-scale Latino and Asian immigration contributes to an increasingly bilingual society, creates substantial problems in schools, and changes our national identity in unwelcome ways. Social, political, and cultural issues are now "uppermost in the minds of many Americans concerned about the consequences of immigration."[21] English-only initiatives have become increasingly common,[22] and their advocates voice the following sentiments:

> Summer has ended and school bells are ringing once again. But what
> will your children or grandchildren learn in our schools this year? . . .
> [T]hey may soon be taught that America is a hateful place founded
> by racists and murderers. Or that holidays like Columbus Day or
> Thanksgiving   celebrate   genocide   and   slavery   and   should   be

banned . . . [or] that they are descendants of the European "ice people" whose lack of skin color identifies them as an inferior race! . . . Many of these educational "experts" are also behind the drive for so-called "bilingualism." I put it in quotes because these people really want to do away with English and everything European. . . . America has a language, a history and a culture. It does not want or need to import others. For two hundred years immigrants have come to our shores looking for something better than what they were leaving behind. . . . They neither expect nor want America to turn itself into a banana republic so they can feel more at home.[23]

Underlying this ferocious rhetoric is the fear that immigrants will leave their nonwhite mark on the American landscape: that there will be revisionist histories outlining the full story of how America developed through genocide, slavery, oppression, imperialism, and expansionism as well as through commitment to independence, justice, and individual rights; that our language will expand to include new terms and idioms, not all of Anglo-European extraction.

At bottom, cultural assimilationists envision America in terms as narrow and racially exclusive as do the race assimilationists such as Buchanan and Brimelow. Despite the difference in diction and approach, both groups share the same philosophical race-based core. They believe that the United States has a Western European cultural heritage that must be maintained, and that current levels of immigration threaten to alter or dilute that culture. This concern for "our" culture and heritage is the essential normative premise of cultural assimilationists and Euro-immigrationists.

Nonetheless, the distinction between the Euro-immigrationists' racist rhetoric and the cultural assimilationists' cries for preserving the English language and American culture serves an important purpose. It allows us to dismiss the racist, inflammatory rhetoric of people like Patrick Buchanan and Peter Brimelow as the views of politically expedient extremists and to begin the task of seriously examining the issues behind the rhetoric of both the cultural assimilationists and cultural pluralists.

America's Multiracial and Multicultural Heritage

The Euro-immigrationist and cultural assimilationist positions are flawed in two important ways. The first flaw is the essentially normative premise that America has a strictly white, Christian, European heritage. The second is their misguided claim that immigrants of color fail to acculturate.

While Buchanan and others dismiss multiculturalism as "landfill," multiculturalism challenges the premise that America is a white, English-speaking, Western Christian nation. Not only did Native American tribes long predate the arrival of white Christians, but the early European settlers spoke Spanish, German, Dutch, French, and Polish in addition to English. Before Chinese exclusion laws became permanent near the turn of the twentieth century, about 300,000 Chinese had entered the country. Filipinos established a community in Louisiana as early as 1565. Spanish-Portuguese Jews, the Sephardim, settled in the New World in the mid-1600s.[24]

Mexicans, initially propelled by Mexico's historical territorial claims in the Southwest, have long established patterns of migration to the United States.[25] Over 9.5 million Africans were captured and brought to the Western Hemisphere as slaves.[26] In the first decade of this century, about 2 million Italians, 1.6 million Russians, and 800,000 Hungarians immigrated.[27] In short, the heritage of the United States does not derive solely from people who are white, English-speaking, Christian, and European. Nonwhite peoples have a long history in America, most of which is unflattering to the white, European Christians that Buchanan and others extol. The genocide of Native Americans, brutal enslavement of African Americans, and exploitation and oppression of Asian and Latino Americans are harsh reminders of our nation's past. In spite of the oppression, people of color have contributed to America's history and development and are a vital part of its heritage.[28]

IMMIGRANT ACCULTURATION

While the race assimilationists tend to focus on the theory that America is a white, European-based society that should stay that way, the culture-based critics of immigration tend to focus on acculturation. Many of the Simpson, Lamm, and FAIR arguments consist of complaints that immigrants fail to absorb American culture. Buchanan, for example, has called for a five-year moratorium on immigration as a "time-out" that will allow the nation to "Americanize and assimilate the people who [have] come."[29]

Study after study demonstrates, however, that the vast majority of immigrants take on cultural traits of the host community. Some traits replace old ones, but most are simply added.[30] For example, immigrants entering the United States today learn English *at the same rate* as other immigrant groups before them. First-generation immigrants tend to learn English and pass it along to their children, who become bilingual. Immigrants want and encourage their children to learn English. By the third generation, the original language is often lost.[31] Throughout the United States, the demand for English as a Second Language (ESL) training far outstrips supply, leading adult newcomers to encounter long lines and waiting lists before gaining access to classes.[32]

Cultural assimilationists frequently accuse the Latino community in particular of not assimilating or learning English. Yet Spanish-speaking immigrants residing in the country for fifteen years regularly speak English. They usually read English fluently within ten years, and most from Mexico and Central America read English- rather than Spanish-language newspapers. In addition, about 93 percent of all Mexican immigrants agree that U.S. residents should learn English.[33]

Although complete acculturation of all immigrants is impossible, immigrants and refugees of all ages become acculturated to some extent. Even before coming to the United States, some adult immigrants and refugees have been exposed to American culture due to its pervasiveness in the global media. Upon arriving in the United States, most adult immigrants and refugees work, learn English, and often strive to pick up U.S. cultural habits and customs. Many young Asian and Latino immigrants, in particular, aggressively strive to be "American." They are eager to learn English, to get a job, to work hard; in short they seek to achieve a part of the American dream.[34] Their aspirations are similar to those of the Jewish, Irish, and southern and eastern European immigrants who came in earlier years. Due to school attendance, interaction with peers, and exposure to the media, the children of immigrants, even foreign-born children, generally become fully acculturated. These children speak English, and their customs, habits, and values are nearly indistinguishable from those of their peers.

Aside from their complaint that new immigrants fail to adopt our society's cultural traits, cultural assimilationists also contend that immigrants threaten to dilute our Western cultural heritage. In truth, immigrants *do* affect our culture, but surely not as much as our culture affects them. To describe this process as a dilution shows an ignorance of how culture in America has developed throughout our history: not as some monolith unmoved by the waves of immigration in the eighteenth, nineteenth, and twentieth centuries, but as an ever-evolving understanding of what it means to be American. As immigrants acculturate, U.S. society in general has absorbed their customs, cuisine, interests, and values. Our culture and our definition of what it means to be American is constantly evolving. Immigrants play an integral role in helping to create that definition.[35]

Changes in U.S. culture are of course not solely nor even mainly attributable to the influence of immigrants. Improved technologies, social movements, and economic developments are also crucial. However, a melting pot of sorts does exist. Immigrants do not displace American culture, but they help develop a distinctively new and constantly evolving and expanding U.S. culture.

MULTICULTURALISM AND ASSIMILATION BY CHOICE

In contrast to the assimilationist approach, cultural pluralism focuses on the benefits immigrants bring. In the historical dispute over immigration policy and assimilation, liberal intellectuals challenged the Anglo-conformity approach with a model of cultural pluralism that actually encouraged ethnic groups to retain their cultural heritage.[36] Ethnic enclaves such as Little Italys and Chinatowns exemplify such preservation. Cultural pluralists envisioned that, while native cultural patterns could be preserved, the groups would continue to evolve as Americans and would eventually take part in democratic institutions.[37]

Historically, cultural pluralism was not diametrically opposed to assimilationist sentiment. In fact, cultural pluralists believed that English should be the common language and that all citizens should share and participate in the general society's political and economic life. For pluralists, this seemed to represent a common core of values.[38] The minimum expectations of English-language competence and acceptance of the nation's political and economic framework by immigrants were important assumptions shared by both assimilationists and cultural pluralists. The similarities end there, however.

Cultural pluralists believed that each nationality and ethnic group should retain its own individuality in language, religion, and culture. Promoting an early version of bilingualism and biculturalism, they felt that both immigrants and minority groups had a right to preserve their primary identities, and they insisted on the value of the ethnic group "as a permanent asset in American life." The pluralists suggested that each ethnic group should be permitted a communal life, "preserving and developing its cultural heritage while at the same time participating effectively in the broader life of the nation as a whole." Pluralists accepted the disintegration of ethnic groups and their subsequent assimilation into American life as long as it resulted from the free choice of individuals and not from coercion.[39]

Although it needs refinement, much of the historical cultural pluralist paradigm remains valid today. Many, myself included to a degree, subscribe to these conventional views of cultural pluralism and dismiss the concerns of cultural assimilationists as well as the racism of Buchanan and Duke. In celebrating multiculturalism, we offer our own rhetoric, arguing that "[a] rambunctious America is a strong America,"[40] and that "[d]espite the costs—and even the pain—that may be caused by immigration, the benefits are incalculable."[41] Behind the rhetoric, moreover, lies substance: pluralism has real advantages.

CONSTITUTIONAL PRINCIPLES

One of the strengths of cultural pluralism is its connection to constitutional principles. Some of the central tenets of liberal democracy—the principles of religious freedom, freedom of speech and assembly, and privacy—encourage and protect diversity. We pride ourselves in maintaining and exercising these constitutional rights, and they are a major reason why so many people seek U.S. residency and citizenship.

Promoting and maintaining one's own ethnic culture—a fundamental premise of pluralism—is therefore consistent with constitutional principles. Not only do individuals possess a broad zone of autonomy regarding how they think, speak, worship, and behave, but the Constitution prohibits the government from endorsing any one religion or political orthodoxy as "correct."[42] The liberal system, aside from controlling substantive subversion (actual violence, disobedience of valid laws, and the like), arguably is prohibited even from proclaiming itself the "best" or only "correct" system. By preserving the "marketplace of ideas," our system protects those who choose to promote their own ethnic culture.

These traditional liberal principles suggest that government should not demand that immigrants subscribe to any particular language or cultural norm any more than to any particular religion. Rather, the ideological principles of the U.S. system require a hands-off, laissez-faire attitude toward shifting cultural boundaries and attitudes. Liberal democrats may desire that new immigrants assimilate into a certain image, but the process is left to market forces rather than state intervention.

Historically, however, the Supreme Court and Congress have acted at times in ways that conflict with these principles. The Supreme Court has espoused assimilationist thought in several opinions. In *Reynolds v. United States*,[43] the Court seemed to support the establishment of a Protestant hegemony by sustaining state antipolygamy laws; the decision reflected "both a tolerance for the legislative efforts at regulating custom and morality, and a distinct preference for European observances."[44] In *United States v. Joseph*,[45] the Court felt that because Pueblo Indians held land as private owners and had adopted agriculture and Christianity, they had become so advanced, enlightened, and civilized as to escape the confines of Indian status.

Congress, meanwhile, helped institutionalize the assimilationist position through the enactment of restrictive immigration laws in place from 1882 to 1965.[46] These provisions specifically established racial categories of immigrants barred from entering the United States. The Supreme Court upheld these provisions under Congress's plenary power over aliens.[47] McCarthy-era ideologically based exclusion provisions, eased only recently,[48] also conflicted with liberal democracy. Congress, however, still has the power to implement new assimilationist changes to the law, a concern given current efforts in the legislature to cut back the number of immigrants admitted to this country and their rights as residents while they are here.[49]

ECONOMIC DIVERSITY AND COMPETITION

One argument advanced in favor of assimilation is that efficiency and competitiveness in the world marketplace demand a common national culture and language. This proposition seems misguided. A multicultural United States provides many advantages in the increasingly interdependent global economy.

Even casual attention to current events of the last decade has taught

us that political and economic developments all over the world—in
Europe, Latin America, Africa, Asia, and the Middle East—affect the
U.S. economy. The Dow Jones, interest rates, production, the dollar's
value, and economic growth all reacted to democracy movements in
Asia and eastern Europe, the Persian Gulf War, South Africa, NAFTA,
Bosnia, and economic problems in Brazil and Mexico. Certainly the
United States will remain economically linked to Europe, but Europe is
only one of many regions that are vital to our economy. The blinders of
a Eurocentric view of America limit our vision and viability in the
international economic community. There are simply too many cultural
differences that have to be considered for the United States to be effective
globally. The economy increasingly demands expertise in more than
American or Eurocentric ways and customs.

Since Asia and the industrializing nations of Latin America are new
areas of economic power, bicultural and multicultural U.S. residents will
prove invaluable as American companies develop private trade
agreements and cooperative business ventures with the nations and corporations of these regions. Many businesses, advertising agencies, and
law firms have already recognized the benefits of taking a multicultural
approach in their Latin American and Asian endeavors. Some have
established branches abroad, most have invested in culture and language
training for employees, and even more have hired bicultural employees.
In the age of jet travel, E-mail, teleconferencing, cellular phones, and fax
machines, multicultural businesses are engaged in daily transactions in
Tokyo, Singapore, Hong Kong, Manila, Beijing, Mexico City, Brasilia,
and Caracas as well as London, Paris, and Frankfurt.

The Advantage of a Diverse Workforce in Domestic Markets

A diverse workforce is an advantage domestically as well. As the ethnic
makeup and demographics of the country change, smart business managers make changes and innovations in response to the needs of the
changing population. In short, responding to demographic changes can
help increase profits. However, producing commercials with slogans like
"se habla español" and advertising in the *Asian Yellow Pages* in order to
attract new business must be coupled with the cultivation of a staff that
can develop a rapport with the new customers. Thus, more and more

employers are coming to view diversity as good business as well as good public relations.

For example, the success of an AT&T service called Language Line which allows companies in the United States to communicate with their non-English speaking customers and business contacts illustrates the benefits of a diverse workforce. Through a staff of interpreters on conference calls, Language Line allows businesses such as Whirlpool, Lands' End, Pepsi, and Gerber to communicate with U.S. and foreign customers who do not speak English. As the director of communications for the service explains, "Business is beginning to appreciate there are over 30 million people in this country who prefer to use a language other than English. . . . The U.S. business community is becoming increasingly attuned to the fact that not every customer speaks English." [50]

Moreover, the gains from a diverse workplace are also independent of the changing demographics. A diverse workplace is also a more innovative workplace. For example, Burger King has implemented diversity and multicultural training seminars for its employees while increasing the percentage of people of color in its workforce from 12 percent in 1986 to 28 percent in 1991. At Burger King and other businesses that have sought diversity, there is "a growing sentiment that diverse employee teams tend to outperform homogeneous teams of any composition. . . . [H]omogeneous groups may reach consensus more quickly, but often they are not as successful in generating new ideas or solving problems, because their collective perspective is narrower." [51] Thus, the old adage that "two heads are better than one" holds true, except that the more appropriate phrase might be "multiple ethnic perspectives are better than one."

OTHER BENEFITS OF CULTURAL DIVERSITY

Cultural pluralists rightly argue that the country continues to benefit from new immigrants. Although many question the economic benefit of immigrants, new immigrants, like their predecessors, have the drive and willingness to make a better life for themselves and their families. As a class, immigrants and refugees could very well represent the most determined class of people from their sending nations. [52] Many have had to survive treacherous journeys and overcome severe obstacles. All have had to demonstrate the courage and fortitude needed to follow through on the difficult decision of uprooting themselves and often their families, by winding their way through immigration mazes and the logistical facets of relocation. With our native workforce often charged with laziness and lack of drive, we stand to learn and to benefit from the hard work ethic of the immigrants and refugees who continue to enter.

More generally, immigrants represent a potential resource for adding to, rather than diluting, American culture. While the United States continues to be an innovative leader on many business, political, scientific, and social fronts, it is not the sole innovative leader in all these realms. We should be open to new ideas from people of different cultures who may have better ways of approaching the gamut of issues facing us, including business operations, protection of the environment, stress, interpersonal relations, and education.[53]

The ultimate benefit from interaction with those of different cultures does not necessarily flow from learning about new innovations, however. Rather, by learning about other cultures through social interaction with people of other cultures, we begin to learn more about other people. We begin to understand their customs, attitudes, and values, as well as to share information about our own cultures. In this process, we begin to develop tolerance and respect for other cultures and backgrounds. This type of education provides the foundation for a peaceful, productive pluralism that must be fostered throughout the world.[54]

chapter 9

The Challenge to Cultural Pluralists:
Interethnic Group Conflict and Separatism

Some nations encourage the development of more than one culture and, in the process, lose some sense of community. Canada is such a nation. There, both the English and the French cultures are deemed equal. Embattled Yugoslavia presents an extreme example. It has two alphabets, three major religions, four major languages, five major nationalities, and until recently, was divided into six major republics. One can legitimately inquire: "What is a Yugoslavian?" Canada, Yugoslavia, Belgium and sundry other countries differ enormously from countries like Japan and Sweden where cultural diversity is minimal and a sense of community is resent[ed]. Multilingual countries often exhibit a tendency toward disintegration. The current situation in the Soviet Union is perhaps the most extreme example of such a situation. . . .

Too many countries have failed to attain true national consciousness because of bilingual and even multilingual controversies. In so many instances, the ethnic minority identifies first with its own subculture rather than the national culture. . . . Canada has experienced considerable difficulty in getting all of its citizens to be "Canadians." Many residents of French-speaking Quebec call themselves "Quebecois" first, and "Canadiens" second.

—LEON F. BOUVIER, *Peaceful Invasions:
Immigration and Changing America* (1992)

In addition to fearing that current levels of immigration threaten to alter our Western cultural heritage, Euro-immigrationists and cultural assimilationists share two beliefs that are not as easily dismissed by cultural pluralists: first, that racial and ethnic conflicts have resulted from changes in the racial and ethnic character of the country, since the amendments to the immigration laws in 1965 permitted so many non-European immigrants to enter; and second, that these changes foster linguistic and cultural separatism which could threaten "the unity and political stability of the nation." [1] The race assimilationist AIC insists that "[n]o one cause of American institutional disarray is more important than ethnic conflict." [2] To Buchanan, ethnic conflict is why "America [is] so vulgar and coarse, so uncivil and angry." He signals a warning by pointing to hostile relations between African Americans and whites: "Look over our country's history. . . . Dred Scott. Gettysburg. Brown vs. the Board of Education. Watts. [And now South Central Los Angeles.] These are all about our effort, successful by and large, but still failed, to assimilate into our society that 10 or 12 percent of Americans who are Afro-Americans. It has been a very, very difficult thing, and we've had great turmoil and a civil war over it." [3] The more culture-conscious Senator Simpson fears that "[i]f immigration is continued at a high level and yet a substantial portion of the newcomers and their descendants do not assimilate, they may create in America some of the same social, political and economic problems which existed in the country which they have chosen to depart." [4]

Cultural pluralists cannot ignore the issues of intergroup conflict and separatism. Despite the very real excesses of the assimilationist view, cultural pluralists are hard-pressed to dispute the serious interethnic group conflict and separatist sentiment among immigrants and other groups of color. The Buchanan, Simpson, and AIC position that the influx of non-English-speaking immigrants of color dooms our culture as we know it to destruction is exaggerated. As we have seen, the United States has a multiracial, multicultural heritage in which new immigrants continue to be highly acculturated. However, the response of some cultural pluralists, celebrating multiculturalism and envisioning the peaceful coexistence of different ethnic groups who are able to retain their cultures yet work together, is no less hyperbolic left unpacked. Multiracial communities that get along well do exist, and the majority of people of color continue to seek integration in conventional terms. Nonetheless, the significance of intergroup conflict and separatist sentiment demand earnest reflection beyond the simplistic viewpoint that "a rambunctious America is a strong America." [5]

INTERETHNIC GROUP CONFLICT

Conflicts involving immigrant groups attract banner headlines today. The aftermath of the first Rodney King verdict brought considerable attention to the conflict between the Korean American and African American communities in South Central Los Angeles. Many Korean American businesses were destroyed and one member of the community was killed. Such conflicts were not new to the popular media, but were magnified as images of Koreans arming themselves to protect their businesses against arson and looting aired throughout the nation.

In the aftermath of Rodney King, diversity of opinion and reaction formed within the Korean American community. Some Koreans denounced the rioters, appearing to feel nothing but anger toward them. Others, while expressing sympathy for fellow Koreans who lost property and livelihoods, denounced the jury's verdict, vilified the judicial system as racist, and supported the social and political motives of the protesters. In Korean American and other Asian American community conversations and meetings, differences along lines of class, generation, and place of birth (native or foreign-born) emerged. Some, but not all, older immigrant Koreans did not want to work or talk with African Americans. Younger Korean Americans often advocated building bridges between the two communities.[6]

Among African Americans, an assortment of attitudes about Korean Americans surfaced. Some blamed Korean Americans for taking business opportunities from African Americans, for gouging customers, and removing money from the community, leaving little for local economic development. Some viewed Korean Americans as the tool of an economic system—a petite bourgeoisie—that had long oppressed African Americans. Others urged African Americans to work with Korean Americans in the development of the African American community.[7]

The tension between the Korean American and African American communities in South Central Los Angeles was not all racial. Much had to do with economic class divisions, as demonstrated by the similar destruction of Latino and African American owned businesses. Understandably, many pluralists and coalitionists argue that we must redesign our economic and social system to create more opportunities because a major factor contributing to intergroup tensions is the competition for limited resources.[8] Thus, what appears to be a racial conflict may actually be a class dispute, or a mixture of racial and class elements.

Yet racial difference has played a role throughout the United States: in San Francisco housing project clashes, in conflicts between Vietnamese and Latinos in Denver, Latinos and African Americans in Compton, and Pacific Islanders and Latinos in East Palo Alto. Violence between whites and people of color is still common, but tension and violence between groups of color is widespread as well. When we consider Korean American-African American conflict in South Central Los Angeles, African American-Jewish tension in Crown Heights, or Latino-African American friction in Miami, much of the time we are faced squarely with the intersection of race and class.[9] Competition for jobs, educational resources, and access to social programs often becomes defined in simplistic terms that ignore the multitude of causes. Recognizing the complexities will begin to help us formulate solutions to the tension and conflict.

SEPARATISM

The existence of linguistic and cultural separatism, about which Euro-immigrationists and cultural assimilationists complain, is undeniable. Latino barrios, Chinatowns, Little Indias, and Little Saigons have grown dramatically in number and size during the last twenty years. But before considering the factors that give rise to separatist communities and separatist sentiment, let us recognize that race and racism are at the root of many of the objections to these communities. When Euro-immigrationists and cultural assimilationists complain about the separatist threat to the unity and stability of the nation today, they are directing their charges against Asian and Latino immigration. Few, if any, of the charges question the presence of distinct communities of Italians, Poles, Hasidic Jews, and even Irish nationals in many U.S. cities. Racial difference appears to be the determinative factor.

As part of thinking seriously about separatism, we must begin by considering what separatism is. There are at least two different types of separatism: an ideological or political version, and a sociological version.

The ideological or political version can stem from anger over or disappointment in a system perceived to be weighted against certain classes or groups. For many, the anger provides an impetus to urge the community to engage in self-help and self-determination. Ideological separatism can result in physical separation, but it can also simply be a state of mind.

The sociological version arises from those who find comfort in a neighborhood with people of the same cultural and linguistic backgrounds. Many people in these neighborhoods want to retain their cultural identity for themselves and for their children. A sense of safety might also be a factor for those who feel physically threatened by the dominant culture. The sociological version could also include those who find the ghetto the most affordable place to live.[10]

Both political and sociological separatists might include some who judge others by race and wish to maintain barriers along those lines. For example, certain people of color may distrust or be bitter about past treatment by whites and wish to avoid contact. Others may believe racial and ethnic stereotypes that reinforce avoidance and separatism.

In my experience, immigrants who reside or work in ethnic enclaves do so less for ideological reasons than for reasons of comfort or affordability, or because of housing and employment discrimination. I have the same sense regarding, but less experience in, the African American community. For those African Americans who appear to have a choice, the ideology-comfort dichotomy is apparent. Thus, in Prince George's County, Maryland, a predominantly African American middle-class suburb of Washington, D.C., some African American residents are there out of "a profound sense of disillusionment." In the words of one resident, "You want to call me a separatist, so be it. I think of myself as a pragmatist. Why should I beg some cracker to integrate me into his society when he doesn't want to? Why keep beating my head up against a wall, especially when I've been there?" But others in the same neighborhood are less ideological: "I don't want to come home and always have my guard up. . . . After I work eight hours or more a day . . . I don't want to come home and work another eight."[11] Another person agrees: "When I'm socializing with people who are not African-American, I have to do a lot of explaining. . . . It's stressful because you know it's your responsibility to educate whites who have a sincere interest in understanding an issue. But it's more like work when you should just be socializing. If it's a black social setting, it's more like sharing ideas than educating."[12]

These comments illustrate the varied motivations for separatism epitomized by African Americans in Prince George's County. Some are there because of political disillusionment. Others are there for comfort and serenity, preferring to socialize and interact with friends and family rather than shoulder the burden of educating non-African Americans about African American culture, life, and perspectives.

Similar types of separatist sentiment no doubt exist in certain white ethnic communities—for example, Jewish, Italian, and Irish—as well. Some may be race-based, but much of it derives from ethnicity. However, Asian or Latino separatism receives much closer scrutiny because it involves immigrants of color who are easier to identify and target. Somehow ethnic separatism represented by Little Italys or Irish neighborhoods escapes criticism.

For Buchanan, Simpson, and FAIR, separatism by immigrants of color provides a reason for immigration restrictions. By their reasoning, the fewer immigrants (who today happen to be mostly Asians and Latinos) that we allow in, the easier it is to limit separatism. This restrictionist approach does not address the understandable separatist reaction to exclusion and discrimination and the desire for ethnic community comfort. It also underestimates the strength of ideological and sociological separatism among many immigrant groups of color who already live in the United States. The restrictionist response to separatism fails to recognize that much of the rationale behind separatism is not related to numbers. For many, separatist sentiment is a response to racism, exclusion, discrimination, and violence. Exclusionary laws and attacks on the Chinese in the late 1800s made the Chinese feel insecure, and Chinatowns correspondingly became more attractive. Exclusion leads to separatism, and dwindling numbers are only more likely to reinforce the trend.

The antiseparatist attack on immigration provides a convenient forum for attacks on separatism by people of color generally. Buchanan reveals his displeasure with African American separatism when he cites the hostile relations between whites and African Americans and the latter group's failure "to assimilate into our society."[13] Buchanan and other assimilationists simply do not like separatism among groups of color, which they see as resulting from immigration: the greater the influx of immigrants, the greater the flight into ethnic enclaves. For the assimilationists, then, the problem only gets worse because the very existence and growth of separate ethnic communities decreases incentives to integrate and threatens the viability of liberalism's solution to race relations. The end result is increased pressure for restrictive immigration laws directed at Asians, Latinos, and Haitians. In the pro-

cess, the underlying basis and rationale for the strong separatist sentiment among immigrants of color, as well as African Americans and
Native Americans, goes unaddressed, and society's ability to progress on
issues of race relations is hampered.

Although the flaws in Buchanan's extremist approach are easy to
identify, separatism also continues to trouble many who consider themselves cultural pluralists, especially those who supported integration as a
fundamental component of the struggle for civil rights and social justice.
While not motivated by the racism of Buchanan, an integration-minded
pluralist such as Todd Gitlin can relate to a Buchanan-like concern about
"cultural balkanization":

> Partly to resist homogenization and antisocial pressures, people identify
> with their separate tribes. Having learned not to have faith in central
> authorities, having grown skeptical of any reform politics that might
> build bridges, many altruists take refuge in their segregated communi-
> ties, competing for resources. The tribe—the ethnic or religious group,
> the profession, the affinity network—becomes the source of identity.
> But the tremendous vitality that results can become self-undermining.
> The sense of the common good is precarious. The commons is being
> paved over.[14]

Many cultural pluralists are ambivalent about separatism. They may
reject assimilationist-driven calls for immigration restrictions but still
worry that separatism means rejecting integration.[15] Make no mistake,
cultural pluralists like Gitlin might not mind Chinatowns or Latino
districts, but they are troubled when such communities "pave over the
commons" by declining to build bridges and participate in a larger
national identity. When separatist ideology appears to reject a common
national identity, the cultural pluralist experiences dissonance.

As a pluralist, I share this dissonance. But it makes me wonder
whether there is not a way of structuring or viewing our society within
its current democratic and economic framework that is respectful of
separatist sentiment. After all, it would not be the first time that dissonance, tension, or pressure led to something positive, including a better
understanding of our society.

1. UNDERSTANDING SEPARATISM

Treatment of interethnic group conflict and separatism may affect the development of immigration policies, but these issues have relevance far beyond immigration concerns. They are related to questions of how we live as a society, how we are structured racially and ethnically, and how we perceive what it means to be an American. On one level, taking a closer look at separatism is important because of the dissonance it causes to both assimilationists and pluralists in the maintenance of a common national identity, however that identity is constructed. On another level, understanding separatism is critical because separatism can and does contribute to hostility toward other groups, resulting in interethnic group conflict. This conflict can lead to the type of anti-immigrant sentiment epitomized by Buchanan, which in turn can reinforce separatist sentiment and interethnic conflict.

a. Ideological Separatism

Consider first those with strong ideologically based separatist sentiment. The perpetuation of racism in the post-civil rights era has understandably led communities of color to focus on achieving political and economic viability. This largely represents their disappointment and disillusionment with liberalism's promise of rights and formal equality. A theory based at least partially on race to explain the rise in separatist tendencies is not new. In his description of 1960s assimilation, sociologist Milton Gordon found racial exclusion to be an obstacle to full assimilation. In his paradigm, assimilation involves two distinct enterprises: acculturation, or behavioral assimilation; and structural assimilation, or social assimilation. Acculturation is the change of immigrant cultural patterns to those of the host society, while social or structural assimilation is the immigrants' large-scale entry into the general civic life of the receiving society, exemplified by social cliques, clubs, and institutions.[16] Unlike acculturation, structural assimilation requires the dominant group to accept the immigrant group. Thus, mainstream acceptance is the decisive element in long-term adaptation.

Gordon concluded that although considerable acculturation had occurred for most immigrants, structural assimilation was limited. This was particularly true for newer immigrants and racial minorities, such as Italians, Poles, Mexicans, African Americans, and Puerto Ricans. Gordon attributed the retardation of structural assimilation to religious and racial differences between immigrants and the mainstream.[17]

There continue to be serious questions about whether current power structures permit immigrants of color large-scale entry into the general civic or "primary group" life of the receiving society. Separatist sentiment cannot simply be equated with a lack of preference for acculturation. Many communities of color have become separatist only after having sought acceptance in mainstream institutions and having been rejected. After decades, even centuries, of unsuccessfully trying to break into the social and political structures of the country, many concluded that they must take things into their own hands, forgo reliance on the power structure, and look out for their own interests. Ideological separatists often encourage their communities to work, spend, and live in the community in a self-help political fashion.[18] Their priority is taking care of themselves, since coalition work with other communities seems to have generated few rewards.[19]

The ideological separatists do have a point. To Buchanan, FAIR, and their ilk, the proportionate increase in the number of people of color in the United States over the last twenty-five years, particularly among Latinos and Asian Americans, has led to more separatism. From the viewpoint of ideological separatists, however, the change has served only to highlight racial differences in the United States. As we have seen, although immigrants of color continue to acculturate and adopt distinctive American behavioral traits, many mainstream institutions refuse to accept them. Certainly culture and language differences serve as a partial explanation for why today's immigrant groups continue to be excluded from certain social and economic institutions. But the race factor cannot be ignored. We read constantly about all-white country clubs that continue to balk at admitting members from other racial groups.[20] Studies reveal glass ceilings that Asian Americans, Latinos, and African Americans encounter on the corporate ladder irrespective of acculturation and English-speaking ability.[21] It is natural, then, for some to turn away from the mainstream in response to rejection by the dominant power structure.

In addition to changing demographics, changing societal attitudes are also important to the foundation of ideological separatism. The patchwork of ethnic groups in the United States has grown even more diverse with increased immigration, contributing to greater diversity of opinion even within Latino and Asian American communities. Meanwhile, two new generations have emerged—one whose beliefs and attitudes were shaped during the civil rights movement, and a subsequent one whose expectations were influenced by that movement. The earlier generation guided the civil rights movement. The latter generation has developed its own interpretation of what has occurred over the last thirty years and is defining new civil rights strategies for the struggles ahead. Consciousness about civil and human rights has increased over the last thirty years, and in institutional arenas tolerance of racism has decreased. This is not to deny that there has been retrenchment on many of these fronts. A backlash against affirmative action and forced busing, as epitomized by the *Bakke* case in the 1970s and by the move to dismantle preferential programs today that began in the 1980s, is also unmistakable. The combination of progress and retrenchment has fostered an environment ripe for ideological separatism.

b. Sociological Separatism

For those who seek separate ethnic and racial communities for reasons of comfort, the choice is often a simple matter of familiarity with language, culture, and behavior. If there were more mainstream social and institutional acceptance of various ethnic groups, there would be less need for nonideological separatists to seek enclaves for comfort. The historical development of Chinatowns is a useful model for understanding this sociological separatist sentiment, as well as ideological separatist sentiment.

Ineligible for citizenship, and targeted by harsh discrimination and an array of repressive state and local laws, the Chinese found themselves segregated and excluded from white mainstream society. Many laborers resettled in urban Chinatowns. Some needed jobs as gold mining waned and the transcontinental railroad was completed in 1869, but others had spent their lives working the land. Often they knew little of urban life, and even feared it, but were forced to move nonetheless. An 1879 California law (soon after declared unconstitutional) required incorporated towns and cities to remove Chinese residents from city limits. In 1885, a Tucson petition urged that Chinese be required to live in a Chinatown. Landlords and realtors refused to rent and sell to Chinese outside the Chinatown, and whites threatened violence against those who passed certain boundaries.[22]

The white mainstream and the Chinese understood this forced migration to Chinatowns in two quite contrasting ways. For white mainstream citizens, Chinatowns helped resolve the dilemma of simultaneously needing the Chinese, or some foreign group like them, for domestic and service jobs, and fearing their unknown "oriental" powers. Chinatowns meant whites could keep an eye on the Chinese—check their wanderings and aspirations, their capacity to "infiltrate" white society, and their economy and politics—yet remain at arm's length.

For the Chinese, Chinatowns provided a measure of much-needed security and comfort. The Chinese frequently suffered mob attacks during the anti-Chinese furor of the late nineteenth and early twentieth centuries. In the relative safety and comfort of their own enclaves, they created formal associations based on geographic origin and family clans that helped meet their economic, social, religious, educational, and political needs. These networks were particularly important to the men, who needed a substitute for the traditional families they were denied. With the advent of exclusion laws, the Chinese population dropped, making the need for Chinatowns even more compelling.[23]

Other minority groups, such as Koreans, Japanese, and Vietnamese, have followed the same pattern as the Chinese. The pattern cuts across racial lines as well. Jews, Poles, and Italians are examples of white immigrants who have established their own enclaves.

The notion that one might prefer segregation because it provides a more comfortable environment, can be unsettling. We may understand the reasons behind separatist sentiment, but still experience dissonance. If whites say they want to live among themselves exclusively, or even in a predominantly white neighborhood, we construe such sentiment as segregation and racism. Is the analogous preference among people of color different? Is it more justifiable? Perhaps it is. For example, if an exclusively Japanese American California community, including elders interned during World War II, chooses to live in a segregated neighborhood because of its bitterness over internment and the safety and comfort of being around other Japanese Americans, we might find such a reaction understandable. If we can empathize with previously interned Japanese Americans who want to live together, then we might begin to understand a similar sentiment among other groups of color.

2. RACISM, LACK OF CONTROL, IDENTITY, AND DIVERSITY

Advocates of conventional cultural pluralism disquieted by separatist ideology must not ignore the realities of past and present racial discrimination. It is quite appealing for progressives to support the retention of culture by people of color, respect for differences by the power structure, and the sharing of power and equal access to institutions, in which case separatism might not be necessary. The problem is that things have not worked out that way. First, immigrants of color have yet to be fully incorporated into the social and political structures of our society. Many immigrants and groups of color think inclusion in the power structures of Wall Street, corporate boardrooms, elite educational institutions, and certain social institutions is not a realistic possibility. Certainly some people are quite happy in their communities and do not desire acceptance in mainstream institutions. Within a broad paradigm of cultural pluralism, this presents no fundamental problem. For those who do desire inclusion within the mainstream society, however, exclusion is grievous and harmful. Exclusion from the mainstream power structure is most obvious because it encompasses the major social, political, and economic institutions of the country. At the local level, exclusion is no less harmful; exclusion from neighborhood, school, and formal social groups can make all the difference to an individual or community trying to be part of that social group.[24]

Separatist sentiment has everything to do with racial discrimination. Today's immigrants face hostilities similar to those faced by their white predecessors. The biggest difference between today's Asian, Latino, and Haitian immigrants and Irish, Italian, and southern and eastern European immigrants of decades past is race. Certainly, all these groups faced hostilities, discrimination, and even violence, but eventually the Irish and Europeans became part of the mainstream.[25] Eventually, European immigrants coalesced for identity purposes into the new monolithic European-American category. By contrast, for "racial minorities, there was not even the pretense of an invitation" to join the power structure.[26] While Jews are still excluded from certain levels of business and social circles, they have achieved some success in entering the professional structure.[27] But new immigrants of color are generally ostracized from business, government, and social circles. The lack of social acceptance, in particular, plagues new immigrants of color and contributes to separatism.

A desire for self-determination is particularly understandable given the continuing economic struggles of many within communities of color.[28] It is easy to assume that this does not apply to all people of color, particularly Asian Americans. A popular misconception is that Asian Americans (as well as professionals of color) do not experience the effects of discrimination and racial and economic stratification. On the contrary, the few professionals of color who are successful in mainstream society often bear the burden of having white society treat them as ambassadors or representatives of their entire race. Thus, even in professional circles, white society's expectations of people of color are often quite different from its expectations of those of European ancestry.

White Americans continue to control the principal economic, social, and political institutions of the country. We continue to read about the all-white country clubs to which political and business leaders and judges belong. It does not take long for communities of color to become skeptical about the willingness of a power structure dominated by whites to permit full assimilation. The fact that many poor whites are also excluded does not diminish these doubts. Racism permeates the lower socioeconomic classes just as surely as it does the higher ones. If racism persists, more people of color will react in separatist ways. Certainly many whites do not feel they are in control of the power structure, but people of color see that even outside the boardrooms and the political elite, whites are primarily in control of the clubs, the leagues, and other social organizations. Moreover, people of color who feel excluded from those institutions see whites as responsible for the exclusion. Although many whites are not part of the power structure, it is whites who have institutional control in most instances. While people of color can be found in positions of control in some mainstream institutions, these cases are rare.

Since people of color generally lack control over mainstream institutions, they ought to be allowed to maintain an environment where they can function autonomously. If white Americans have control over most mainstream structures, why shouldn't people of color be allowed to seek alternative structures, even separatist ones, to control at least part of their world and advance and provide for their families? To be sure, the anger that impels a community to self-help can lead to more destructive speech and behavior that is based strictly on race or ethnicity, such as anti-Asian sentiment or anti-Semitism. At this point, separatism becomes indefensible. However, apart from this, a philosophy of separatism that is based on self-help should be fostered and defended.

Respect for separatism also flows from understanding that for many people of color, separatism plays a critical role in their identity. Many people of color are isolated or have no sense of identity in the mainstream, for example, at work, at school, or in social settings.[29] They need their ethnic community to develop a sense of self. Their communities may provide a better chance to learn about and develop a respect for their own race and culture. Like the family, the ethnic community often supports an individual's emotional, social, and political development, when that person would otherwise flounder in the mainstream.[30] Certainly this is not true for all people of color, but for many the ethnic community makes a huge positive difference. At the very least, the availability of the option is vital.

Understanding separatism also means understanding that each community is comprised of members with diverse points of view about separatism, pluralism, coalition building, race, and assimilation. Some who are not separatists may downplay or cast aside their race and submerge themselves in the mainstream culture and its promise of a true meritocracy. Some may form coalitions with other groups of color. Still others reject their own racial community's mainstream culture as thoroughly as they reject mainstream white culture.[31]

Understanding separatism means recognizing that immigrant adaptation should not rest solely on the shoulders of immigrants. In order to elicit some commitment from separatist communities to participate in a core or central culture, it is necessary to view immigrant adaptation as a dual responsibility. Those in control of the power structure and mainstream social institutions have a duty as well.

Some may look for a simple, idealistic form of cultural pluralism that preserves different groups' ethnic identities but also advocates participation in a common political, social, and economic identity. The reality of the diversity of opinions within communities of color is likely to frustrate such idealists. Perhaps by understanding the thinking behind these varied views we can begin to accept a form of cultural pluralism that recognizes the validity of even the most ideological separatist sentiment.

chapter 10

A New Way of Looking
at America

Each generation of Americans must define what it means to be an American.

— PRESIDENT BILL CLINTON
Inauguration Speech
Jan. 20, 1993

Cultural pluralism is alive in the United States. Its advocates have tired of the assimilationist stridency which envisions a narrow, anachronistic, and European American notion of what it means to be an American. At the moment, a modified pluralism controls an immigration policy which, except for certain restrictive refugee policies, is more open than ever.[1] Asians and Latinos dominate the predominantly family-based immigration system. Recently available diversity visa programs are designed to permit Africans to use them, and many Latinos and some Haitians and Cubans were granted amnesty under a 1986 law. The government is no longer engaged in official Americanization programs aimed at supplanting immigrants' cultures.

While cultural pluralism is alive, it may not be well. Assimilationists have tired of what they view as a fanciful, doctrinaire vision of a multicultural society. After experiencing some progress in the areas of social acceptance, political influence, and economic development, ideological segments of ethnic and racial minorities in the United States have moved away from the dream of a cultural plurality, toward separatism.[2] Most of these separatists are searching for a society in which they are valued and have a level of control over the institutions that influence their lives.

If some manifestations of separatism are regarded as evil—such as the rejection of a common core culture or set of values—then the biggest share of the blame should be placed at the feet of those who have excluded people of color from the power structure. Thus, the anti-immigrant statements of Brimelow, Buchanan, and FAIR are not only misguided in their refusal to deal with the tension created by interethnic violence or separatism, but also counterproductive to the adaptation process of the very immigrants that concern them. The nativist Euro-conformity doctrine is irrelevant to an already multiracial nation grappling with separatism and ethnic conflict. Furthermore, their divisive and spiteful attack on immigration may discourage immigrants from striving to acculturate. Urging the revision of immigration laws to allow only European immigrants or English speakers is to tell over 80 percent of our immigrants that we do not like them; that there is something about their race and language that is offensive; that because of their race, language, and culture they do not belong in this country.

We all share to varying degrees the blame for a culture that gives rise to protests epitomized by the uprising in South Central Los Angeles. Every time we engage in even subtle racism or the fostering of stereotypes, we perpetuate that culture. As much as each of us shares the blame, each of us also has the opportunity to be part of the solution. Every time we reach out to others whom we have been conditioned to distrust, fear, or subordinate because of race or class, we begin to chip away at the wicked culture that gives rise to irrational hatred, animosity, and violence.[3]

DEFINING AMERICA

An important part of any nation's cultural and social life is the way its citizens conceive of themselves. We have seen the narrow racial provincialism of the assimilationists fail to take into account the rich diversity in America's past and present. At the same time, assimilationists may also foster increased separatism, as minorities who did not fit the assimilationists' mold for being an American become angry and frustrated by their exclusion in society. Since we are becoming an increasingly multiracial and multicultural nation, we need to find new ways of looking at what it means to be an American.

The idea of "being an American" signifies different things to different people. Recognition of these differences helps develop a respect for other cultures and sets the groundwork for a workable multiracial society. This groundwork can help us counter the human tendency to divide and distinguish in binary terms of superiority and inferiority based on racial or ethnic criteria. We must overcome that tendency if we wish to fashion a new vision of pluralism that respects diverse viewpoints and backgrounds. Neither Euro-conformity nor conventional pluralism adequately describes what is happening. A multiracial process that accommodates separatism for those people of color who choose it demands new ways of thinking. Under a new version of pluralism, separatists would be welcomed when their separatism was based on self-help, self-determination, and comfort, rather than destructive racial or ethnic sentiments aimed at other groups. Concepts of what it means to be an American must include the diversity of new generations of Americans—foreign-born, native-born, white, and of color—and be cognizant of the tension that accompanies diversity. Catch phrases like *melting pot* or *salad bowl* fail to describe our complex society in a useful way.

Clinging to a Euro-conformity paradigm of what constitutes an American is simultaneously fruitless and dangerous. When culture and race assimilationists advocate their positions, they ignore the demographic realities of the nation. About a quarter of the nation is comprised of people of color: 12 percent African American; 10.2 percent Latino; 3.3 percent Asian American; and 1 percent Native American. By the year 2050, the population will be almost evenly divided between Anglos and people of color. Already certain states and localities are quite diverse.[4]

With these demographic changes, we cannot forget that acculturation will also continue. Left to market forces, immigrants are indeed Americanized, picking up the habits, cultural traits, values, interests, and languages of the dominant group. However, market forces have also worked in a manner that constantly changes American culture and redefines what an American is. As immigrants become more "American" due to these market forces, their native cultural traits also influence existing social norms. Thus, just as the process of Americanization has evolved from one of Anglo-conformity to Euro-conformity, it is evolving now and in the future into a multicultural-conformity that requires us to look at our society in broader perspective. This change has been gradual because of the strength and ubiquity of the dominant culture. Yet change has occurred, and the futility of defining what an American is in purely Eurocentric terms should be apparent.

Just as the advocacy of white-only immigration is counterproductive to the adaptation process of nonwhite immigrants, the continued definition of an American in Eurocentric terms is fraught with danger. Indeed, the rhetoric of Buchanan and Duke suggests that this is their purpose. Expressions of Euro-Americanization help racists confirm their views of racial superiority over people of color. White supremacists feed on this type of sentiment and manipulate the advocacy for Euro-conformity to their benefit by finding new recruits initially attracted to the more benign notion of strengthening the nation through unity. The hazards of such a process are clear. Resentment of immigrants is engendered, scapegoating of people of color becomes easier, racial and ethnic epithets remain commonplace, and hate-motivated violence ensues.

Immigrants *do* acculturate. Assimilation is a fluid and evolving process rather than a static one. Furthermore, the presence of immigrants also influences the ongoing evolution of American culture. As a result, the definition of what an American is must be expanded. The concept must be one of addition rather than omission. It must embrace differences rather than attack them. It must respect diversity rather than disregard it. It must appeal to a sense of unity that incorporates multiculturalism rather than the illusion of Eurocentric unity, which often serves as a pretext or mask for ostracizing other cultures.

Thus, the new definition of "what it means to be an American," which President Clinton has challenged us to provide, is one of inclusion rather than exclusion. It respects the history, the traditions, the culture, the literature, the values, the language, and the music of Native Americans, African Americans, Latinos, Asian Americans, Pacific Islanders, and others as those cultural qualities have distinctly evolved within our borders. This modern vision recognizes that the Navajo's respect for the earth and its natural resources is an American value; that the African American-led civil rights movement of the 1960s represents a powerful moment in our American history; that the continuing nightmares of torture, death, and heartache endured by Cambodian refugees is a component of the American psyche; that the folklore and labor of Mexican farmworkers is an American experience. It recognizes that the American experience is broad and diverse. In short, it recognizes not only that being an American can mean different things to different people, but also that each experience contributes to the national story and each achievement leads the nation forward.

A New Commitment

In light of this new dynamic, we clearly need a new commitment to race relations and multiculturalism. Less than twenty years ago, little in the way of an environmental movement existed in the United States. Yet with leadership, planning, commitment, and persistence, we have become an environmentally conscious society. Schoolchildren are taught about the environment. We devote local government efforts to recycling and reducing waste. Water conservation is a high priority in some states. The federal Environmental Protection Agency has state counterparts with staffs devoted to environmental issues. An entire lexicon—recycling, pollution, air quality, biodegradable, greenhouse effect, global warming, ozone depletion, rain forest—has developed during this time.[5] Many of us do not act without thinking about the possible impact on the environment.

The same kind of commitment is needed for race relations and multiculturalism.[6] We need to promote constant awareness of interethnic group relations, elimination of conscious and unconscious racism,[7] and social acceptance of people of color. We must reach a new level of consciousness, strive to develop a new inclusive vocabulary, explore new ways of being American, and recognize the variety of racial and ethnic issues that face our society. As Martin Luther King urged, we must judge people by the content of their character rather than by skin color.[8] Although we are not all environmentalists, and we are committed to the environment in different degrees, even that level of awareness in a new commitment to interracial relationships would be much better than what we have today, where interracial dialogue is minimal and positive discussion even within communities about other communities receives low priority.

A viable multiethnic, multiracial society that recognizes a need for separatism in certain sectors, yet simultaneously urges some form of common American political identity, is not impossible or inconsistent.

Diversity of opinion runs deep. Even among separatists, significant differences arise concerning the degree of separatism desired, often based on class, experience, education, and economic background. For example, some may seek more active coalition building, while others may reject it. Those within a particular ethnic community, as well as nonmembers, should recognize and respect the diversity within each community and recognize the care that must be exercised in purporting to speak on behalf of a community.[9]

Make no mistake. The ability to maintain ethnic communities need not give way to a new commitment toward establishing a common political identity. Some who are committed to multiculturalism are also troubled by interethnic tension and what they label "identity politics."[10] But they should not ignore the good relationships between ethnic groups that are easy to find, as well as the social and economic benefits that accrue to the entire society when individuals are able to preserve their identities through their communities.

A new perspective on pluralism would encourage interaction between the mainstream and people of color in the following ways. First, immigrants should be encouraged, but not required, to move back and forth between their ethnic communities and the mainstream community. This process might entail becoming completely bicultural—that is, able to operate in both spheres smoothly—but it might not. Knowledge of enough English and Euro-American culture to get by in the mainstream world would be adequate. Ethnic media and bicultural community members can keep people sufficiently informed to participate indirectly in the mainstream community.[11]

Second, and perhaps most important, the mainstream should be encouraged to learn to be bicultural (or multicultural) as well. In a multicultural society, the mainstream should be responsible for developing an understanding and knowledge of other cultures. Today, shrewd retailers and business managers already aim to do so, not unlike the situation in Europe where students learn more than one language, an example of successful multiculturalism Euro-immigrationists seem to ignore. Indeed, failing to learn more than one language or more about other cultures could be regarded as imprudent. This perspective recognizes that culture, ethnicity, and identity are neither static nor exclusive. One can be 100 percent Chinese American and also 100 percent loyal to the United States and its political and economic institutions.

FINDING CORE VALUES

Even a multicultural society must share a core of values, or a culture, to provide a means to live together as a society. Without a commitment to a common core, balkanization into assorted factions is likely. Without a core, it will be more difficult to eliminate interethnic group violence and tension. This core, however, need not be more than a common nucleus. It should respect the need for separatist sentiment so long as that sentiment does not violate the core values. It should not be an all-encompassing concept that defines each person's or each community's total identity. The image, rather, is one of many communities, some more separate than others, some overlapping, but all interlinked at the core.

The common core of values encompasses the essence of good citizenship. It includes respect for the nation's laws, for its democratic political and economic system, and for equal opportunity.[12] But this common nucleus is part of a modern vision of being an American. The requirement of inclusion and respect for diversity is reciprocal and applies not only to those in control of the power structure, but also to those at the margin and how they should regard one another. Thus, as part of this core, I would urge others to consider adopting a particular set of values—which some would regard as American, but which I regard as human values—so that we might move toward a peaceful multiracial society. Basically, these values are to repudiate racism, sexism, heterosexism, and class distinctions in our daily activities; to be open, caring, and fair; and to be accepting of diversity and respectful of others.[13]

At first it might seem hypocritical on the one hand to criticize assimilationists for urging immigrants to become a certain type of American, but on the other hand to come up with my own set of normative standards. However, these values are not simply a matter of "political correctness." My standards have to do with respect for the lives, identities, and cultures of others. They are standards which promote understanding, unity, and camaraderie, rather than divisiveness, hatred, and violence. Assimilationists only promote a Euro-American lifestyle and culture and are intolerant of others;[14] my core would seek to promote racial and class harmony, the cornerstone of a multicultural society. I would urge my nucleus set of values on all Americans, not just immigrants.[15]

These core values must be followed at the highest levels of government and society, by political leaders, government officials, business executives, educators, community representatives, and public figures. Their example through words and day-to-day activity is critical. Not only can they set the tone for the repudiation of racism, sexism, heterosexism, and class distinctions, but their actions will demonstrate their sincerity about welcoming everyone into the mainstream. The values of respect for the law, support of the democratic political and economic system, fairness, and respect for differences are dependent on the power structure's acceptance of a new vision of pluralism. Without the power structure's imprimatur and resolve, the likelihood of broad-based endorsement of a common core by those at the margin may be impossible to realize.

chapter 11

Back to Superior

Modern-day advocates of immigration restrictions often advance popular, but negative, images of immigrants and the economy. But people like my client Rodolfo Martinez Padilla do not hurt—and most likely help—the U.S. economy. While sometimes contradictory and inconclusive, the empirical results as a whole suggest that current levels of immigration—documented or undocumented—do not create massive job dislocation or depression of wages, nor result in net costs in the public sector as a whole. The fever-pitch charges aimed at immigrants are simply not justified by economic studies.

Indeed, the presence of immigrants—both documented and undocumented—may actually boost or sustain jobs and wages for most native workers. The selection bias of many regional and sectoral studies which specifically focus on areas or industries with significant immigrant concentrations provides further evidence that the overall impact of immigrants is not a negative one.

Labor market reports about New York, Los Angeles, Miami, and

Texas consistently find that immigrants do not negatively impact the jobs and wages of native workers, and are credited with the viability of certain industries. In Miami, jobs and wages of native workers were not damaged even on the heels of a major influx of low-wage, low-skilled Cubans. The plight of poor whites, African Americans, and Puerto Ricans in Chicago had little to do with the presence of Mexican immigrants and more to do with conventional human capital and social issues.

The sectoral studies are equally positive, providing evidence that immigrants do not cause massive job displacement. In fact the evidence shows that immigrants create jobs through their complementary rather than competitive role in some industries, and that they contribute to the very survival of many U.S. industries. The flexibility of an immigrant workforce—documented or undocumented, willing to take low-wage, low-skilled, and unstable employment opportunities—has enabled certain industries to stay in the United States rather than close down or relocate their factories in countries with cheap labor. While this country's reliance on immigrant workers in agriculture is long and well-known, the food processing industry has also sought out immigrant workers as the industry has changed. Similarly, the service and construction industries have turned to low-wage immigrant workers especially during the recessionary 1980s.

Individual labor market studies that suggest some negative impact (i.e., the study of janitors in Los Angeles) as definitive indictments of immigrants, though the fodder for attention-grabbing headlines, rarely constitute representative results. Policymakers must recognize the context of these studies, and should view the empirical work as a whole, especially in light of the favorable impact suggested by most studies.

Of course the issues are not simple. Consider the economic status of African Americans. African Americans in New York and Los Angeles have enjoyed expanded access to white-collar and public sector jobs at the same time as immigrants have come to dominate many of the low-wage, low-skilled sectors. What then do diminishing funds for public sector employment mean to African Americans? How should we respond to survey results that indicate that many employers prefer (or discriminate in favor of) immigrant workers over African American workers? In service and food packing industries where African Americans were once dominant, is their displacement by immigrant workers a clear sign of injury at the hands of immigrants? On the other hand, is it

not important to recognize that immigration restrictions are not necessarily the most direct way to deal with tough economic issues? In fact,
might not such restrictions be counterproductive for our economy? And
does attempting to remove one group of exploitable low-wage workers
really represent an intellectually honest and logistically effective approach to racism and discrimination directed at African Americans?

In addition to thinking about native workers who might have taken
at least some of the low-wage jobs now held by immigrants, we must
also consider the prospect that the low-wage immigrant workers themselves are being exploited. Can we determine whether maintaining low-
wage jobs through an available pool of immigrant workers is better for
the economy than automation or mechanization? Does the use of low-
wage jobs depend on the industry, the location, or levels of competition?
Similarly, it is still unclear how unionization and the presence of immigrants interact to affect the U.S. economy; this should be further studied.
Research in Texas and Los Angeles revealed little negative impact. In
any event, we do know that immigrants—including the undocumented—have rights under the National Labor Relations Act and actively participate in many unions, but we still need to know more about
this relationship.

In terms of public sector costs, despite the headlines about the so-
called "cost" of immigrants, the most reliable studies on public sector
consumption and tax contributions demonstrate that immigrants—documented and undocumented—are net contributors. Even though Los
Angeles County researchers—whose methodology and assumptions
have been criticized as being biased toward a finding of high fiscal
costs associated with immigrants—found that immigrants ultimately
put more into the system through federal and state tax contributions
than they extract. While Huddle's work has been heavily cited by anti-
immigrant groups and attracts media attention, his methodology has
been shown to be highly suspect and as such lacks credibility. On the
other hand, the detailed, careful, and meticulously explained research of
the Urban Institute is the most reliable work available, and consistently
supports the understanding of immigrants as net contributors. More
systematic research also counters Huddle Report findings and public
perceptions of immigrants as welfare abusers. When broken down, Government Accounting Office figures cannot be used to support an image
of inordinate welfare use by lawful permanent residents either.

As with empirical work on the labor market, these cost studies raise important questions. That immigrants, while serving as net contributors when all levels of government are taken into account, resemble their native counterparts in being net consumers at the local level suggests that attention should be paid to the various gubernatorial claims that federal tax contributions by immigrants are being maldistributed. We might wonder about the increasing poverty rate among immigrants even as we recognize that the usage rates of long-term immigrants might be lower than those of the native population. And intuition might cause us concern about places that appear to be crowded already: Does the inflow of more immigrants begin to approach a congestion problem which should be addressed? And can true economic congestion be tested?

Thus, while the empirical work speaks to much of the theoretical framework discussed in chapters 4 and 5, some of these theories have not been subject to or certainly would defy easy empirical testing. For example, while some of the labor market studies (including the Alexis de Toqueville Institution's analysis of unemployment statistics) support the theory that immigration actually creates jobs, and that immigrants are complementary actors rather than competitors, the job-creation effects of immigrants as consumers who stimulate the economy is not so easily measured.

Likewise, if we view spending on education as loans against future human capital, can we empirically approximate the payback? Can we calculate the value of immigrants as additions to the stock of useful knowledge or human potential? As the stimulus for investment and technology? Or measure their job-creation and tax contributions as entrepreneurs? It is also not clear how we are to assess the value of immigrants in terms of trade theory or our nation's role in the global economy. Defying quantitative calculation as well are the psychic advantages that immigrants contribute to their relatives and the rest of the nation.

Advocates of immigration policy as a tool to address state or national economic woes are misguided. There is much that empirical work cannot tell us about the impact of immigrants on our nation's health and future; but what it does tell us is mostly positive. Overall what we know so far simply does not support the image of immigrants as the cause of massive job displacement and wage depression, as welfare-dependent burdens, or as inflicting inordinate costs on the public sector. Indeed, the evidence suggests that restrictions on immigration or immigrants' participation in the economy and public sector could have significantly negative economic effects.

The truth about Rodolfo Martinez Padilla is that he and his family are net contributors to our national and global economy. He is young and hardworking. In terms of capital investment, we did not have to invest much in his schooling (a year of high school). His on-the-job training has prepared him to be the productive worker he is now. In the labor market Rodolfo has contributed income taxes since his teens, paid into the Social Security fund, and been a steady consumer. No one in his family has ever received welfare. Even if a family member looks to public assistance in the future, given the family's entire work history the benefits would likely be covered by its contributions.

We may not all be willing to work the sixteen-hour, two-job days that Rodolfo Martinez Padilla has endured, but we all have something to learn from him. The lesson reaches beyond the overworn claim of the immigrant work ethic or willingness to take anything available. Rather, the lesson is about his willingness to take chances, to look for better ways, and to insist on better wages. Although he has held a large number of jobs over a fifteen-year period, he has been able to recognize oppressive situations, cope, look for other options, and, when necessary, move on. He has accepted and offered help from friends and family in locating work. He has shown initiative, starting a janitorial service and helping his father establish an automobile refurbishing business. He volunteers—sometimes out of altruism, other times to learn. He seeks out and is willing to take advice.

But Rodolfo Martinez Padilla also teaches us that economic considerations should not be the sole basis for decisions related to immigration policy or to immigrants. Immigrants have much more to offer than what can be measured in surveys and graphs. Think only of the role model and avuncular support Rodolfo provides for his nephews and nieces, or of his emotional sustenance for his parents.

Those who support measures for more rigorous border enforcement, measures such as Proposition 187 directed at undocumented migrants, efforts to cut legal immigrants off public benefits, stricter standards for refugee and asylum admissions, and reductions in the number of legal immigrants are a diverse group. Their proposals do not reflect a consistent or monolithic philosophy. Some are directed at undocumenteds, while others are aimed at legal immigrants. Certain individuals are motivated by economic concerns related to jobs, wages, and burdens on public coffers. This may well be the expression of a working class and middle class that is comfortable, but has little indication that its members are getting ahead.[1] These anxieties are rooted in social interests related to assimilation, language, or the perception of societal changes over which they sense a lack of control. Still others are troubled by environmental or population concerns. Many who are focused on the undocumented are upset by the integrity of the border—the immigration laws have been broken, so something must be done. Some are simply racists.

I have here strived to clarify many of the issues swirling in the immigration debate by recognizing the complexities involved, acknowledging areas of reasonable conflicting interpretations, and pointing out that more needs to be known about specific topics. Unfortunately this nuanced approach may do little to quiet restrictionists who will no doubt note that I cannot come up with simple one-line answers or solutions to their allegations. My textured analysis can also be easily misquoted, taken out of context, or mischaracterized. But hopefully more well-meaning observers will begin to understand the complexities as well as the bigger picture and begin to question the simplistic hyperbole offered up by most leaders of the modern-day restrictionist movement.

Important policy decisions on many subjects are made on a daily basis without regard to the full picture or a fair understanding of the context in which social phenomena occur. Would those decisions have been changed, influenced, or modified with more complete information and contextualization? The answer lies in our own decision-making experiences. Sometimes we reach the same conclusion irrespective of additional information. But no doubt we have all changed our minds or influenced others at some time or another with more information. Certainly when it comes to immigration policy, as with most questions of public policy, we will advocate and act on our own notions of justice or personal sense of values. We are hard-pressed to limit the ability of others to advance their views based on their own notions of fairness and justice. But what I ask here is that we acknowledge the complexities of the issue, be aware of the multitude of factors at play, and be honest about the consequences of proposals before acting on them. The soundness of these decisions may not be tested until years from now when future generations of Americans look back on this era. Will they look back with pride, or will this era be regarded as a shameful period of scapegoating?

In this book I have especially urged us to consider anew our vision of pluralism, of what it means to be an American, and of what it would take to live in a more peaceful multiracial society. Given demographic changes in the last generation and conservative estimates of what is to come, we must begin by recognizing the dangers and the narrow-mindedness of racial and cultural assimilationists who demand an exclusively Eurocentric vision of America. We should not fear the social impact of new members in our society. While immigrants do gradually influence our culture, market forces cause them to acculturate in rather conventional terms. Furthermore, their influence is positive; like generations of immigrants before them, they represent a class of people who contribute greatly to society and from whom we can learn. Although some espouse separatist sentiment, we should be open to their views in a new vision of pluralism. Developing a new commitment to the elimination of racism at all levels must be a chief priority. We must broaden our vision of what an American is as we strive for a common core of values.

A new understanding of and respect for separatism represents an important starting point for the resolution of interethnic group conflict, as does recognizing that much of the conflict is between the "haves" and "have-nots." This forces us to realize that many communities need creative and meaningful economic assistance and job-training programs.

As much as many of us revel in and thrive on multiculturalism and the drive that diversity provides, we cannot deny the tensions that multiculturalism causes. Ignoring or glossing over conflict and tension would be a mistake. We must constantly reevaluate and reassess our efforts.[2] We cannot be overly romantic in our pursuit of a peaceful and productive diversity. Yet to advance we must not be demoralized or paralyzed by the tension either. Those working to resolve tension and conflict between and within groups of color, and between communities of color and the power structure and the white working class should be supported. To deal with the tension, we must understand its sources. We must remain alert, ever mindful that things can be improved. Ignoring the pressure breeds complacency about inequities and tolerance of racism. Understanding and addressing the tension and pressure allows us to advance as a society.

Thus, for example, the racism within communities of color directed at other communities cannot be ignored. There is much room for improving racial understanding in communities of color as well as across all communities and classes. Every community must take the responsibility for educating its members about the evils of racial hatred. If the primary disagreement is over economic exploitation or political differences, let that be the debate without distorting the discussion with racial enmity.

The problems that communities share can provide a basis for addressing their own racism. Communities of color have all experienced various forms of subordination in the United States. The poor among them face similar housing and employment problems. Their middle classes encounter the same economic struggles related to mortgage payments, car loans, and the challenge of saving for the future. Their professionals face the same glass ceiling in promotions. Certainly Native American and African American communities share a uniquely grim history of oppression in the United States because of the involuntary nature of their place in a society dominated by European Americans. Rather than ranking or comparing degrees of subordination, these groups might find that the similarities are sufficient cause for understanding. Then, by working together on common problems, interracial understanding may be promoted, and judging others by their character rather than by stereotypes based on skin color, may be facilitated.

The responsibility for working on solutions lies with all sides if racism and violence are to be eliminated. Dialogue is the first step. Despite the obstacles and problems, dialogue among communities of color is possible. Amazingly, only three weeks after the uprising in Los Angeles, Korean American grocers agreed to hire African American gang members.[3] It took cooperation on both sides to reach this accord, and more progress is being made in spite of the difficulties. The communities have also joined together in peace marches. In San Diego, a coalition of African Americans and Latinos provide a model for engendering mutual respect and cooperation. Working with churches, community groups, and local government, they combat common problems such as drug use, the lack of low-income housing and job training, and violence.[4]

Although the challenges before us are extraordinary and the approaches proffered are preliminary, I hope to contribute to the energy needed to overcome our society's inertia. The solutions to these challenges are not simple, and my call to action may be utopian and naive,[5] but we are foolish to stand by idly.

In contrast, Buchanan's and Brimelow's proposals, and those of

Euro-immigrationists who call for severe immigration restrictions, do little to address the issues of interethnic conflict and separatism. Their proposals skirt the harder issues presented by a social and economic system which has failed groups of color and poor whites. They commit a foolish error by running from the tension hoping that it will go away if it is ignored for long enough. Assimilationists represent many Americans who are unwilling to shoulder the hard work and strain of developing a multicultural society, who cling to an exclusively Euro-conformist definition of an American, or who are just plain racist. Instead, we need to fashion an approach with hope. Just as we know that culture is constantly changing, the meaning of being an American is also changing to embrace diverse groups. Just as mainstream intolerance of religious discrimination eventually prevailed, the idea of permitting people of color to become Americans on their own terms can also permeate American culture, but only if the racism at the core of exclusionist proposals is exposed and rejected.

Ethnic conflict, divided neighborhoods, economic competitiveness, and militant separatism raise immense challenges. But the neonativist solution to those challenges is not the proposal of a country willing to respond thoughtfully and constructively to racial and ethnic tensions. The right response involves the willingness of all of us—especially the educated, those with influence, and those who have tapped into the economic and political power structures—to acknowledge our responsibility and to fulfill it. Those in control and with options have the power to initiate change. They can set the example for others.

Our nation's slow progress on multiracial and multiethnic issues is bound to spark further separatism. Yet if we remember that separatism is not all evil—especially in its emphasis on self-help, identity, and a sense of community—events such as the South Central Los Angeles uprising should reinforce our commitment to continue the struggle for a viable multicultural society. South Central was an ugly manifestation of a society that has failed in many respects—not simply in terms of interethnic group relations. But it reminds us that we cannot continue to ignore the problem. It jolts us into considering new ways of looking at our responsibilities as members of society.

I know that the notions I advocate can work. I have experienced much of this vision. In my hometown of Superior, I witnessed a community of different classes, backgrounds, and ethnicities thrive. There were political and sociological separatists among the Chinese, Navajos,

Apaches, and Mexican Americans. At the same time, however, they were bicultural: they accepted the premise of being part of a larger community. Languages, foods, and values were shared. People of all colors were part of the community, men and women; Mexicans, Navajos, Chinese, Syrians, and whites; bankers, lawyers, copper miners, mine bosses, ranchers, ranch hands, beauticians, grocers, and barbers; Catholics, Mormons, Baptists, Protestants, Jehovah's Witnesses, Episcopalians, Jews, and Buddhists. We worked, laughed, played, ate, celebrated, prayed, mourned, achieved, failed, and learned together. We benefited from one another. Of course there were tensions along racial, gender, generational, and class lines, but none proved insurmountable.

This perspective on race, culture, self-determination, and separatism has significant ramifications not only for Americanization and immigration policies, but also for issues such as affirmative action, integration, the educational curriculum, and educational methods.[6] How does a modern vision of being an American influence these issues? How does respecting separatist sentiment influence racial preferences and school busing? How does a new pluralism affect what and how students learn? The issues will become no less complicated when, early in the next century, no single racial group comprises a majority of the population and biracial marriages become more and more common. But we can continue to make sense of these issues, as well as deal with the many tensions we face, if we build an increasing respect for diversity and think in terms of inclusion rather than exclusion.[7] Our multicultural society can thrive if we all take responsibility, remaining mindful of who wields power and control, how that power is used, and who has been subordinated and oppressed by that power.

Notes

NOTES TO THE INTRODUCTION

1. See chapter 2.
2. A total of 4,326,335 immigrants entered from Asia and 4,466,064 from Latin America. These figures are calculated from the IMMIGRATION AND NATURALIZATION SERVICE, 1990 STATISTICAL YEARBOOK (1991), table 2, at 50.
3. Proposition 187 was the voter initiative passed by California voters in November 1994 that, among other things, would make undocumented children ineligible for public schooling, and prevent public health care facilities from rendering most medical care to all undocumented immigrants. Its provisions have not gone into effect, as their constitutionality is being tested in court.

NOTES TO CHAPTER 1

1. As chapter 3 relates, my mother was actually born in Scranton, Pennsylvania, in 1901, but accompanied her mother to China at the age of three to care for an ailing grandmother. My mother did not return to the United States until 1925, as the spouse of my father who was born in Guangdong, China, but who had false documents indicating that he was the son of a U.S. citizen. Many Chinese immigrants entered the United States as "paper sons" in response to exclusionary laws. *See* BILL ONG HING, MAKING AND REMAKING ASIAN AMERICA THROUGH IMMIGRATION POLICY 1850–1990 74 (1993); RONALD TAKAKI, STRANGERS FROM A DIFFERENT SHORE 110–12, 234–37 (1989).
2. See chapter 3.

NOTES TO CHAPTER 2

1. BEVERLY J. ARMENTO, ET AL., AMERICA WILL BE (1991).
2. EDITH ABBOTT, HISTORICAL ASPECTS OF THE IMMIGRATION PROBLEM 125 (1969), Garrett Davis, speech delivered to the Convention to Revise the Constitution of Kentucky, December 15, 1849.

3. SHIH-SHAN H. TSAI, THE CHINESE EXPERIENCE IN AMERICA 60 (1986); R. J. Mooney, *Matthew Keady and the Federal Judicial Response to Racism in the Early West*, 63 ORE. L. REV. 561, 571 (1984); ALEXANDER SAXTON, THE INDISPENSABLE ENEMY: LABOR AND THE ANTI-CHINESE MOVEMENT IN CALIFORNIA 60–65 (1971); BILL ONG HING, MAKING AND REMAKING ASIAN AMERICA THROUGH IMMIGRATION POLICY 1850–1990 20 (1993).

4. E. SANDMEYER, THE ANTI-CHINESE MOVEMENT IN CALIFORNIA 47–48 (1939). Placards in the parade carried messages such as "Women's Rights and no more Chinese Chambermaids," "Our Women are degraded by Coolie Labor," "No Servile Labor shall Pollute our Land," "American Trade Needs no Coolie Labor," "We want no Slaves or Aristocrats," and "The Coolie Labor System leaves us no Alternative—Starvation or Disgrace." The interest of eastern laborers was being aroused by Henry George's strong article in the *New York Tribune* and by the shipping of Chinese to North Adams, Massachusetts, to break a strike at a shoemaking facility. *Id.* at 48; STUART C. MILLER, THE UNWELCOME IMMIGRANT 8 (1969).

5. SAXTON, *supra* note 3, at 19–20. Under the Nationality Act of 1790, citizenship through naturalization was limited to "free white persons." By 1870, naturalization benefits were extended to persons of "African descent." EDWARD P. HUTCHINSON, LEGISLATIVE HISTORY OF AMERICAN IMMIGRATION POLICY 1798–1965 58–60, 212 (1981).

6. SAXTON, *supra* note 3, at 44–45, 104–5, 112–20. For the early Republican Party, nativism was a critically important element. The fear of foreign immigration had three parts: a strong attraction for certain groups of workingmen, the nondiminution among immigrants who were as menaced by further immigration as was the native American, and a pattern of organized violence. The Democratic Party initially advanced a strong sentiment for racial tolerance because of the need for a supply of cheap labor. However, pressure from white workingmen eventually moved the Democratic Party to adopt platforms recognizing Chinese as inferior and degrading to American labor. The Workingman's Party of California should be distinguished from the Workingman's Party of the United States. The California party was headed by Dennis Kearney who gained notoriety for urging not only Chinese exclusion but that Californians should organize their own new party. By 1878, the party was a strong force in California. At the California constitutional convention that year, the Workingman's Party advanced several anti-Chinese clauses. One clause read, "No native of China, no idiot, insane person or person convicted of any infamous crime shall ever exercise the privileges of an elector of the state." *Id.* at 32–34, 83–84, 87–89, 116–20, 128–29.

7. MILLER, *supra* note 4, at 191–200; SAXTON, *supra* note 3, at 103. One anti-Chinese piece of legislation introduced in the forty-fifth Congress (1977) was the so-called "fifteen-passenger" bill. It was based on the belief that Chinese lacked morality and could not assimilate, even though they were obedient and hardworking. Although the bill passed both the House and Senate, President Hayes vetoed the legislation after intensive lobbying by Chinese and Chinese supporters such as the Yale College faculty. TSAI, *supra* note 3, at 45–48.

One commentator of the time described the Chinese in this manner:

> The Chinaman, it is claimed, and apparently with truth, will learn any given mechanical operation in one-third of the time required by a white workman. He has no family; he lives in the most frugal manner; he lodges upon a wooden bench; he has been used at home to wages that would hardly more than sustain life. His sole ambition is to accumulate two hundred to four hundred dollars. . . . By means of all this he is enabled to live as no white man could live. . . . The result has been to prevent the immigration of a strong and healthy laboring class of kindred and easily affiliated races from the Eastern States and from Europe.

J. WHITNEY, THE CHINESE AND THE CHINESE QUESTION 113–14 (1888).

8. HUTCHINSON, *supra* note 5, at 69–70; MARY COOLIDGE, CHINESE IMMIGRATION 105 (1909); MILLER, *supra* note 4, at 191–200. Relying on the minority findings of one commission member and a review of the testimonial transcripts, Coolidge observed that the report was distorted and failed to clear up any disputed points. *Id.* at 104–8. A select committee report issued in 1880 concluded that the people of California had just cause for complaint and that it would be impossible for the Chinese ever to meet on common ground with American citizens or occupy the same social level. The committee called for the annulment of the treaties with China that permitted immigration. An accompanying minority report expressed doubt as to whether the depression of business and labor in California was due to the presence of Chinese; some questioned the conclusions which were based on biased testimony. HUTCHINSON, *supra* note 5, at 75–76. The report also recommended revisions of the Burlingame Treaty with China. SAXTON, *supra* note 3, at 137.

9. 92 U.S. 275 (1875); *see also Henderson v. Mayor of New York*, 92 U.S. 259 (1875).

10. COOLIDGE, *supra* note 8, at 58. If asked about their program, its members were instructed to answer, "I know nothing about it." JOHN F. KENNEDY, NATION OF IMMIGRANTS 70 (1964).

11. Gerald P. López, *Undocumented Mexican Migration: In Search of a Just Immigration Law and Policy*, 28 UCLA L. REV. 615, 642–43 (1981); U.S. COMMISSION ON CIVIL RIGHTS, THE TARNISHED GOLDEN DOOR 11, 13–19 (1980); IMMIGRATION AND NATURALIZATION SERVICE, 1976 ANNUAL REPORT 87–88 (1977).

12. López, *supra* note 11, at 647.

13. George J. Sanchez, *"Go After the Women": Americanization and the Mexican Immigrant Woman, 1915–1929*, in ELLEN C. DuBOIS AND VICKIE L. RUIZ, EDS., UNEQUAL SISTERS: A MULTICULTURAL READER IN U.S. WOMEN'S HISTORY 250, 254 (1990).

> Though governmental bodies and private organizations in other states also sought to Americanize Mexicans, California's program was the most complete attempt to bring together government,

business, and private citizens to deal with the "problem of the immigrant" in a scientific and rational fashion. The Commission successfully recruited university academics, religious social workers, government bureaucrats, and middle-class volunteers.

Id. at 254.

14. *Id.* at 256–59.

15. *Id.* at 255–57.

16. *Id.* at 259–61.

17. *See* John W. Ragsdale, Jr., *The Movement to Assimilate the American Indians: A Jurisprudential Study,* 57 UMKC L. Rev. 399, 401–2 (1989).

18. *Id.*

19. *Id.* at 403–5.

20. *Id.* at 407–8.

21. *Id.* at 410.

22. *Id.*

23. *Id.* at 422–23.

24. López, *supra* note 11, at 632–33.

25. *See* Charles Gordon and Stanley Mailman, Immigration Law and Procedure § 1.4c (1993); Memorandum for the Associate Attorney General, Re: Allocation of Visas under *Silva v. Levi,* Deputy Assistant Attorney General, Office of Legal Counsel, Department of Justice, 3 (May 15, 1978).

26. *See* The Tarnished Golden Door, *supra* note 11, at 12; *Silva v. Bell,* 605 F.2d 978, 980–82 (7th Cir. 1979); Gordon and Mailman, *supra* note 25, at § 7.9e.

27. Act of Oct. 20, 1976, Pub.L. No. 94–571, 90 Stat. 2703 (1976); *Silva v. Bell,* 605 F.2d at 980–82.

28. *Silva v. Bell,* No. 76C 4268 (N.D. Ill. Oct. 10, 1978), order granting permanent injunction; *see also* No. 76C 1456 (N.D. Ill. June 21, 1977), final judgment order—visas recaptured.

29. Telegraphic Message of Hugh J. Brian, Asst. Commr. Detention and Deportation, Central Office Immigration and Naturalization Service, CO 242.4–P (Aug. 20, 1982); Memorandum from E. B. Duarte, Jr, Director, Outreach Program, Central Office Immigration and Naturalization Service, To Outreach Centers, Subject: Silva Update (Feb. 3, 1983).

30. 643 F.2d 471, 476 (7th Cir. 1981).

31. *See* Visa Bulletin, Visa Office, Bureau of Consular Affairs, U.S. Department of State, Vol. VII. No. 52 (July 1995).

32. *See* David Castro, *Dragnet for Illegal Workers,* Time, May 10, 1982, at 16; International Molders and Allied Workers' Local Union, 799 F.2d 547 (9th Cir. 1986).

33. *See Illegal Alien Raids Trigger Local Lawsuits,* Argus-Courier, Aug. 16, 1982, at 2.

34. *See, e.g., ILGWU v. Sureck,* 681 F.2d (9th Cir. 1982); *Illinois Council v. Pilliod,* 531 F.Supp. 1011 (N.D. Ill. 1982).

35. Immigration and Naturalization Service, 1977 Annual Report 14 (1978).

36. 422 U.S. 873 (1975).

37. 428 U.S. 543 (1976).

38. 468 U.S. 1032 (1984).

39. 413 U.S. 717 (1973).

40. 413 U.S. 634 (1973).

41. 435 U.S. 291 (1978).

42. 441 U.S. 68 (1978).

43. In *Cabell v. Chavez-Salido*, 454 U.S. 432 (1982), the Court also ruled that probation officer positions in California could be limited to U.S. citizens. In the federal civil service area, the Supreme Court has refused to review lower court decisions that have upheld an executive order limiting federal civil service jobs to U.S. citizens. *Mow Sun Wong v. Campbell*, 626 F.2d 739 (9th Cir. 1980), *cert. denied*, 450 U.S. 959 (1981); *Vergara v. Hampton*, 581 F.2d 1281 (7th Cir. 1978), *cert. denied*, 441 U.S. 905 (1979).

44. *Haitian Refugee Center v. Smith*, 676 F.2d 1023 (5th Cir. 1982).

45. *American Baptist Churches v. Thornburgh*, 760 F.Supp. 796 (N.D. Cal. 1991).

46. *See generally* Bill Ong Hing, *The Immigration and Naturalization Service, Community-Based Organizations, and the Legalization Experience: Lessons for the Self-Help Immigration Phenomenon*, 6 Georgetown Immig. L. J. 413, 475–91 (1992).

NOTES TO CHAPTER 3

1. Immigration and Naturalization Service, 1993 Statistical Yearbook 159 (1994), at table 60.

2. Rodolfo's name has been changed for this book.

3. Bill Ong Hing, Handling Immigration Cases 371–72 (1995); 8 U.S.C. § 1254.

4. Helping family and friends in their jobs without receiving any compensation seems to be fairly common. He says that oftentimes people do it because they want to do something fun with a friend, but the friend is unable to because he has to work. Rodolfo says that in those cases he will volunteer to help the friend get the job done faster. Doing this has helped Rodolfo because, as in the case of Le Lumiere, the owners have noticed and liked his work and eventually have hired him. Also, helping a friend in this way has helped him learn the janitorial contracting business, which he will put to use as he starts his own janitorial service.

NOTES TO CHAPTER 4

1. Charles Bierbauer, *Transcript No. 164–10,* CNN NEWS1, Sept. 27, 1995.
2. Rick Gladstone, *The Economics of Immigration,* S.F. EXAMINER, June 13, 1993, at E3.
3. JULIAN SIMON, THE ECONOMIC CONSEQUENCES OF IMMIGRATION 218–19 (1989); GEORGE BORJAS, FRIENDS OR STRANGERS 82 (1990); THOMAS MULLER, IMMIGRANTS AND THE AMERICAN CITY 10 (1993).
4. SIMON, *supra* note 3, at 225.
5. MICHAEL J. PIORE, BIRDS OF PASSAGE ch. 2 (1979). According to Piore, the division into two sectors results from two economic facts: some sectors are more capital-intensive than others, and some sectors have a greater variation in demand. *See also* Robert Aponte, *Ethnicity and Male Employment in the Inner City: A Test of Two Theories,* unpublished paper prepared for presentation at the Chicago Urban Poverty and Family Life Conference, University of Chicago, October 1991 (paper dated Sept. 16, 1991), at 11.
6. ECONOMIC REPORT OF THE PRESIDENT, the Annual Report of the Council of Economic Advisers, Feb. 1986, at 223.
7. This view, based largely on research by Herbert Gans, connects the process of settlement with the status of jobs. If jobs are of low status and conform to the social hierarchy theory of the labor market, the creation of ethnic enclaves facilitates the employment of migrants in socially inferior jobs. Piore emphasizes that the enclave phenomenon occurs outside both the dual labor market and conventional theories of jobs.

Piore is careful to point out that social conflict and differences may occur among the immigrant population. Therefore, relegation to socially inferior jobs may not be acceptable to all immigrants in the ethnic enclave. For some, the ethnic enclave may be just a stepping stone for further assimilation and social advancement. PIORE, *supra* note 5, at ch. 3.
8. BORJAS, *supra* note 3, at 82–84.
9. SIMON, *supra* note 3, at 249, 255, 347–48.
10. PRESIDENT'S COUNCIL, *supra* note 6, at 23, 221–22.
11. *Id.* at 222; BORJAS, *supra* note 3, at 84–86.
12. U.S. DEPARTMENT OF LABOR, THE EFFECTS OF IMMIGRATION ON THE U.S. ECONOMY AND LABOR MARKET 51, 54–55, 58–59 (1989).
13. Donald Huddle, *The Costs of Immigration,* Carrying Capacity Network, July 1993, at 1.
14. *Id.* at 12–14.
15. Apparently this was a small survey Huddle conducted in the Houston area.
16. Internal Services Division, Los Angeles County, *Impact of Undocumented Persons and Other Immigrants on Costs, Revenues and Services in Los Angeles County; A Report Prepared for Los Angeles County Board of Supervisors,* Nov. 1992, at 13 (hereinafter "Los Angeles County"). For example, in their well-documented analysis of the effects of immigration on less skilled natives using 1970 and 1980 census data, Joseph Altonji and David Card found "little evi-

dence that inflows of immigrants are associated with large or systematic effects on the employment or unemployment rates of less-skilled natives." Joseph G. Altonji and David Card, *The Effects of Immigration on the Labor Market Outcomes of Less-Skilled Natives,* in JOHN M. ABOWD AND RICHARD B. FREEMAN, EDS., IMMIGRATION, TRADE, AND THE LABOR MARKET 226 (1991).

17. *See generally* MICHAEL FIX AND JEFFREY S. PASSEL, IMMIGRATION AND IMMIGRANTS: SETTING THE RECORD STRAIGHT (1994).

18. However, increases in unemployment would not necessarily disprove the theory that immigrants create more jobs than they take. For instance, take the following (overly simplified) example: suppose that a small city whose population includes 100,000 job seekers has an unemployment rate of 5 percent, meaning that 95,000 individuals in the labor pool are employed, while 5,000 are unemployed. Suppose that the city experiences an influx of 2,000 job-seeking immigrants, and that this influx results in the creation of 880 more jobs (which are filled) and 1,120 more unemployed persons. The result would be (1) an increase in the unemployment rate from 5 percent to 6 percent (6,200 unemployed persons out of 102,000 job seekers); and (2) an increase in the total number of jobs (by 880). So increased immigration created more jobs than it took, even though unemployment rose as a result. This illustration demonstrates the limitations of using unemployment figures as an absolute guide to whether or not immigrants create jobs; it also shows the limitation of using job creation, in and of itself, as the primary indicator of whether increased immigration has a "good" economic effect.

19. Richard Vedder, Lowell Gallaway, and Stephen Moore, *Immigration and Unemployment: New Evidence,* for the Alexis de Tocqueville Institution (Mar. 1994), at 7–10.

To test for the relationship between immigrant presence and unemployment, the researchers incorporated into their model a variable measuring the estimated percentage of the total U.S. resident population that was foreign-born for each year. Then using an ordinary regression procedure, they ascertained the relationship between immigration (and other control variables) and unemployment. After running regressions from several perspectives, they could not find "any statistically meaningful positive relationship between immigration and unemployment." *Id.* at 14.

The details of their basic labor market model are contained in RICHARD D. VEDDER AND LOWELL E. GALLAWAY, OUT OF WORK: UNEMPLOYMENT AND GOVERNMENT IN TWENTIETH-CENTURY AMERICA ch. 3 (1993).

20. The ten states with the highest unemployment were West Virginia, Michigan, Louisiana, Alabama, Mississippi, Alaska, Kentucky, Ohio, Arkansas, and Illinois. The ten states with the lowest unemployment were New Hampshire, Nebraska, South Dakota, Hawaii, Connecticut, Kansas, Vermont, Virginia, North Dakota, and Massachusetts.

The ten states with the largest proportion of immigrants were California, Florida, New Jersey, New York, Hawaii, Massachusetts, Rhode Island, Connecticut, District of Columbia, and Illinois. The ten states with the lowest proportion of immigrants were Mississippi, Kentucky, West Virginia, Alabama, Arkansas, Tennessee, South Dakota, South Carolina, Iowa, and Missouri.

21. *See* Altonji and Card, *supra* note 16, at 221; Robert J. LaLonde and Robert H. Topel, *Economic Impact of International Migration and the Economic Performance of Migrants* (Aug. 1994), at 53 (Center for the Study of the Economy and the State, Univ. of Chicago, Working Paper no. 96). A different set of researchers' quantitative comparisons between high-immigration cities— Miami, New York, San Antonio, Houston, and Los Angeles—and low-immigration cities—Dayton, Memphis, Minneapolis, Pittsburgh, and Birmingham— shows that while the number of white-collar workers tended to increase with immigration, the number of blue-collar workers declined. The extent of out-migration was surprisingly high: for every seven immigrants, one native worker moved. Robert Walker, Mark Ellis, and Richard Barff, *Linked Migration Systems: Immigration and Internal Labor Flows in the United States*, 68 ECONOMIC GEOGRAPHY, at 234 (1992). This finding suggests that the decline in wages for working-class natives is spread by internal migration throughout the nation. Thus, a comparison of wage levels alone in high- and low-immigration areas would understate, or perhaps miss entirely, the effects of immigration, which are national. This work at least forces us to raise the question—perhaps unanswerable—as to whether the physical presence of immigrants, rather than wage and job competition, causes people to move.

22. Vedder, et al., *supra* note 19, at 15. Thomas Muller describes the situation as follows:

> Some of the jobs that immigrants help to create—notably in retail trade and personal services—are taken by other immigrants. But in many other areas—utilities, banking, finance, real estate, and communications—new jobs tend to be filled by natives. Similarly, added economic activity creates new demand for nontechnical professionals—lawyers, accountants, and bankers—primarily natives because language and licensing requirements make it difficult for immigrants to enter these fields.

MULLER, *supra* note 3, at 142.

23. U.S. DEPARTMENT OF LABOR, *supra* note 12, at 67–68, 70. Nearly 70 percent of male immigrants from Latin America, 62 percent from the Caribbean, and 40 percent from Asian are so employed. *Id.; see also* MULLER, *supra* note 3, at 143.

24. U.S. DEPARTMENT OF LABOR, *supra* note 12, at 13, 72.

25. *Id.* at 6, 76–77; *see also* Paul Ong and Abel Valenzuela, Jr., *The Political Economy of Job Competition between Immigrants and African Americans* (1994 Draft), at 16–17.

26. MULLER, *supra* note 3, at 143.

27. *See* Robert H. Topel, *Regional Labor Markets and the Determinants of Wage Inequality*, 84 AMERICAN ECON. REV. 17, 21 (1994). This is consistent with the findings of researchers that looked at 1970 and 1980 census data who

found that, depending on the method of calculation, a 1 percentage point increase in the fraction of immigrants in metropolitan areas reduced less-skilled native wages from 0.3 to 1.2 percent. Altonji and Card, *supra* note 16, at 226. But when Altonji and Card look at cross-sectional data at two points in time, this reverses the negative relationship between employment outcomes and the fraction of immigrants across cities. *Id.* at 221. In earlier work that treated immigrants as a homogeneous group, Topel and Robert LaLonde found that the "wages and earnings of young blacks and Hispanics are not very sensitive to immigration. . . . [I]mmigrants are rather easily absorbed into the American labor market." Robert J. LaLonde and Robert H. Topel, *Labor Market Adjustments to Increased Immigration,* in JOHN M. ABOWD AND RICHARD B. FREEMAN, EDS., IMMIGRATION, TRADE AND THE LABOR MARKET 190–91 (1991); *see also* LaLonde and Topel, *supra* note 21. Topel's findings that unskilled immigrants from Asia and Latin America result in wages among unskilled workers that are 10 percent lower than in other parts of the country are a bit distorted. The data were taken from the Current Population Survey which records broad ethnic categories rather than immigration status. To make his calculations on the impact of immigrants, he excluded all "Hispanics and Asians." Topel, *supra,* at 21. The problem of course is that not all "Hispanics and Asians" are immigrants, so the 10 percent effect is clearly overstated.

28. U.S. DEPARTMENT OF LABOR, *supra* note 12, at 84.

29. David Card, *The Impact of the Mariel Boatlift on the Miami Labor Market,* 40 INDUSTRIAL AND LABOR RELATIONS REV. (1990), at 255–57.

30. IMMIGRATION AND NATURALIZATION SERVICE, 1991 STATISTICAL YEARBOOK (1992), TABLES 9 AND 10.

31. U.S. DEPARTMENT OF LABOR, *supra* note 12, at 79, 83.

32. Aponte, *supra* note 5, at 8–9, 20–21, 27, 34–35, 40–42.

33. U.S. DEPARTMENT OF LABOR, *supra* note 12, at 86–87.

34. The industry has been able to rely on skilled weavers from the British Isles, Ireland, Greece, Poland, Italy, Portugal and, since World War II, French Canada, Brazil, Mexico, Cuba and, most recently, Columbia. U.S. DEPARTMENT OF LABOR, *supra* note 12, at 113.

35. *Id.* at 114–15.

36. Rebecca Morales, *Transitional Labor: Undocumented Workers in the Los Angeles Automobile Industry,* 17 INTERNATIONAL MIGRATION REV. 570, 571–75, 579–81, 586 (1983). Morales conducted case studies on the auto parts companies in order to observe hiring practices. She then looked at additional companies in the Los Angeles area to complement the data in order to perform a statistical analysis of the practice of hiring undocumented workers and differentiating various workers in terms of wages. While her study was completed more than a decade ago, its findings appear quite relevant to the way businesses and industries are currently evolving in a more global environment.

37. *Id.* at 580–81. In fact workers believed that Company B had paid higher wages to prevent unionization.

38. U.S. DEPARTMENT OF LABOR, *supra* note 12, at 106–7.

39. *Id.* at 107; Edward Jang-Woo Park, *Asians Matter: Asian American En-*

trepreneurs in the Silicon Valley High Technology Industry, in BILL ONG HING AND RONALD LEE, EDS., REFRAMING THE IMMIGRATION DEBATE (1996).

40. U.S. DEPARTMENT OF Labor, *supra* note 12, at 107–8.

41. *Id.* at 108–9.

42. As the Department of Labor recounts:

> From its inception, the U.S. garment industry has been inextricably tied to immigration. With the advent of a ready-to-wear clothing industry in the 1880s, Irish, German and Swedish dressmakers were succeeded by Italians and Eastern Europeans. By 1900 the industry was already ethnically and functionally differentiated. Men's clothing was produced by Italian women working out of the home; other apparel came from factories owned and operated by Europeans (most of whom were Jewish). As European immigration slowed in the 1930s other groups, especially native-born black women from the South and Puerto Ricans, took over production roles. The latest groups of women to succeed them in the industry are Chinese, Korean, Dominican and Mexican immigrants.

Id. at 109.

43. *Id.* at 109–13.

44. *Id.* at 131–36.

45. *Id.* at 132–33.

46. U.S. GENERAL ACCOUNTING OFFICE, ILLEGAL ALIENS: INFLUENCE OF ILLEGAL WORKERS ON WAGES AND WORKING CONDITIONS OF LEGAL WORKERS 39–41 (1988).

47. Interview with Eric Pierson, former organizer for Justice for Janitors, April 8, 1996. *See also* Bob Baker, *Unions Try Bilingual Recruiting,* L.A. Times, Mar. 25, 1991.

48. U.S. DEPARTMENT OF LABOR, *supra* note 12, at 137–40.

49. *Id.* at 118–19. As the Department of Labor notes, "One outcome of the relocation process has been a decline in union involvement in the meatpacking industry. The time and effort spent in organizing workers is lost each time a plant closes or moves. Meatpacking plants have tended to settle in right-to-work states, hire primarily rural natives and the foreign born, and thus minimize the threat of subsequent organization." *Id.* at 120.

50. *Id.* at 120–21; BILL ONG HING, MAKING AND REMAKING ASIAN AMERICA THROUGH IMMIGRATION POLICY 1850–1990 128–33 (1993).

51. U.S. DEPARTMENT OF LABOR, *supra* note 12, at 121–24.

52. HING, *supra* note 50, at 20–23; U.S. DEPARTMENT OF LABOR, *supra* note 12, at 126–27.

53. *Id.* at 127–29; Eli Setencich, *Future for UFW Is Growing Brighter,* FRESNO BEE, June 3, 1993, at B1; Channel 2 News, KTVU, San Francisco, 10 O'clock News, April 24, 1994 (story on UFW March to Sacramento).

54. As of 1994, union membership stood at 15.5 percent of the workforce, down from a third in 1955. Carl Horowitz, *New Militancy at the AFL-CIO?* INVESTOR'S BUS. DAILY, Nov. 14, 1995.

55. Bob Baker, *Unions Try Bilingual Recruiting*, L.A. TIMES, Mar. 25, 1991.

56. *Id.*; Steven Lerner, *Let's Get Moving: Labor Survival Depends on Organizing Industry-Wide for Justice and Power*, 18 LAB. RES. REV. 1 (1991).

57. Alan Hyde, et al., *After Smyrna: Rights and Powers of Unions That Represent Less than a Majority*, 45 RUTGERS L. REV. 637, 639 note 5 (1993).

58. Lane Kirkland, *Organized Labor and Civil Rights*, L.A. TIMES, Apr. 28, 1991; Baker, *supra* note 55.

59. Morales, *supra* note 36, at 584–85.

60. Peter Kuhn and Ian Wooton, *Immigration, International Trade, and the Wages of Native Workers*, in JOHN M. ABOWD AND RICHARD B. FREEMAN, EDS., IMMIGRATION, TRADE AND THE LABOR MARKET 300 (1991).

NOTES TO CHAPTER 5

1. Letter to The President from Governor Pete Wilson, Aug. 9, 1993.

2. Richard L. Berke, *Politicians Discovering An Issue: Immigration*, N.Y. TIMES, Mar. 18, 1994, at A14.

3. Amy Chance, *Immigration Contributing to California's Decline, Groups Say*, SACRAMENTO BEE, Feb. 1993.

4. Wilson is claiming "reimbursement of $377 million in incarceration costs and approximately $1.6 billion for prison construction costs associated with jailing 16,700 undocumented aliens who have committed felonies." Nancy E. Roman, *Florida Expects Surge of Illegals to Sail from Haiti*, WASHINGTON TIMES, May 10, 1994, at A15. His second suit demands nearly "$370 million in federal reimbursement for emergency health care provided to undocumented residents" in one year. *Wilson Files Second Immigration Suit*, UNITED PRESS INTERNATIONAL, May 31, 1994; Larry Rohter, *Florida Wants U.S. Aid For Illegal Immigrants*, N.Y. TIMES, Dec. 31, 1993, at A7; Berke, *supra* note 2.

5. Internal Services Division, Los Angeles County, *Impact of Undocumented Persons and Other Immigrants on Costs, Revenues and Services in Los Angeles County; A Report Prepared for Los Angeles County Board of Supervisors*, Nov. 1992; Donald Huddle, *The Costs of Immigration*, Carrying Capacity Network, July 1993.

6. ECONOMIC REPORT OF THE PRESIDENT, the Annual Report of the Council of Economic Advisers, Feb. 1986, at 233–34.

7. This results from the political reality that Social Security will not fund future Social Security payments at a level reflecting the rate of savings of the current generation of workers' contributions.

8. JULIAN SIMON, THE ECONOMIC CONSEQUENCES OF IMMIGRATION 152 (1989). In 1945, for each of the 1 million beneficiaries collecting Social Security benefits, forty-six workers contributed. By 1950, just five years later, coverage included so many new categories of beneficiaries (such as door-to-door salesmen and home workers) that there were only sixteen workers for every beneficiary. Today, for each of the 41 million individuals collecting Social Security benefits,

only three workers are contributing. By the time the "baby boomers"—those born from 1946 to 1964—begin to retire en masse (around 2025), only two workers will be contributing for each of the 70 million beneficiaries collecting. Already, entitlement programs (including Social Security, Medicare and Medicaid, unemployment compensation, and veterans' benefits) eat up 49 percent of every federal tax dollar. Jack Anderson, *Why Should I Pay for People Who Don't Need It?* PARADE MAGAZINE, Feb. 21, 1993, at 4–7.

9. Ronald D. Lee, *Race-Ethnicity and Social Security Transfers: Who Gains and Who Loses?* (unpublished paper, on file with author), May 16, 1994.

10. Eric S. Rothman and Thomas J. Espenshade, *Fiscal Impacts of Immigration to the United States,* 58 POPULATION INDEX 381–415 (1992).

11. Alan O. Sykes, *The Welfare Economics of Immigration Law: A Theoretical Survey With An Analysis of U.S. Policy,* in WARREN F. SCHWARTZ, ED., JUSTICE IN IMMIGRATION 161 (1995); PRESIDENT'S COUNCIL, *supra* note 6, at 221. Simon points out that a native Nobel laureate can be more productive if she has good immigrant graduate students to work with. But if a foreign Nobel laureate immigrates and competes for good graduate students, the native laureate's productivity might be reduced. Simon, *supra* note 8, at 147. In the view of the President's Council and Sykes, even the latter situation could result in greater total productivity. The President's Council points out:

> Inputs to production can become more effective as they acquire greater quantities of labor with which to work. This concept may be illustrated by several examples. A bulldozer on a road construction project is more productive if there are workers to keep it running for multiple shifts, repair it, and redirect traffic away from the construction site. A scientist is more productive if there are assistants to wash the test tubes and type manuscripts. A worker with family responsibilities is more productive if there are others in the household to help with child care and home maintenance.

PRESIDENT'S COUNCIL, *supra* note 6, at 221.

12. Edward Jang-Woo Park, *Asians Matter: Asian American Entrepreneurs in the Silicon Valley High Technology Industry,* and Melanie Erasmus, *Immigrant Entrepreneurs in the High-Tech Industry,* in BILL ONG HING AND RONALD LEE, EDS., REFRAMING THE IMMIGRATION DEBATE (1996).

13. SIMON, *supra* note 8, at 147, 163, 174–75.

> For example, foreign graduate students raise the productivity of American university scientists, and directly contribute their own new ideas and discoveries. Furthermore, many technological advances come from people who are neither well educated nor well paid: the dispatcher who develops a slightly better way of deploying the taxis; the shipper who discovers that garbage cans make excellent cheap containers; the supermarket manager who finds a way to display more merchandise in a given space; the clerk who

finds a quicker way to stamp prices on cans. A larger population
of scientific workers could also facilitate the development of cost-
effective and available nuclear power.

Id. at 175.

14. *Id.* at 177–79.

15. *Id.* at 168–69, 176.

16. Internal Services Division, Los Angeles County, *supra* note 5, at 1–2.

17. Recent legal immigrants: 630,000; amnestied persons: 720,000; undocumenteds: 700,000; citizen children of undocumenteds: 250,000. There were also
an estimated 1.1 million other foreign-born residents in the county comprised of
pre-1980 legal immigrants and persons on temporary non-immigrant visas (e.g.,
students and temporary workers). The total population of Los Angeles County
as of the study date, January 1, 1992, was estimated at 9.2 million. *Id.* at 15.

18. *Id.* at 29. The specific figures were: $365 million (68 percent) of net
county costs for the Department of Health Services; $351 million (23 percent) of
net county costs for justice-related departments; $102 million (21 percent) of net
county costs for the Department of Public Social Services; and $5.5 million (16
percent) of net county costs for the Department of Mental Health. The researchers also attempt to measure consumption tax through consumer expenditures.
Id.

19. Rebecca L. Clark and Jeffrey S. Passell, *How Much Do Immigrants Pay
in Taxes? Evidence From Los Angeles County* (unpublished working paper,
Urban Institute, August 1993). The study starts by pointing out a few of the
more notorious mistakes in present empirical studies. It criticizes the focus on
recent arrivals only rather than all immigrants. Also, the researchers note that
the costs of immigrants are much easier to gauge than are the benefits (e.g.,
benefits are in a stream that can often only be indirectly measured). Cost estimates are generally based on administrative data, with a proportion of the cost
assigned to the immigrant populations. The proportions sometimes come from
administrative counts of immigrants, but more often from census or survey
estimates. Estimating revenues derived from immigrants is usually more difficult
because most administrative data sources do not identify nativity and even those
that do are usually inaccessible to researchers. They also criticize the common
use of small sample size for estimating tax revenues, and the typical disregard
for some other types of tax revenue (e.g., taxes of immigrant-owned businesses
or jobs created by these businesses) or indirect benefits of immigrants such as
jobs created because of economic activity generated by immigrants.

20. Clark and Passel looked at five taxes: federal and state income taxes,
FICA (old age, survivor, disability, and health insurance portions of the Social
Security tax), unemployment insurance, and property tax. These five sources of
revenue account for 81 percent of all revenues collected from residents. For their
estimates of taxes (except property tax), Clark and Passel used "TRIM2," the
Transfer Income Model Version 2 (the Urban Institute's tax simulation program)
based on data from the March 1990 Current Population Survey (CPS). TRIM2,
a microsimulation computer program, applies tax rules based on detailed infor-

mation from federal and state tax codes to individuals, families, or households to determine their tax liability. Property taxes, calculated separately for owners and renters, are based on relationships between income, housing costs, and property tax. For each household, property and income taxes are apportioned to recent immigrants, long-term immigrants, and natives according to the immigrant status of the household members. Clark and Passel, *supra* note 19, at 6. The CPS is a monthly survey of approximately 57,000 households, designed primarily to gather data on employment, unemployment, and demographic characteristics. It includes occasional special purpose supplements, and for this study the researchers used all March 1990 CPS cases from Los Angeles County— 6,286 individuals in 2,020 households. The nativity information was developed from a November 1989 CPS Immigration Supplement and multivariate models. To assign nativity and year of immigration, they matched "Hispanic" households in the November 1989 CPS to the same household in March 1990 and used the immigrant status reported in November (which asked about country of birth, year of immigration, etc.). Then they fit logistic regression models to the full November 1989 CPS Los Angeles sample to model nativity and year of immigration. Finally, they applied these regression models to the March 1990 CPS to assign nativity and year of immigration to persons not matched directly to the November sample. They weighted their sample so the number of adults and children in each immigrant status category matched the 1990 census. *Id.* at 7.

21. *Id.* at 4. While the per capita tax payments for adults are higher for natives ($6,902) than for immigrants ($4,264), on the whole, long-term and short-term immigrant groups, which comprise 32.2 percent of the LA County population, account for 28 percent of the tax revenue coming out of the LA County area in aggregate taxes.

22. In my view, this might not have much effect on recent immigrants. Because this is perceived as a large amount of revenue, the omission of such a factor severely undercuts the local "benefits" or contribution levels of immigrant populations. Internal Services Division, Los Angeles County, *supra* note 5, at 43. Indeed, the researchers note that in competitive industries, owners of capital bear a large portion of these taxes. Commercial and industrial property accounts for 37 percent of the county's tax base. If many immigrants are entering into competitive industries (such as grocery stores), then the omission of these estimates from the study is significant. The study ignored revenues from immigrant-owned businesses, because calculating those "would take a gargantuan effort," submitted LA Study coauthor Nancy Bolton. Steve Johnson, *Immigration Fears Disputed,* SAN JOSE MERCURY NEWS, Dec. 31, 1992, at A1, A18.

23. Internal Services Division, Los Angeles County, *supra* note 5, at 2, 6, 44. Often immigrant workers assist in supporting their families in the sending country. Because this represents capital flight from the host country, a potential cost of immigration was ignored. Exactly how this measure should be treated is not clear. On the one hand, it represents a transfer payment, but on the other it could be regarded as a capital "leak" from the host country. However, note two factors in response to this argument. First, immigrants still have to subsist in this

country, and therefore must spend a substantial amount of their wages domestically (especially since those wages are fairly low). Second, and more importantly,
to the extent that immigration is a proxy form of international trade (see the
trade theory discussion *infra*) the amount of capital "flight" to the sending
country is simply a lower limit of the resources that would be going there
anyway if a trade mechanism were used instead of an immigration mechanism.
In other words, it simply measures gains from trade due to immigration.

24. Over one in three immigrants in Los Angeles County (35 percent of the
immigrant population) were not included. For example, the study did not include immigrants who entered the United States before April 1, 1980 or those
immigrants who are now U.S. citizens. By excluding the long-term immigrants,
the study almost certainly understates the contributions of immigrants and
overstates the per capita costs. It is very likely that immigrants who have resided
in the country for longer periods have higher incomes and pay more taxes than
the new arrivals. Also, the earlier immigrants are known to use few social
services.

25. In a subsequent report that examined similar fiscal concerns on a state-
wide basis in California, the Urban Institute researchers also found that undocumented aliens cost the state more than they put in in state and local taxes. *See
generally* REBECCA L. CLARK, ET AL., FISCAL IMPACTS OF UNDOCUMENTED
ALIENS: SELECTED ESTIMATES FOR SEVEN STATES (1994). But they are quick to
note that their study did not include federal tax contributions, nor the impact of
undocumented immigrants on the economy as workers, business owners, or
consumers.

26. Huddle, *supra* note 5, at 1.

27. *Id.* at 3.

28. The probability of immigrant assistance use was based on the determination of the overall national recipiency rate stated as a percentage of the particular
subpopulation at risk and an estimation of the extent of variation in immigrant
recipiency rates from the overall rate, although how he makes this estimation is
not explained.

29. The federal income tax is the largest single source of revenue from immigrants, commanding 43.2 percent of revenues. State sales taxes rank second,
representing 21.8 percent of all immigrant tax payments.

30. He also apparently assumes that displaced workers and dependents stay
unemployed forever. Because this is not likely the case, and because the length
of unemployment is likely shorter for U.S.-born workers, the study likely overes-
timates the cost of displacement assuming any displacement exists.

31. As to future costs, assuming no changes in policy or enforcement, Huddle
estimates that the post-1970 legal immigrant population will grow by 810,000
persons annually—to 21.8 million by 2002. The undocumented population will
grow by 300,000 annually, reaching 7.8 million by 2002. He also assumes that
current growth trajectories of per capita costs for public assistance and educational categories will persist, and that tax collections will grow by 5.2 percent
annually.

32. Huddle calculated that public education (K-12) was 25.9 percent of all

outlays on immigrants. Medicaid consumed 16.8 percent, while county social and health services, including medical care, accounted for 15.3 percent of costs. These three programs, together with AFDC, unemployment compensation, public higher education, and bilingual and English-deficient instruction comprised over 80 percent of total public outlays for immigrants. Huddle, *supra* note 5, at 9.

33. Richard L. Berke, *Politicians Discovering an Issue: Immigration,* N.Y. Times, Mar. 6, 1994, at A14.

34. Huddle, *supra* note 5, at 10–11.

35. *Id.* at 11.

36. Jeffrey S. Passel, *Immigrants and Taxes: A Reappraisal of Huddle's "The Cost of Immigrants,"* Program for Research on Immigration Policy, Urban Institute, Jan. 1994.

37. *Id.* at 4. Legal immigrants to LA County entering between 1980–90 have a per capita income of about $9,700, according to the assumptions underlying the LA Study figures used by Huddle. But the Urban Institute's estimates show that legal immigrants to the United States entering between 1970–90 have an average per capita income exceeding $14,000.

38. The average income of immigrants nationally is 45 percent greater than Huddle's assumption of 10 percent less. *Id.* at 4–5.

39. *Id.* at 8. *See also* Shubha Ghosh, *Understanding Immigrant Entrepreneurs: Theoretical and Empirical Issues,* in Bill Ong Hing and Ronald Lee, eds., Reframing the Immigration Debate (1996).

40. *See* Clark, et al., *supra* note 25.

41. Apparently they did not use the 250,000 citizen category.

42. Internal Services Division, Los Angeles County, *supra* note 5, at 62. Remember that education is the largest single expenditure in the state's budget. Because education is so expensive, most parents who use the public school system, immigrant or native, do not pay the full cost of educating their children while their children attend school. With the passage of Proposition 98 in 1988, state schools are guaranteed approximately 40 percent of the California budget, making education the largest single expenditure in the state budget. State procedures for allocations assured LA County school districts roughly $3,000 to $3,200 per ADA. *Id.* at 59.

43. Without more specific identifiers within school districts about immigrant students, estimates about cost must be viewed as crude measures at best, of the level of educational funds diverted to immigrants.

44. Sykes, *supra* note 11, at 172.

45. 457 U.S. 202 (1982).

46. Sykes, *supra* note 11, at 172–73.

47. Paul Ong and Linda Wing, *The Social Contract to Educate All Children,* in Bill Ong Hing and Ronald Lee, eds., Reframing the Immigration Debate (1996).

48. Huddle, *supra* note 5, at 5.

49. PUS data are large stratified samples of housing units enumerated in the U.S. census that contain sociodemographic information on housing units and

each person residing within them. From these samples, special household-level data files were constructed, one each for 1960, 1970, and 1980. Referred to as "family files," they were parallel in structure. Data for these files were drawn from the PUSs using a stratified sampling strategy. As many as possible, but no more than 10,000 households were sought among the following groups: foreign Asian, foreign Hispanic, foreign black, other foreign, native Asian, native Hispanic, native black, and other native. LEIF JENSEN, THE NEW IMMIGRATION 37–38 (1989).

50. This included Old-Age Assistance, Aid to the Blind, and Aid to the Permanently and Totally Disabled.

51. Absolute poverty, which is a measure widely used in government and research documents, places the poverty threshold at the annual income needed to maintain a minimally acceptable standard of living. Families are defined as poor if their posttransfer annual income is less than the absolute poverty threshold. Whereas absolute poverty relates income to a minimum standard, relative poverty relates income to average income in the population. The former reflects whether people do not have enough to get by, the latter whether people have much less than average. In the relative measure adopted by Jensen, a household is defined as poor if its total income is less than 44 percent of the median nonnegative household income of whites. JENSEN, *supra* note 49, at 39–41.

52. Remember too that Jensen has mixed refugees, asylum seekers, and undocumenteds with immigrants! JENSEN, *supra* note 49, at 105.

53. This does raise the question, however, of whether public assistance was more readily available in 1979.

54. *Id.* at 106, 141, 145, 176–77.

55. *Id.* at 177.

56. Michael Fix and Jeffrey S. Passel, *Immigrants and Welfare: New Myths, New Realities,* Urban Institute, Testimony before the U.S. House of Representatives Committee on Ways and Means, Subcommittee on Human Resources, Nov. 15, 1993, at 4–5.

57. Afghanistan, Cambodia, Laos, Iraq, Vietnam, Ethiopia, Albania, Poland, Romania, U.S.S.R., and Cuba.

58. Michael Fix, Jeffrey S. Passel, and Wendy Zimmermann, *The Use of SSI and Other Welfare Programs by Immigrants,* Testimony before the U.S. Senate Subcommittee on Immigration, Feb. 6, 1996, at 2–3.

59. Larry Hajime Shinagawa, *The Impact of Immigration on the Demography of Asian Pacific Americans,* in BILL ONG HING AND RONALD LEE, EDS., REFRAMING THE IMMIGRATION DEBATE (1996), at 81.

60. Jonathan Marshall, *Study Backs Fears About Immigrants, Report Shows Higher Welfare Dependence,* SAN FRANCISCO CHRONICLE, Feb. 26, 1996, at D1.

61. GENERAL ACCOUNTING OFFICE, WELFARE REFORM: IMPLICATIONS OF PROPOSALS ON LEGAL IMMIGRANTS' BENEFITS 2 (1995).

62. I made the calculation in this manner: (1) GAO reported that 1.4 million "legal immigrants" were receiving AFDC or SSI, which amounted to 6 percent of all immigrants. *Id.* at 6. An algebraic calculation [1.4 million $= 0.06x$, where

x is the total number of immigrants] means that x = 23.3 million total immigrants, but GAO does not inform the reader what proportion of all "legal immigrants" are lawful permanent residents. (2) The GAO reported that 683,150 "legal immigrants" were receiving SSI, and that 76 percent of those receiving SSI were lawful permanent residents. *Id.* at 8, 10. Seventy-six percent of 683,150 means 519,194 lawful permanent residents were receiving SSI. (3) The GAO reported that about 471,000 lawful permanent residents were receiving AFDC, amounting to 65 percent of all "legal immigrants" receiving AFDC. *Id.* at 11–12. (4) The number of lawful permanent residents receiving SSI (519,194) plus those receiving AFDC (471,000) totals 990,194. (4) The total number of lawful permanent residents receiving SSI and AFDC (990,194) divided by the total number of legal immigrants (23.3 million) yields 4.3 percent. But we do not know from the GAO information what the total number of lawful permanent residents is. (5) From other sources, we know that about 84 percent of all entrants to the United States from 1986 to 1993 were preference immigrants, immediate relatives of citizens or legalized aliens admitted as lawful permanent residents. About 10 percent were refugees or asylees. Calculation based on IMMIGRATION AND NATURALIZATION SERVICE, 1993 STATISTICAL YEARBOOK (1994), table 4. Taking 84 percent of the GAO's 23.3 million figure for "legal immigrants," about 19.6 million are lawful permanent residents. The total number of lawful permanent residents receiving SSI and AFDC (990,194) divided by my figure of 19.6 million lawful permanent residents yields about 5 percent.

63. Interview with Cynthia M. Fagnoni, Assistant Director, General Accounting Office, Feb. 10, 1995. Refugees are eligible to apply for lawful permanent resident status one year after admission as refugees.

64. PRESIDENT'S COUNCIL, *supra* note 6, at 6, at 229; SIMON, *supra* note 8, at 124, 156–58.

65. PRESIDENT'S COUNCIL, *supra* note 6, at 233; Ronald Lee, *supra* note 9.

66. Sykes, *supra* note 11, at 190–91.

67. PRESIDENT'S COUNCIL, *supra* note 6, at 233.

68. Fix and Passel, *supra* note 56, at 3.

69. For SSI, this deeming period has been extended to five years on a temporary basis.

70. PRESIDENT'S COUNCIL, *supra* note 6, at 228.

71. SIMON, *supra* note 8, at 144–46, 149.

72. *Id.* at 144, 152, 160.

73. Sykes, *supra* note 11, at 173–74.

74. Ghosh, *supra,* note 39; Park, *supra* note 12; Erasmus, *supra* note 12; Craig Huynh, *Vietnamese-Owned Manicure Businesses in Los Angeles,* and Gen L. Lee, *Cambodian-Owned Donut Shops,* in BILL ONG HING AND RONALD LEE, EDS., REFRAMING THE IMMIGRATION DEBATE (1996).

75. President's Council, *supra* note 6, at 213–27.

76. Sykes, *supra* note 11, at 175.

77. *Id.* at 109; PRESIDENT'S COUNCIL, *supra* note 6, at 222.

78. U.S. Department of Labor, The Effects of Immigration on the U.S. Economy and Labor Market 11–12 (1989).

79. Sykes, *supra* note 11, at 180–81.

80. U.S. Department of Labor, *supra* note 78, at 5.

NOTES TO CHAPTER 6

1. Neal R. Peirce, *California's Recovery: What Now?* National Journal, Jan. 20, 1996, at 135; Ed Mendel, *California's Bond Rating Shows Gain,* San Diego Union-Tribune, Feb. 28, 1996, at C2.

2. Mendel, *supra* note 1; Peirce, *supra* note 1; Dave McNary, *California Homes Sales up 4.3 Percent,* u.p.i., BC Cycle, Feb. 28, 1996; Stuart Silverstein and Robert A. Rosenblatt, *State Job Rate Hits Best Level Since '89 as U.S. Holds Firm,* L.A. Times, Jan. 20, 1996, at A1; *The Wilson Agenda Prospects Improved For Tax Cut, Social Reform,* San Diego Union-Tribune, Jan. 10, 1996, at B8.

3. Center on Budget and Policy Priorities, A Tale of Two Futures: Restructuring California's Finances to Boost Economic Growth (1994).

4. *Id.* at 11–12, 51–54, 64–66. Of course, this does follow the federal rule, as does the treatment of mortgage interest. While I criticize the state's treatment of Social Security payments as not following the federal rule, my point is that the state has minimized its tax revenues in several areas by following the federal rule in some cases and choosing not to in others.

5. *Id.* at 75–91.

6. Richard Reeves, *The Tax Revolt That Ruined California,* San Francisco Chronicle, Jan. 23, 1994, This World section, at 5; Paul Ben-Itzak, *Budget Squeeze Hits Once-Wealthy California Schools,* Reuters World Service, Sept. 28, 1992.

7. Louis Uchitelle, *Job Losses Don't Let Up Even as Hard Times Ease,* N.Y. Times, Mar. 22, 1994, at A1, C4; David Dishneau, *Sara Lee to Trim Work Force by 6%,* S.F. Examiner, June 6, 1994, at D1, D5.

8. *Downsizing Downsizing,* Business Wire, Apr. 14, 1996 (quoting Joseph Stiglitz, chairman of President Clinton's Council of Economic Advisors).

9. Dishneau, *supra* note 7 (quoting Laurence C. Siefert, a vice-president at AT&T); Dirk Johnson, *Family Struggles to Make Do after Fall From Middle Class,* N.Y. Times, Mar. 11, 1994, at A1, A10.

10. Uchitelle, *supra* note 7; Caren Bohan, *U.S. Job Growth Dispels Doubts,* S.F. Examiner, Apr. 8, 1996, at B1, B3.

11. Marc Levinson, *Help Wanted—Reluctantly,* Newsweek, Mar. 14, 1994, at 36.

12. Martin Crutsinger, *Jobless Rate Sinks to 5.3%, 6-Year Low,* S.F. Examiner, July 5, 1996, at A1, A20; Thomas L. Friedman, *World's Big Economies Turn to the Jobs Issue,* N.Y. Times, Mar, 14, 1994, at C1, C4 (citing Secretary of Labor Robert B. Reich).

13. *Id.*

14. Peter T. Kilborn, *For High School Graduates, A Job Market of Dead Ends,* N.Y. TIMES, May 30, 1994, at 1, 29. In the first quarter of 1994, California had a net gain of 29,000 jobs. But that "is pittance compared with the 600,000 to 800,000 jobs lost during the long recession, and most of it comes in low-paying service and construction jobs." Jane Gross, *California Shows Signs of Recovery as Jobs Increase,* N.Y. TIMES, Apr. 11, 1994, at A1, A12.

15. Kilborn, *supra* note 14.

16. Suzanne Berger, et al., *Toward a New Industrial America; Massachusetts Institute of Technology Commission on Industrial Productivity Study,* SCIENTIFIC AMERICAN, June 1989, vol. 260, no. 6, at 39.

17. Marc Levinson, *Hey, You're Doing Great,* NEWSWEEK, Jan. 30, 1995, at 42.

18. Berger, et al., *supra* note 16, at 39; *see also* Bill Ong Hing, *Immigration Policies: Messages of Exclusion to African Americans,* 37 HOWARD L. J. 237 (1994).

19. David E. Sanger, *Clinton Offers $20 Billion to Mexico for Peso Rescue; Action Sidesteps Congress,* N.Y. TIMES, Feb. 1, 1995, at A1, A10.

20. U.S. DEPARTMENT OF LABOR, THE EFFECTS OF IMMIGRATION ON THE U.S. ECONOMY AND LABOR MARKET 125–26 (1989).

21. The market for frozen fruits and vegetables has remained much stronger than that for canned goods. As such, that segment of the industry has not suffered such serious problems.

22. Interview with Peter Rosset, Executive Director, Food First, April 8, 1994.

23. Karen Rothmyer, *Everyone's Talking About It. . . . But Why? From NAFTA to GATT, Free Trade Becomes a Dinner-Table Issue,* NEWSDAY, Dec. 12, 1993, at 96.

24. Ravi Batra, a professor at Southern Methodist University and author of *The Myth of Free Trade* puts it this way: "If the U.S. had a 50 percent tariff on manufacturing imports, all foreign companies would have to produce here using American labor." Rothmyer, *supra* note 23.

25. Allen R. Myerson, *U.S.-Mexico Trade Advances Sharply Under New Accord,* N.Y. TIMES, June 6, 1994, at A1, C2.

26. James Sterngold, *In Nafta's Complex Trade-Off, Some Jobs Lost, Others Gained,* N.Y. TIMES, Oct. 9, 1995, at A1; S. P. Dinnen, *Government and Labor Debate NAFTA's Effect on Employment,* INDIANAPOLIS STAR, Mar. 24, 1996, at E2.

27. Laurence C. Seifert, *The Myth of Cheap Foreign Labor,* CHI. TRIB., Oct. 15, 1992, at A27. One business representative suggests:

> The federal government could be doing more to make the United States an attractive choice for manufacturers. This country needs favorable tax and trade incentives, and should avoid any restrictions that inhibit U.S. producers' access to new technology, whatever the source. It also must ensure that its workers are better educated and have the job skills that manufacturers require. Pro-

tecting the jobs of underskilled workers through political means is
an equation for long-term economic disaster.

Id.

28. Edward A. Gargan, *For a Furniture Maker, a Taste of a Global Future,*
N.Y. Times, Mar. 17, 1994, at C1, C3.

29. Dorothy E. Logie and Jessica Woodroffe, *Structural Adjustment: The
Wrong Prescription for Africa?* 307 Brit. Med. J. 41 (july 3, 1993); nancy
dunne, *Poor Hit Back at Structural Adjustments,* Fin. Times, Sept. 24, 1992, at
7.

30. Peter Brimelow, *Time to Rethink Immigration?* National Review, June
22, 1992, 30–46.

31. I understand, of course, that this may depend upon market price, at the
point where increased supply and demand intersect.

32. *See generally* Berger, et al., *supra* note 16; Elizabeth Corcoran and Paul
Wallich, *The Analytical Economist: The Cost of Capital,* Scientific American,
Oct. 1989, vol. 261, no. 4, at 79. I understand that an argument can be made
that the cost of capital to Japanese firms is not cheaper than to U.S. firms. All
companies—Japanese, European, American, and others—must compete for the
same capital. Those who obtain it on favorable terms will do so not because
they are Japanese but because they are efficiently organized and governed. In
short, U.S. managers should stop complaining about how much capital costs
and worry more about how to manage it after it's been raised. The evidence
suggests that differences in capital costs in Japan and the United States have
been isolated and temporary, not broad and persistent. Unfortunately, many U.S.
managers propose external, macrolevel schemes to fix the problem. Reduced to
their essentials, most of these schemes involve forcing people to save more,
forcing investors to hold equity investments for long periods (to make them more
"patient"), or restricting foreign companies' trade and investment opportunities.
These managers are too easily satisfied that their cost-of-capital problem is an
external phenomenon caused by Washington's ineptitude, Tokyo's cheating, or
Wall Street's shortsighted greed. Carl W. Kester and Timothy A. Luehrman, *The
Myth of Japan's Low-Cost Capital,* Harv. Bus. Rev., May/June 1992, at 130.

Many have argued that Japanese firms face a considerably lower cost of
capital because of more favorable tax rules. However, differences in corporate
tax rules, or the greater Japanese reliance on tax-favored debt finance, explain
only a relatively small part of the gap. Subsequent study suggests that the lower
Japanese earnings-price ratios need not be associated with lower cost of capital
at all, if share prices reflect the very high market value of corporate landholdings.
Alan J. Auerbach, Nber Rept., Sept. 11, 1993, at 6.

In the same vein, many U.S. managers argue that Japanese banks provide
capital to Japanese manufacturers at advantageous rates. It is true that some
aspects of the relationship between a Japanese bank and its large customers have
the potential to lower borrowing costs. Most Japanese industrial companies
maintain "main bank" relationships—a long-term relationship with one or two
banks characterized by cross-shareholding arrangements, board representation,

and quick intervention in the event of financial distress. The bank has extensive, reliable information about the company and, further, has the capacity to become actively involved should problems arise. This makes it safer to provide capital, which makes it possible to charge less for it. However, Japanese companies explicitly pay for the benefits provided by their main banks. They consistently award them the largest share of their banking business, and they pay a premium for the loans and services provided by main banks—all of which drives up the cost of what may appear, on its face, to be a cheap loan. In addition to their main-bank relationships, Japanese companies tend to maintain enduring business relationships with other commercial stakeholders such as major customers, suppliers, subcontractors, and so forth. The stakeholders in a large Japanese corporation are widely viewed in the United States as "patient" investors who supply cheap capital. However, the commingling of commercial and financial contractual relationships makes it extremely difficult to conclude that this capital is truly cheaper. Kester and Luehrman, *supra,* at 130.

33. Berger, et al., *supra* note 16.

34. Suvendrini Kakuchi, *Illegal Workers Risk Dying to Avoid Deportation,* INTER PRESS SERVICE, Feb. 18, 1993.

35. Editorial, *Social Reform Needed to Cope with Aging Population,* NIKKEI WEEKLY, Nov. 23, 1992; Pang Eng Fong, *Much Ado about Managing Regional Unskilled Labour Flows,* BUSINESS TIMES, Feb. 26, 1994, at 4; Nihon Keizai Shimbun, *The Pros and Cons of Foreign Workers; Experts Discuss Proposed Plan to Admit Some Unskilled Workers,* NIKKEI WEEKLY, Oct. 19, 1992, at 26.

36. Robert R. Rehder, *Sayonara, Uddevalla? Production Methods of Volvo's Uddevalla Plant in Sweden,* BUSINESS HORIZONS, Nov. 1992, vol. 35, no. 6, at 8.

37. *Id.*; Mary Ann Maskery, *Fast Paced Japanese Hit the Expansion Redline,* AUTOMOTIVE NEWS, Sept. 2, 1991, at 1, 34.

38. James Fallows, *What Is an Economy For?* ATLANTIC MONTHLY, Jan. 1994, at 76–92. Japan also does not engage in any military spending.

39. *Id.*

NOTES TO CHAPTER 7

1. AMERICA BECOMING, PBS Documentary, Sept. 16, 1991.

2. Earnest L. Perry, *Violence Is No Answer, But Understanding Can Be a Key,* HOUSTON CHRONICLE, May 10, 1992, Outlook Section, at 1 (editorial opinion).

3. Gene Gibbons, *Clinton to Speak on Race Relations Monday,* REUTERS WORLD SERVICE, Oct. 13, 1995.

4. This percentage dropped from 56.3 percent of black families earning an average income in 1970 to 46.7 percent by 1988. David H. Swinton, *The Economic Status of Black Americans During the 1980's: A Decade of Limited Progress,* in NATIONAL URBAN LEAGUE, THE STATE OF BLACK AMERICA 29 (1990).

5. The percentage of black families living below the poverty level has risen from 33 percent in 1970 to 39.2 percent in 1988. Thus, another generation of black children has been born into poverty. The number of black children under eighteen born in poverty is now 44.1 percent, up from 41.5 percent in 1970. *Id.* at 29, 34. Those born in poverty today will also more than likely remain in poverty because of changes in the economy which make it more difficult than ever for poor Americans to become upwardly mobile. One in four black men in their twenties is in jail, on probation or out on parole, while only one in five are in college. Dirk Johnson, *Milwaukee Creating 2 Schools Just for Black Boys,* N.Y. TIMES, Sept. 30, 1990, § 1, at 1. At least 30 percent of black youth are not graduating from high school, and more than half of all suspensions, expulsions, and dropouts in metropolitan school districts are of black youth. Antoine Garibaldi, *Black School Pushouts and Dropouts: Strategies for Reduction,* in WILLY D. SMITH AND EVA W. CHUNN, EDS., BLACK EDUCATION: A QUEST FOR EQUITY AND EXCELLENCE 227, 227–29 (1989). *See also* Laura J. Young and Susan L. Melnick, *Forsaken Lives, Abandoned Dreams: What Will Compel Us to Act?* 58 HARV. EDUC. REV. 389 (1988), reviewing WILLIAM J. WILSON, THE TRULY DISADVANTAGED: THE INNER CITY, THE UNDERCLASS, AND PUBLIC POLICY (1987), which analyzes social dislocation and poverty in America's inner cities. In 1986, African Americans constituted 44 percent of the murder victims although they comprised only 12 to 15 percent of the U.S. population. Carl C. Bell, *Preventing Black Homicide,* in NATIONAL URBAN LEAGUE, THE STATE OF BLACK AMERICA 143 (1990).

6. Swinton, *supra* note 4, at 47. Kevin Phillips has shown that the official employment figures tabulated by the government are often "underflated" by not reporting the numbers of people who have ceased looking for work, reporting underemployed workers along with fully employed workers, and reclassifying some people who are still looking for work as "unemployable" in order to exclude them from the statistical tables. KEVIN PHILLIPS, POLITICS FOR RICH AND POOR 20 (1990).

Therefore, the low unemployment figures (around 5.3 percent) during the years of the "Reagan Miracle" were misleading because of the tactic of excluding certain definitions from "unemployment." For example, in 1988 in New York City, "45.3% of the city's residents over the age of 16 could not be counted as labor force participants because of poverty, lack of skills, drug use, apathy or other problems. . . . [The number] of uncountables for the nation as a whole was 34.5%. Thus the paradox: *millions of jobs might be going begging, but huge numbers of Americans remained either unemployed or unemployable.*" *Id.* (emphasis in original).

7. JOHN W. WORK, RACE, ECONOMICS, AND CORPORATE AMERICA 89–97 (1984). The lower-level white-collar occupations include positions in the mailroom, secretarial, and low-level clerical positions. Although this finding may not seem profound, it is crucial. In these days of widespread sentiment that black Americans have made "enough progress, and should just stop complaining," empirical proof to the contrary is significant. Work also discovered that corpo-

rate America has created a "caste" system that perpetuates the notion of certain jobs being "Negro jobs." *Id.* at 47–49.

8. *Id.* at 3, 25, 112–17.

9. Stephen S. Cohen, *Where the Jobs Were; Unemployment Isn't Equal—It's in L.A.,* WASHINGTON POST, Mar. 14, 1993, at C5; Donald Woutat, *L.A. Left Behind As State Revs Up,* L.A. TIMES, Dec. 25, 1993, at D1.

10. Patrice Apodaca, *L.A. Makes Its Last Car,* L.A. TIMES, Aug. 28, 1992, at D1; Richard W. Stevenson, *After the Riots; Riots Inflamed a Festering South-Central Economy,* N.Y. TIMES, May 6, 1992, at A23; Benjamin Mark, *Rioting Highlights Concern for City's Future,* L.A. BUS. J., May 4, 1992, at 1–1; Rochelle Sharpe, *In Latest Recession, Only Blacks Suffered Net Employment Loss,* WALL STREET JOURNAL, Sept. 14, 1993, at A1.

11. Sharpe, *supra* note 10.

12. *Id.* Jobs outside the inner city add to the difficulties of finding and maintaining jobs because of commuting costs and inconveniences. For some inner-city residents, public transportation is not always available, the cost of fares high, the time involved in traveling to the suburbs is great, and many transfers are needed. Those with low reading skills have trouble with the complex signs and instructions in the transportation systems of cities. WILLIAM L. HENDERSON AND LARRY C. LEDEBUR, ECONOMIC DISPARITY: PROBLEMS AND STRATEGIES FOR BLACK AMERICA 5, 305 (1970).

13. *Id.* at 5.

14. Neal R. Peirce, *Low-Skill Jobs Flee the Cities,* L.A. TIMES, Aug. 14, 1988. For most inner-city poor African Americans, the suburbs are a place they "can't afford to live, and often fear to go." *Id.* Recall that for African Americans, Aponte found that education is a human capital characteristic highly relevant to employment. The flight of companies from the inner city is consistent with the premise of Aponte's analysis of the "spatial mismatch" explanation for urban joblessness among African Americans.

15. 347 U.S. 483 (1954).

16. *See, e.g.,* ROBERT CRAIN AND JACK STRAUSS, SCHOOL DESEGREGATION AND BLACK OCCUPATIONAL ATTAINMENTS: RESULTS FROM A LONG-TERM EXPERIMENT 1–2 (1985); *America's Blacks—A World Apart,* ECONOMIST, Mar. 30, 1991, at 17, 21.

17. *See generally* JONATHAN KOZOL, SAVAGE INEQUALITIES (1991), evaluating the disparities in education between poor and wealthy children.

18. HENDERSON AND LEDEBUR, *supra* note 12, at 6, 11.

19. Muriel L. Whetstone, *The Story Behind the Explosive Statistics: Why Blacks Are Losing Ground In The Workforce,* EBONY, Dec. 1993, at 102–6.

20. Sharpe, *supra* note 10.

21. HENDERSON AND LEDEBUR, *supra* note 12, at 5–6, 53, 132.

22. Interview with Eva Jefferson Patterson, Executive Director, Lawyers' Committee for Civil Rights, San Francisco, California, June 6, 1994.

23. Michael Piore, *Can International Migration be Controlled?* in SUSAN POZO, ED., ESSAYS ON LEGAL AND ILLEGAL IMMIGRATION 38–39 (1986).

24. David Card, *The Impact of the Mariel Boatlift on the Miami Labor Market,* 40 INDUSTRIAL AND LABOR RELATIONS REV. (1990), at 245–46.

25. *Id.* at 249–50.

26. Paul Ong and Abel Valenzuela, Jr., *The Political Economy of Job Competition between Immigrants and African Americans* (1994 Draft), at 14, 17–19.

27. Robert Aponte, *Ethnicity and Male Employment in the Inner City: A Test of Two Theories,* unpublished paper prepared for presentation at the Chicago Urban Poverty and Family Life Conference, University of Chicago, October 1991 (paper dated Sept. 16, 1991), at 8, 20–21, 25, 27, 34–35.

28. *Id.* at 40–42.

29. Roger Waldinger, *Who Makes the Beds? Who Washes the Dishes? Black/ Immigrant Competition Reassessed,* Draft, Feb. 1992, Dept. of Sociology, UCLA, at 4, 18, 26.

30. *Id.* at 2, citing Jolene Kirschenman and Kathryn Neckerman, *"We'd Love to Hire Them, But...": The Meaning of Race for Employers,* in CHRISTOPHER JENCKS AND PAUL PETERSON, EDS., THE URBAN UNDERCLASS 203–34 (1991).

31. Aponte, *supra* note 27, at 44–45.

32. The IRCA may have pervasive effects within the restaurant industry. It could necessitate a substantial reduction in the number of back-of-the-house jobs, now held primarily by undocumented workers. But ironically, by compelling the industry to restructure toward less labor-intensive operations, it could also phase out many of the (numerically more significant) front-of-the-house positions predominantly held by native workers. U.S. DEPARTMENT OF LABOR, THE EFFECTS OF IMMIGRATION ON THE U.S. ECONOMY AND LABOR MARKET 137 (1989).

33. What does discouraging mechanization really mean to the economy? Is it possible that this is sometimes good and sometimes bad, depending on the situation? In reviewing California's fruit and vegetable processing industries, Martin argues that the industry's ease of access to undocumenteds has slowed the introduction of technology and has depressed wages relative to other seasonal industries such as construction. U.S. DEPARTMENT OF LABOR, *supra* note 32, at 77.

34. Interview with Katherine Brady, Staff Attorney, Immigrant Legal Resource Center, San Francisco, California, June 2, 1993.

35. U.S. DEPARTMENT OF LABOR, *supra* note 32, at 131.

NOTES TO CHAPTER 8

1. John Hanchette, *Sharp Tongue, Quick Wit, Could Come Back to Haunt Buchanan,* GANNETT NEWS SERVICE, Feb. 26, 1992; *see also* Patrick J. McDonnel, *California's Immigration Hot Button Awaits GOP Candidates,* L.A. TIMES, Mar. 2, 1996, at A10; William Branigin, *Congress to Confront GOP Immigration Split,* WASHINGTON POST, Feb. 29, 1996, at A11.

2. Harry Shearer, *Man Bites Town: Our Teeming Shore,* L.A. TIMES, Jan. 5, 1992, (Magazine), at 8 (quoting David Duke).

3. PETER BRIMELOW, ALIEN NATION (1995), at 221, 232.

4. Alan K. Simpson, *Foreword*, 20 SAN DIEGO L. REV. 1, 1 (1982); SELECT COMM'N ON IMMIGRATION & REFUGEE POL'Y, U.S. IMMIGRATION POLICY AND THE NATIONAL INTEREST, 412–13 (1981), statement of Commissioner Alan K. Simpson, United States Senator; Eric Schmitt, *Debate on Immigration Bill Yields Deep Division and Unusual Allies*, N.Y. TIMES, Feb. 26, 1996, at A1, A7; Steven A. Chin, *Asian American Power Tested*, S.F. EXAMINER, May 26, 1992, at A6 (quoting Dick Day, Simpson's chief counsel on the Senate Judiciary Committee).

5. Morton M. Kondracke, *Borderline Cases*, NEW REPUBLIC, Apr. 10, 1989, at 8, 9. FAIR describes itself as a "centrist" organization with a membership that includes environmentalists and people with a wide range of political philosophies, including Eugene McCarthy. Telephone interview with Anna Weinroth, lobbyist for FAIR, Nov. 4, 1991.

6. *Hearings before the Subcomm. on Economic Resources, Competitiveness, and Security Economics of the Joint Economic Comm.*, 99th Cong., 2d Sess. 397 (1986) [hereinafter *Hearings*], statement of Otis L. Graham, Jr., Professor, Center for Advanced Studies, Stanford University.

7. *Id.* at 359. Statement of Governor Richard D. Lamm.

8. LEON F. BOUVIER, PEACEFUL INVASIONS: IMMIGRATION AND CHANGING AMERICA 184–86 (1992). In his acknowledgments, Bouvier states, "It has been a rewarding and challenging experience, and in one sense, troublesome as well. Here I am, a self-proclaimed and proud Liberal advocating reduced levels of immigration!" *Id.* at iii. *See also* SCHLESINGER, THE DISUNITING OF AMERICA (1992).

9. "Anglo-conformity," along with the "melting pot" and "cultural pluralism," constitute the three main conceptual models of assimilation in the United States. These categories may provide a mere description of the process, or an ideal, or both. The Anglo-conformity model assumes the "desirability of maintaining English institutions (as modified by the American Revolution), the English language, and English-oriented cultural patterns as dominant and standard in American life." Milton M. Gordon, *Assimilation in America: Theory and Reality*, 90 DAEDALUS 263, 263, 265 (1961). Restrictionists, who were adamantly opposed to the melting pot idea, embraced Anglo-conformity. Their Anglo-conformity aimed to strip the immigrant of his or her homeland culture and "make him over into an American along Anglo-Saxon lines." Leon F. Bouvier and Robert W. Gardner, *Immigration to the United States: The Unfinished Story*, 41 POPULATION BULL. 1, 33 (1986).

The melting pot model is based on the belief that immigrants of all cultures together form a new national character. *See* Gordon, *supra*, at 271. I later argue that a de facto sort of melting pot actually occurs today, with the culture of new immigrants constantly affecting the definition and character of the national character; *see infra* text accompanying notes 34 and 35.

Philosopher Horace Kallen coined the term "cultural pluralism" in the 1920s. In proposing cultural pluralism, Kallen argued that the nation should "consciously allow and encourage its groups to develop democratically, each emphasizing its particular cultural heritage." Bouvier and Gardner, *supra*, at 33 (quoting Horace Kallen); *see also* Gordon, *supra*, at 277–78.

The traditional strict assimilationist sentiments merged racial and nonracial issues and embodied racial and cultural prejudices. This philosophy has a long heritage. Prior to the arrival of the Chinese in the late 1800s, some American opinion leaders promoted the melting pot notion of blending races and cultures, although Native Americans and African Americans were excluded from this vision. *See* STUART C. MILLER, THE UNWELCOME IMMIGRANT: THE AMERICAN IMAGE OF THE CHINESE, 1785–1882 192 (1969). However, restrictionists adamantly opposed the melting pot concept, embracing instead a cauldron concept of Anglo-conformity. Becoming an American involved stripping the immigrants of their homeland culture to make them over "into an American along Anglo-Saxon lines." Bouvier and Gardner, *supra,* at 33.

This movement, evident as far back as colonial times (*see* Gordon, *supra,* at 266–67), was fueled by the influential 1911 Dillingham Commission report. *See* William P. Adams, *A Dubious Host,* WILSON Q. 101, 107 (1983), AND A GENERAL SENTIMENT EXEMPLIFIED IN 1917 BY PRESIDENT WOODROW WILSON: "A MAN WHO THINKS OF HIMSELF AS BELONGING TO A PARTICULAR NATIONAL GROUP IN AMERICA HAS NOT YET BECOME AN AMERICAN." *Id.* at 111. For a more recent example, see Patrick Buchanan, *New Hampshire: The National Window to '96* (broadcast on WMUR-TV, Manchester, N.H., Oct. 11, 1995, 8:00 P.M.), arguing "we've got to get away from this idea of hyphenated Americanism." This Anglo-conformity philosophy was part of the foundation for exclusionary laws aimed at Asian immigrants. *See* BILL ONG HING, MAKING AND REMAKING ASIAN AMERICA THROUGH IMMIGRATION POLICY 1850–1990 17–42 (1993), discussing national origins quota restrictions on southern and eastern Europeans; EDWARD P. HUTCHINSON, LEGISLATIVE HISTORY OF AMERICAN IMMIGRATION POLICY 1798–1965 180–94 (1981); JOHN HIGHAM, STRANGERS IN THE LAND 316–24 (1955). *See also* BOUVIER, *supra* note 8, at 180, asserting that, as European Americans gradually gained acceptance by conforming to Anglo norms, "[w]hat had been an Anglo-conformity umbrella had become a European-American umbrella."

10. I use the terms "race assimilationists," "race-based assimilationists," and "Euro-immigrationists" interchangeably to describe Buchanan, Brimelow, Duke, and others who correlate race and immigration. Conservative Republican Senator Alan Simpson also labels Buchanan's immigration proposals racist: "Buchanan's promise to shut off illegal immigration in six months is . . . an impossible thing and it's also racist. It is very unfortunate to play to the base emotions of the American public, and that is what that is." Peter Kenyon, *Senate Judiciary Committee to Vote on Immigration Bill,* NATIONAL PUBLIC RADIO: MORNING EDITION, Feb. 29, 1996 (quoting Senator Alan Simpson). Buchanan's racially conscious policies tend to attract intolerant people on the fringes of politics, including white supremicist David Duke. Ken Herman, *A Loss in Louisiana Could Swamp Gramm's Hope,* AUSTIN AMERICAN-STATESMAN, Feb. 5, 1996, at A1; Carl M. Cannon and Ann LoLordo, *Furor Follows Buchanan,* BALTIMORE SUN, Feb. 24, 1996, at 1A.

11. Samuel Francis, *Wake-up Alarm on Illegal Immigration,* WASHINGTON TIMES, Dec. 10, 1991, at F1 (quoting David Duke); Robert Shogan, *Duke Will*

Run Against Bush in Primaries, L.A. TIMES, Dec. 5, 1991, at A1, A34 (quoting David Duke); Judy Keen, *Immigration Fast Becoming Issue for '92,* USA TODAY, Jan. 3, 1992, at 4A (quoting David Duke).

12. *A Nasty Campaign of "Us" vs. "Them": Buchanan's Appeal to Voters' Fears,* L.A. TIMES, Mar. 5, 1992, at B6.

13. *See generally* RONALD TAKAKI, A DIFFERENT MIRROR: A HISTORY OF MULTICULTURAL AMERICA (1994).

14. One wonders whether Buchanan and Duke would permit non-English-speaking white Europeans to immigrate, since both are concerned with insuring the monopoly of English. Professor Stephen Carter points out that "Mr. Buchanan might be surprised at how many Zulus in multi-lingual South Africa speak better English than most of the Europeans of whom he is so enamored." Stephen L. Carter, *Nativism and Its Discontents,* N.Y. TIMES, Mar. 8, 1992, at E15.

15. *Environmentalist Hits Immigration,* IMMIGRATION WATCH (Americans for Immigration Control, Monterey, Va.), Oct. 1989, at 8 (quoting American environmentalist Edward Abbey); Chilton Williamson, Jr., *The Right Books,* NAT'L REV., Apr. 21, 1989, at 48, reviewing and quoting GLAISTER A. ELMER AND EVELYN E. ELMER, ETHNIC CONFLICTS ABROAD: CLUES TO AMERICA'S FUTURE? (1989).

16. *Hearings, supra* note 6, at 359 (statement of Governor Richard D. Lamm). The cultural assimilation rhetoric of FAIR complains that "large-scale" immigration lowers American living standards and dilutes American culture. *See* Dan Stein, *The New Americans* (letter to the editor), ECONOMIST, June 22, 1991, at 6.

17. SELECT COMM'N ON IMMIGRATION & REFUGEE POL'Y, *supra* note 4, at 413 (1981), statement of Commissioner Alan K. Simpson, United States Senator.

18. *See* Stein, *supra* note 16.

19. Richard Estrada, *National Language Has to Begin at U.S. Borders,* CHI. TRIB., Sept. 23, 1995, at 17.

20. Isola Foster, *CNN & Company* (CNN broadcast, May 26, 1994, 4:30 p.m.). One wonders whether the "good-heartedness" that supposedly makes our culture superior has been undermined by efforts of people like Foster to cut back on educational and medical services available to illegal immigrants.

21. *See* THOMAS MULLER AND THOMAS J. ESPENSHADE, THE FOURTH WAVE: CALIFORNIA'S NEWEST IMMIGRANTS 187 (1985); *Hearings, supra* note 6, at 370–73 (statement of Governor Richard D. Lamm).

22. Twenty-three states have made English their official language. Joan Biskupic, *English-Only Case to Get Court Review,* WASHINGTON POST, Mar. 26, 1996, at A5.

23. Memorandum from Gary Rubin and Frank Sharry, National Immigration, Refugee & Citizenship Forum, to Forum Members & Colleagues 3, Apr. 1, 1992, quoting George Tryfiates, Executive Director, English First (on file with author).

24. Diego Castellanos, *A Polyglot Nation,* in JAMES CRAWFORD, ED., LANGUAGE LOYALTIES: A SOURCE BOOK ON THE OFFICIAL ENGLISH CONTROVERSY

13–18 (1992); BILL ONG HING, MAKING AND REMAKING ASIAN AMERICA THROUGH IMMIGRATION POLICY 1850–1990 48, 61 (1993).

25. Gerald P. López, *Undocumented Mexican Migration: In Search of a Just Immigration Law and Policy,* 28 UCLA L. REV. 615, 641–72 (1981); ALFREDO MIRANDE, GRINGO JUSTICE 100–16 (1987).

26. *See* JOHN HOPE FRANKLIN, FROM SLAVERY TO FREEDOM: A HISTORY OF NEGRO AMERICANS 59 (3d ed. 1967).

27. IMMIGRATION AND NATURALIZATION SERVICE, 1990 STATISTICAL YEAR-BOOK, table 2, at 49 (1991).

28. *See generally* TAKAKI, *supra* note 13.

29. Patrick Buchanan, *Meet the Press* (NBC broadcast, July 16, 1995).

30. Sociological studies on immigrant assimilation show that culture is not a zero-sum quantity where a gain is necessarily accompanied by loss. An individual's culture is not a fixed quantity; it can grow and develop without necessarily displacing another element. For example, post-1965 Asian immigrants have not followed a Euro-conformity model of assimilation. Even a cursory examination of Asian communities shows the maintenance of a vital Asian American community: pockets of residential and economic enclaves of Asian Americans thrive; Asian languages are spoken frequently; Asian language media is on the increase; Asian Americans are demanding a variety of educational and social services from the government. But does this necessarily mean that a cultural pluralist approach has emerged?

In the Korean American community, for instance, immigrants have followed a mode of cultural adaptation that is not accompanied by their detachment from Korean culture. *See* Won Moo Hurh and Kwang Chung Kim, *Adhesive Sociocultural Adaptation of Korean Immigrants in the U.S.: An Alternative Strategy of Minority Adaptation,* 18 INT'L MIG. REV. 188, 205 (1984). Hurh and Kim describe the mode of adaptation as "additive" or "adhesive." Similarly, Erich Rosenthal observed that the high level of acculturation among Jewish immigrants in the Chicago area was not accompanied by a decline in Jewish ethnic consciousness and attachment—a case of "acculturation without assimilation." *See* Erich Rosenthal, *Acculturation Without Assimilation? The Jewish Community of Chicago, Illinois,* 66 AM. J. SOC. 275, 282–88 (1960). A 1979 survey of 615 Korean immigrants in the Los Angeles area found a relatively low degree of adaptation to new American habits, customs, and tastes, with a strong attachment to native culture and society. The data on acculturation had three dimensions: English proficiency, exposure to American-printed mass media, and Anglicization of Korean first names. Social assimilation was examined in terms of the nationality and ethnic background of friends and participation in American voluntary associations. This high degree of ethnic attachment was not related to the length of residence in the United States. On the other hand, length of residence and level of American education were both positively related to the degree of attachment to new American customs. For example, the proportion of respondents who subscribed to American newspapers increased in relation to length of residence in the United States, whereas a great majority subscribed to Korean newspapers regardless of the length of residence. Hurh and Kim, *supra,* at 192–200. Thus, Korean immigrants demonstrated that the two cultures, American and Korean, were not mutually exclusive; they could acculturate while still retaining many of their traditions.

A study of the pattern of Japanese American adaptation yielded similar observations. Japanese Americans maintained their heritage but adopted many aspects of American life. The researcher found significant compatibility, but not identity, between Japanese American and white mainstream values and behavior. *See* Minako Kurokawa, ed., Minority Responses: Comparative Views of Reactions to Subordination (1970). The process of Americanization of Southeast Asian refugees reveals a degree of sociological separatism. The initial government resettlement plan was intended to disperse Vietnamese refugees widely and avoid enclaving. *See* Hing, *supra* note 24. In that respect, it represented a rough outline for Anglo-conformity. However, the refugees ignored the resettlement plans imposed on them, opting instead to relocate to areas closer to former friends, family, and those with similar backgrounds. *See* Paul J. Strand and Woodrow Jones, Jr., Indochinese Refugees in America: Problems of Adaptation and Assimilation 131 (1985).

That Southeast Asians have elected such an assimilation process should come as no surprise. They have had to deal with the shock of relocation to the United States and with the difficulty of adjusting to a new lifestyle. Uprooted by war, they were forced to seek refuge in the United States, rather than make a conscious, planned decision to emigrate. It is natural for them to cling to their community, tradition, and culture. Adaptation through increasing economic power and contact with the mainstream society has not been an avenue followed by most Southeast Asians, due in part to racial prejudice and a lack of English facility and other job skills. *Id.* at 131–38.

Studies of other immigrant groups yield similar findings. In a study of Cuban immigrants in Washington, D.C., fifteen years after the Cuban Revolution in 1959–60, one researcher found that "[i]n spite of similarities in adjustment, each group creates a unique cultural blend. Some traditional values are retained, and other, less useful customs are discarded." Margaret S. Boone, Capital Cubans: Refugee Adaptation in Washington D.C. 1 (1989). A study of 850 Pakistani immigrants who settled in Michigan revealed that the longer the immigrant had resided in the United States, the more noticeable was the change in daily habits and attitudes, and the greater the influence of friends and colleagues. Iftikhar H. Malic, Pakistanis in Michigan: A Study of Third Culture and Acculteration [*sic*] 114–15 (1989). Seldom did these immigrants change their preference for Pakistani food, and some women retained their preference for Pakistani clothes. While religion is a very important social institution in Pakistan, it becomes less institutional to many Pakistani immigrants, although some become more religious and conservative as a result of "strong doubts and suspicions about American moral standards." *Id.* at 117, 130.

31. *See* Frank Sharry, *Why Immigrants Are Good for America*, Orlando Sentinel, Sept. 22, 1991, at G1, G5; Lawrence Kutner, *Parent & Child*, N.Y. Times, Nov. 19, 1992, at C12, describing an Armenian immigrant's bilingual

childhood, and pointing out that "many children who were raised speaking a different language often feel considerable pressure to speak only English at school and in public." In my experience, I have never met an immigrant family that discouraged its children from learning English.

32. Interview with Maria Monet, San Francisco Community College Board of Trustees, in San Francisco, California, Mar. 9, 1993; *see also* Ashley Dunn, *Immigrants Protest English Class Cuts*, L.A. TIMES, June 19, 1991, at B3. Many immigrants, embarrassed by their "accents," have turned to private English diction lessons. *See* Raymond Hernandez, *Immigrants Use Diction Lessons to Counter Bias*, N.Y. TIMES, Mar. 2, 1993, at A12 (national edition); Tracy Wilkinson, *An Accent Could Be an Invitation to Bias*, L.A. TIMES, Apr. 23, 1991, at B1.

33. *See* Sharry, *supra* note 31, at G5. *See also* Patrick J. McDonnell, *Study Shows Immigrants Assimilate Quickly to U.S. Life*, SAN FRANCISCO CHRONICLE, Nov. 3, 1993, at A7. English proficiency among Latino immigrants who entered in the 1970s increased from 13 percent in 1980 to 21 percent in 1990; among Asians, the proportion of English speakers rose from 39 percent in 1980 to 53 percent in 1990; Linda Chavez, *Tequila Sunrise: The Slow But Steady Progress of Hispanic Immigrants*, HERITAGE FOUND. POL'Y REV., Spring 1989, at 64; HARRY PACHON AND LOUIS DeSIPIO, NEW AMERICANS BY CHOICE 76–77 (1994); Roberto Suro, *Hispanic Pragmatism Seen In Survey*, N.Y. TIMES, Dec. 15, 1992, at A20.

34. *See, e.g., Latinos as They See Themselves*, PLAIN DEALER, Dec. 17, 1992, at 10B: "'Even among those on the margins of society we found a desire to gain access to mainstream America.' Just like earlier waves of immigrants from elsewhere" (quoting Rudolpho O. de la Garza).

35. Absorption of the foods, music, and even vocabulary of immigrants into "American" society is most common. A survey by the National Restaurant Association revealed that 25 percent of non-Latino consumers consider Mexican to be their favorite ethnic food and 41 percent of non-Latino people ate Mexican food within the last month of the survey. Salsa outsells ketchup in the United States. Calvin Sims, *Tortillas Gain Aficionados in U.S.*, N.Y. TIMES, Sept. 23, 1992, at D1, D5. In the same vein, Henry Louis Gates regards African American culture as a "model of multiculturalism and plurality":

> Duke Ellington, Miles Davis, and John Coltrane have influenced popular musicians the world over. Wynton Marsalis is as comfortable with Mozart as with jazz. Anthony Davis writes in a musical idiom that combines Bartok with the blues. In dance, Judith Jameson, Alvin Ailey, and Katherine Dunham all excelled at "Western" cultural forms, melding these with African-American styles to produce performances that were neither, and both. In painting, Romare Bearden and Jacob Lawrence, Martin Puryear and Augusta Savage, learned to paint and sculpt by studying Western artists, yet each has pioneered the construction of a distinctly African-Ameri-

can visual art. And in literature, of course, the most formally complex and compelling black writers—such as Jean Toomer, Sterling Brown, Langston Hughes, Zora Hurston, Richard Wright, Ralph Ellison, James Baldwin, Toni Morrison, and Gwendolyn Brooks—have always blended forms of Western literature with African-American vernacular and written traditions. Then again, even a vernacular form like the spirituals took as its texts the King James version of the Old and New Testaments. Morrison's master's thesis was on Virginia Woolf and Faulkner; Rita Dove is as conversant with German literature as she is with that of her own country.

HENRY L. GATES, JR., LOOSE CANONS: NOTES ON THE CULTURE WARS xvi-xvii (1992).
Similarly, Asian American writers such as Maxine Hong Kingston and Frank Chin blend two cultures into a distinct American product, as do Latino writers such as Sandra Cisneros and Luis Valdez.

36. *See* ALEXANDER SAXTON, THE INDISPENSABLE ENEMY: LABOR AND THE ANTI-CHINESE MOVEMENT IN CALIFORNIA 103 (1971); Bouvier and Gardner, *supra* note 8, at 32; Gordon, *supra* note 9, at 277–78; Horace M. Kallen, *Democracy Versus the Melting Pot: A Study of American Nationality* (pt. 2), 100 NATION 190, 217 (1915).

37. *See* Gordon, *supra* note 9, at 274–77.

38. I discuss my own vision of common core values in chapter 10.

39. *See* Raymond A. Mohl, *Cultural Assimilation Versus Cultural Pluralism*, in GEORGE E. POZZETTA, ED., ASSIMILATION, ACCULTURATION, AND SOCIAL MOBILITY 187, 192–93 (1991).

40. Tom Peters, *On Excellence—Give U.S. Chaos or Give It Stagnation*, CHI. TRIB., Apr. 9, 1990, at B11.

41. William Broyles, Jr., *Promise of America*, U.S. NEWS & WORLD REP., July 7, 1986, at 25, 29. Essayist Roger Rosenblatt suggests that:

> America is only America because the country is black, white, tan, beige, yellow, red, pink and all shades not accounted for. What would happen if the bigots got their wish is that we would be stuck in a country unrecognizable to ourselves. To be sure, an all white America would be recognizable to the bigots, but then they would be stuck with themselves, a punishment they probably deserve. The rest of us would have to get out of here, go off in search of a new world, where differences make strength.

MACNEIL/LEHRER NEWSHOUR (WNET television broadcast, Jan. 14, 1992). Author Ellis Cose submits,

> Certainly America is in the process of assembling an array of ethnicities and races unlike anything previously assembled. And if we are wise, we will choose to make that a virtue. We will realize

that the differences various groups bring to the table represent a potential gold mine of fresh ideas, if only we can learn to be open to them.

ELLIS COSE, A NATION OF STRANGERS: PREJUDICE, POLITICS, AND THE POPULATING OF AMERICA 218 (1992).

42. Constitutional law scholar Paul Brest puts it this way:

It is a truism that we are socially constructed beings—defining ourselves and being defined by others in terms of myriad characteristics, including nationality, national origin, race, ethnicity, religion, gender, and sexual orientation, among others. However much or little freedom individuals actually have to choose and change their identities, it is a strong norm of our society that governments, employers, and most public and private institutions should not coerce or constrain such choices. This norm is, for example, embodied in the establishment and free exercise clauses of the first amendment to the Constitution, and in the antidiscrimination principle embodied in the equal protection clause of the fourteenth amendment. It finds voice in state and federal antidiscrimination legislation that applies to private employers, landlords, and organizations.

Paul Brest, *"Diversity" for Whom?* Presentation at the *Stanford Law Review* Symposium on Civic and Legal Education, Mar. 6, 1993 (manuscript at 14–15, on file with author).

43. 98 U.S. 145 (1878), *overruled by Thomas v. Review Bd. of Ind. Employment Sec. Div.,* 450 U.S. 707 (1981).

44. *See* John W. Ragsdale, Jr., *The Movement to Assimilate the American Indians: A Jurisprudential Study,* 57 UMKC L. REV. 399, 416 (1989).

45. 94 U.S. 614 (1877), *overruled by United States v. Sandoval,* 231 U.S. 28 (1913).

46. *See* HING, *supra* note 11, at 17–42.

47. *See e.g., Chae Chan Ping v. United States* (The Chinese Exclusion Case), 130 U.S. 581 (1889).

48. The law continues to allow the exclusion of aliens who have been members of or affiliated with "the Communist or any other totalitarian party." 8 U.S.C.A. § 1182(a)(3)(D)(i) (West Supp. 1993). However, changes made in 1990 (1) eliminated the exclusion for nonimmigrants, (2) provided that immigrants who terminated membership or affiliation two years prior to applying for admission are not excluded, and (3) installed a waiver of excludability for a current party member who has a close family member lawfully in the United States. *See* CHARLES GORDON AND STANLEY MAILMAN, 2 IMMIGRATION LAW AND PROCEDURE § 61.04(4)(d) (1993).

49. Congress's authority to legislate in the area of immigration has been deemed plenary. *See, e.g., Fiallo v. Bell,* 430 U.S. 787, 792 (1977) (asserting that "over no conceivable subject is the legislative power of Congress more complete

than it is over the admission of aliens") (citations omitted). However, modern commentators regard the race-based Chinese exclusion laws of the 1880s to be based on a principle that "emerged in the oppressive shadow of a racist, nativist mood a hundred years ago" and is a "constitutional fossil." Louis Henkin, *The Constitution and United States Sovereignty: A Century of Chinese Exclusion and Its Progeny*, 100 HARV. L. REV. 853, 862 (1987).

However, fears that immigration has grown too large have prompted members of the Republican Congress to introduce numerous bills that would cut back on immigrants' rights and restrict their numbers into this country. *See, e.g.*, Penny Bender and Jim Specht, *Republican Seeking Speedy Reform of Immigration Statutes*, GANNETT NEWS SERVICE, Sept. 14, 1995, *available in* Westlaw, ALL-NEWS file.

50. *See* Jim Cole, *Breaking the Language Barrier*, S.F. EXAMINER, Apr. 18, 1993, at E1, E7 (quoting Michael Cuno, Director of Communications, AT&T Language Line).

51. *See* Lena Williams, *Companies Capitalizing on Worker Diversity*, N.Y. TIMES, Dec. 15, 1992, at A1, D20 (quoting Robert L. Lattimer, Managing Director, Diversity Consultants, Inc.).

52. One commentator writes,

> Contrary to our fears of immigration draining our nation's economy, the truth is that immigrants infuse us with new life, giving more than they take. . . . [N]ew immigrants contribute more in taxes than they consume in public services. Within ten years after arriving in this country, they pass native-born citizens in earning power and their children overtake those born in the United States in academic achievement.

THOMAS BENTZ, NEW IMMIGRANTS: PORTRAITS IN PASSAGE 186 (1981).

Moreover, immigrants today share distinctive characteristics with immigrants of the past:

> Those who seek our shores today are not different. They may come from different places on the globe, but their reasons for coming are strikingly similar to the reasons our ancestors came. Even people who escape penniless from hunger or terror bring with them something of value. They, like the pioneers of old, have determination and courage to overcome hardships. They bring knowledge, creativity, ideas and industry which will reinforce or improve the fiber of a free nation.

Theodore M. Hesburgh, *Preface* to BENTZ, *supra*, at ix-x.

53. It takes little effort to think of the contributions of immigrants and refugees, such as mathematician and physicist Albert Einstein, computer giant An Wang, architect I. M. Pei, Nobel laureate Yuan-tse Lee, educator Jaime Escalante of *Stand and Deliver* fame, and countless others in the arts, theater, sciences, and business. Consider, too, the following citizenship lesson provided by less well-known immigrants and refugees:

Immigrants are not only interested in their own success. They also give us valuable lessons in responsible citizenship. In a Honolulu murder trial last year, all three key witnesses for the prosecution were immigrants. Eyewitness Sui Fong Ngai, a Hong Kong native, testified to what she saw when her boss was slain. The second witness, Zbysek Kocur, had fled Czechoslovakia in 1968. When deputy prosecutor Archibald Kaolulo thanked him, Kocur said, "For what? This is expected of me." And the third witness, Ahmed Rehman, a Pakistani, identified the gunman, after two men had approached him on his way into the courthouse foyer and told him to change his story. Rehman said, "That only made me more determined to testify."

In a nation where most citizens will watch crimes but do nothing to stop them, the courage and determination of [these immigrants] is truly remarkable.

Bentz, *supra* note 52, at 187.

54. Assimilationists who fear the social challenge represented by immigrants should be mindful of the fact that the United States is confronted with more diversity that has little to do with immigration. Differences in class, social status, age, religious beliefs, political values, gender, and sexual orientation also represent challenges to the conventional vision of white Anglo-conformity Americanization. Diversity engenders challenges. Immigrants, both historically and at present, have always been a part of that challenge, but not the sole or central feature. Immigration ought not be the scapegoat for the challenge that diversity presents to the nation.

NOTES TO CHAPTER 9

1. SELECT COMM'N ON IMMIGRATION & REFUGEE POL'Y, U.S. IMMIGRATION POLICY AND THE NATIONAL INTEREST 417 (1981), statement of Commissioner Alan K. Simpson, United States Senator. Former Colorado Governor Richard Lamm notes: "Immigration at massive levels . . . creates societal problems. . . . In the United States, there has been gang warfare between Vietnamese and Hispanics in Denver." RICHARD D. LAMM AND GARY IMHOFF, THE IMMIGRA-TION TIME BOMB: THE FRAGMENTING OF AMERICA 10–11 (1985). *See also* John A. Farrell, *Open Doors/Closing Minds,* BOSTON GLOBE, Feb. 23, 1992, at 61, 63.

2. Chilton Williamson, Jr., *The Right Books,* NAT'L REV., Apr. 21, 1989, at 48, reviewing GLAISTER A. ELMER AND EVELYN E. ELMER, ETHNIC CONFLICTS ABROAD: CLUES TO AMERICA'S FUTURE? (1989) and quoting therefrom.

3. Farrell, *supra* note 1, at 63 (quoting Patrick Buchanan).

4. SELECT COMM'N ON IMMIGRATION & REFUGEE POL'Y, *supra* note 1, at 417 (statement of Commissioner Alan K. Simpson, United States Senator).

5. Tom Peters, *On Excellence—Give U.S. Chaos or Give It Stagnation*, CHI. TRIB., Apr. 9, 1990, at B11. *See* BERNSTEIN, DICTATORSHIP OF VIRTUE (1994).

6. For examples of Korean Americans' varying reactions to the Rodney King aftermath, see Garry Abrams, *Out of Chaos, A New Voice*, L.A. TIMES, July 20, 1992, at E1; Steven A. Chin, *Innocence Lost: L.A.'s Koreans Fight to Be Heard*, S.F. EXAMINER, May 9, 1992, at A1; Susan Moffat, *Splintered Society: U.S. Asians*, L.A. TIMES, July 13, 1992, at A1; Tyson B. Park, *Why Punish the Victims?* L.A. TIMES, July 15, 1992, at B7; Eui-Young Yu, *We Saw Our Dreams Burn for No Reason*, S.F. EXAMINER, May 24, 1992, at A13; Press Release from the Korean American Bar Association of Southern California, Apr. 30, 1992 (on file with author); Statement by Korean Americans for Racial Justice, May 9, 1992 (on file with author). Prominent Chinese American activist, Henry Der, argued:

> As politically volatile as it is, I wonder if we're failing [Korean American merchants] in Los Angeles. . . . the issue is if we go after skinheads or KKK folks—people actually who are responsible for conduct of crime based on hate animosity—I wonder if we are negligent in not raising that issue [here against the black and Latino looters] because [Korean] folks who don't speak English, that's what they're feeling. . . . That is really the largest concern—racial hatred.

AT&T National Asian American Leadership Video Conference, New York, Chicago, Houston, San Francisco, and Los Angeles, June 24, 1992 (videotape on file with author).

See also Chin, *supra*, at A1, A5; Andrea Ford, *Koreans, Blacks Try to Forge Alliance*, L.A. TIMES, Nov. 9, 1992, at B1; Stewart Kwoh et al., *Finding Ways to Salve Intergroup Sore Points*, L.A. TIMES, June 5, 1992, at B7.

7. Rap artist, Sister Souljah, explained:

> I think that we have to look at the fact that black people didn't just run outside and burn up their houses because they were angry. The Beverly Center was wrecked and that's in a white area. Korean businesses were targeted because that Korean woman shot and killed Latasha Harlans and she was convicted of the crime and she did not get one day in jail and we've got 25 percent of our black population behind bars doing exorbitant sentences for small crimes and we don't get justice. These are the reasons why people were attacked.

Listening to America with Bill Moyers (Public Affairs television broadcast, May 5, 1992).

For examples of African Americans' varying reactions to the Rodney King aftermath, *see* Ford, *supra* note 6, at B1; David Freed and Charisse Jones, *Blacks, Koreans Seek Conciliation*, L.A. TIMES, May 26, 1992, at A1; Patrick Lee, *Not Business as Usual*, L.A. TIMES, Aug. 21, 1992, at D1; Seth Mydans,

Accused Looters Are Varied as Greatly as Things Stolen, N.Y. TIMES, May 7, 1992, at A1.

8. *The Emerging New Majority: Black, Asian, Hispanic Relations in the '90s,* AGENDA (Nat'l Council of La Raza, Washington, D.C.), Fall 1992, at 10.

9. Similarly, when unemployed auto workers lash out at Japanese Americans as well as Japan, the motive is ostensibly economic, but racial overtones dominate. Certainly Japan-bashing begins because of the perception of Japanese auto market domination. *See* Ronald Takaki, *Behind the Bashing of Japan,* ASIAN WEEK, Feb. 14, 1992, at 2 (stating that imports of Japanese automobiles "have been denounced as an 'invasion'"). However, even if Germany's autos took a greater market share, it is unlikely that unemployed auto workers would beat German Americans because their race allows them to blend into white American culture and society. *See* RONALD TAKAKI, STRANGERS FROM A DIFFERENT SHORE 13 (1989).

10. Keep in mind, however, that many residents of the ghetto are there because of housing discrimination rather than by choice. *See, e.g.,* Robert Pear, *Bias Is Admitted by New York City in Public Housing,* N.Y. TIMES, July 1, 1992, at A1; Douglas S. Massey and Nancy A. Denton, *Trends in the Residential Segregation of Blacks, Hispanics, and Asians: 1970–1980,* 52 AM. SOC. REV. 802, 823 (1987).

11. David J. Dent, *The New Black Suburbs,* N.Y. TIMES, June 14, 1992, § 6 (Magazine), at 20–21, 23.

12. *Id.* at 23. For similar reasons, African Americans in New Hampshire have formed a "blacks-only club," although its meetings are broadcast on a novel cable TV show for anyone to listen in and observe. As one participant explained, "To be able to eat certain foods. . . . To have somebody say, 'Hey, collard greens. That's good stuff, man, I wish I'd had some,' you know? I don't have to explain that thing. If I want to eat a sweet potato pie and somebody else says, 'Oh, man, I know what you mean,' you know? I don't have to explain that thing." Tovia Smith, *New Hampshire African-Americans Form Support Group,* NATIONAL PUBLIC RADIO, MORNING EDITION, Transcript No. 1816–17, Mar. 4, 1996.

13. Farrell, *supra* note 1, at 63 (quoting Patrick Buchanan).

14. Todd Gitlin, *Uncivil Society,* S.F. EXAMINER (Magazine), Apr. 19, 1992, at 13, 16. Gitlin expands on his concerns about separatism and identity politics in his book, TODD GITLIN, THE TWILIGHT OF COMMON DREAMS (1995). Political commentator Michael Lind raises similar worries in MICHAEL LIND, THE NEXT AMERICAN NATION (1995).

15. *See* Scott Harris, *'Little India,'* L.A. TIMES, Sept. 1, 1992, at B8: "Dhanesh agrees . . . that his fellow Indians need to become assimilated, become more involved in the wider community. 'Many of them, they're not doing their part of integrating'" (quoting Dhanesh Bhindi).

16. Milton Gordon, *Assimilation in America: Theory and Reality,* 90 DAEDALUS 263, 279 (1961).

17. *Id.* at 280–81. As early as the 1930s, sociologists expressed concerns that because of conspicuous color or cultural heritage, immigrants were being tar-

geted as outsiders. *See, e.g.,* E. S. Bogardus, *Anti-Filipino Race Riots* (Report to the Ingram Institute of Social Science, 1930), at 23.

18. In the words of one Korean American leader: "We'll never be white people no matter how long we've lived here. We cannot afford to live in America scattered and isolated. Only through unity can our people protect our rights and pass on a great legacy to our children." KOREATOWN, Oct. 20, 1979, at 5 (statement by Han Mo Koo, President of the Korean Association of Southern California). *See also* Carl McClendon, *Rodney King Redux: Symptoms of a Deeper Malady,* ST. PETERSBURG TIMES, Mar. 21, 1993, at 1D: "The King beating comes on top of a long list of incidents that have intensified blacks' ongoing internal debate over whether a society originally designed to exclude them can ever truly include them."

Although the evolution of the life and philosophy of Malcolm X symbolizes different things to different people, a Gallup poll showed that to 84 percent of African Americans, he represents African Americans helping one another. *See* Mark Whitaker, *Malcolm X,* NEWSWEEK, Nov. 16, 1992, at 66, 72.

19. For example, in Compton, California where Latinos comprise 44 percent of the population, they hold only 9 percent of city jobs. MACNEIL/LEHRER NEWSHOUR (WNET television broadcast, July 30, 1991, statement by Jeffrey Kaye). Because many Latinos felt that the predominantly African American city leaders were not responding to Latino needs, one Latino decided to run for city council saying, "There's a lot of frustration out in the community. We've asked our [predominantly African American] city council to implement an affirmative action program. They have refused. We know what that means. I believe they see the writing on the wall. They see the demography changing very rapidly and do not want to share the power." *Id.* (statement by Pedro Pallan).

20. *See, e.g.,* Jaime Diaz, *Shoal Creek Decision Puts Golf on a New Course,* N.Y. TIMES, Jan. 14, 1991, at C6, discussing exclusion of a Jewish businessman from Kansas City country club, former Vice President Dan Quayle's patronage of Cypress Point, an exclusive club on the Monterey Peninsula that refused to conform to pro golf's antidiscrimination policy, and other clubs which continue to exclude people of color; Lawrence O. Graham, *Invisible Man,* N.Y. MAG., Aug. 17, 1992, at 26, 26–34, discussing his experiences with discrimination at an exclusive country club in Connecticut.

21. *See* CHINESE FOR AFFIRMATIVE ACTION, THE BROKEN LADDER '89: ASIAN AMERICANS IN CITY GOVERNMENT (1989); Veronica Byrd, *The Struggle for Minority Managers,* N.Y. TIMES, Mar. 7, 1993, at A27; Shawn Hubler and Stuart Silverstein, *Schooling Doesn't Close Minority Earning Gap,* L.A. TIMES, Jan. 10, 1993, at A1; Ruben Navarrette, Jr., *Education's Broken Promise to Minorities,* L.A. TIMES, Feb. 14, 1993, at M1.

22. *See, e.g.,* ROSE HUM LEE, THE CHINESE IN THE UNITED STATES OF AMERICA 13 (1960), describing anti-Chinese campaign; SUCHENG CHAN, ASIAN AMERICANS: AN INTERPRETIVE HISTORY 56–57 (1991); John R. Wunder, *Law and the Chinese on the Southwest Frontier, 1850s-1902,* 2 W. LEGAL HIST. 139, 141 (1989).

23. LEE, *supra* note 22, at 142–52; HARRY H.L. KITANO AND ROGER DAN-

IELS, ASIAN AMERICANS: EMERGING MINORITIES 25–26 (1988); VICTOR G. NEE AND BRETT DE BARY NEE, LONGTIME CALIFORN' 13–29 (1972). The overinclusive enforcement of an 1875 law barring the entry of Chinese prostitutes, the intent to exclude women and men under the 1887 Chinese Exclusion law, and antimiscegenation laws in states such as California and Oregon made it very difficult for Chinese male workers to marry and form families. BILL ONG HING, MAKING AND REMAKING ASIAN AMERICA THROUGH IMMIGRATION POLICY 1850–1990 45 (1993). For a detailed account of mob attacks on Chinese, see SHIH-SHAN H. TSAI, THE CHINESE EXPERIENCE IN AMERICA 67–73 (1986). One irony of separatist movements is that while ethnic ghettos have for some time been imposed on people of color, when they themselves advocate separatism those powerful forces that created and perpetuated segregation become particularly upset.

24. This explanation of exclusion underscores the importance of separate communities because within these communities, people of color can find acceptance at the local level: in neighborhood, school, community, and formal social groups. Secure in their identities, they can then enter the mainstream with greater confidence.

25. Replicating the animosities that they had faced on the Atlantic Coast, the Irish led much of the anti-Chinese sentiment on the Pacific Coast in the 1800s. See HING, supra note 23, at 21.

26. Gordon, supra note 16, at 282–83.

27. Interview with Allan Brotsky, Professor at Golden Gate University School of Law, in San Francisco, California (Mar. 18, 1993). In response to exclusion, Jewish men in the past formed their own clubs, yet membership was not limited to Jews. Id.

28. I understand that many whites struggle economically and have little sense of control over the power structure. Theirs is a class fight, as is true for many people of color. But because of higher percentages of poverty in communities of color and exclusion from social institutions and the power structure irrespective of class, communities of color, particularly separatists within those communities, tend to view the problems in terms of race.

29. The mainstream media is of little help because it portrays and perpetuates negative stereotypes of Asian Americans.

> Reporters are not alone in sterotyping Asian Americans and Asian immigrants. Bespectacled math whizzes and buck-toothed businessmen are standard characters on television and in the movies. Often these figures are depicted as fools whose conversation is filled with fortune cookie cliches. Asian women frequently appear as exotic sex objects rather than as multidimensional characters. Asian communities are "filled with thoroughly ruthless ganglords, evil drug rings, secret taverns, and hidden lairs behind neon lights."

HING, supra note 23, at 11–12 (footnotes omitted).
The media does occasionally portray people of color more positively. When

M.I.T. admitted several Mexican American students from a high school in Texas one year, one newspaper profiled them in a highly favorable light. Mark McDonald, *Making the Grade: Five Students from El Paso Are Learning What It Takes to Survive Fabled MIT,* DALLAS MORNING NEWS, Jan. 2, 1993, at 1C.

30. Over the years I have had countless students of color who find law school unbearable until they work or volunteer in a community law office and help people from the same racial background. The community provides these students with a sense of purpose and identity that positively affects their attitude about law school. In fact, this was my own experience when I attended law school in the early 1970s and worked at the Chinatown office of the San Francisco Neighborhood Legal Assistance Foundation.

31.

> Prominent African Americans such as Jesse Jackson and Magic Johnson are no more effective than President Bush in reaching alienated urban black youths. . . .
>
> Houston Baker, director of the Center for the Study of Black Literature and Culture at the University of Pennsylvania . . . was surprised and discouraged by the teenagers' rejection of black culture.
>
> "Even when presented by stunning role models like Magic Johnson, they don't want to hear it."

Young Blacks Reject Black, White Mainstream Culture, S.F. EXAMINER, May 27, 1992, at A2 (quoting Houston Baker).
See also Lyle V. Harris, *Reaching the Hip-Hop Generation,* ATLANTA J.-CONST., Mar. 7, 1993, at C1, C4: "Successful blacks who might otherwise be considered good role models may be rejected because they seem foreign to the hard-core street culture from which hip hop springs."

NOTES TO CHAPTER 10

1. President Bill Clinton has spoken directly about the benefits of immigration and the need for tolerance and understanding. "[W]e should never, ever permit ourselves to get into a position where we forget that almost everybody here came from somewhere else and that America is a set of ideas and values and convictions that make us strong." Maria Alicia Gaura and Edward Epstein, *Clinton Backs Immigrants in Bay Visit: He Pans Divisive Politicians,* SAN FRANCISCO CHRONICLE, Sept. 5, 1995.

2. Critical race theorists, for example, have detailed their disappointment and disillusionment with liberalism. *See* DERRICK BELL, AND WE ARE NOT SAVED: THE ELUSIVE QUEST FOR RACIAL JUSTICE (1987); PATRICIA J. WILLIAMS, THE ALCHEMY OF RACE AND RIGHTS (1991); Richard Delgado, *The Ethereal Scholar: Does Critical Legal Studies Have What Minorities Want?* 22 HARV. C.R.-C.L. L. REV. 301 (1987); Mari J. Matsuda, *Looking to the Bottom: Critical Legal Studies and Reparations,* 22 HARV. C.R.-C.L. L. REV. 323 (1987).

3. On more than one occasion, white acquaintances, friends, and students have confided that they grew up being taught a "we/they" perspective where people of color are "they" and potentially dangerous. It is difficult to rid oneself of those feelings. Thus, it comes as little surprise to learn of the distinctive fear that many non-African Americans have of African American males encountered on the street. *See, e.g.,* ELIJAH ANDERSON, STREETWISE 164 (1990). Similarly, some people claim to be "wary of black men and generally nonchalant with Latinos." Jack Miles, *Blacks vs. Browns,* ATLANTIC MONTHLY, Oct. 1992, at 41, 58. In a Los Angeles Times poll conducted before and after the verdict in the first case against the police who beat Rodney King, only a minority of whites said they would favor living in a neighborhood where half their neighbors were either Asian, African American, or Latino. Amy Wallace, *Riots Changed Few Attitudes, Poll Finds,* L.A. TIMES, Sept. 3, 1992, at B1, B8.

Furthermore, when an African American corporate lawyer took a leave of absence from his $105,000–a-year job to become a $7–an-hour busboy at a Connecticut country club to get a sense of its membership's attitudes toward race, the culture of racist stereotyping became chillingly clear. In one instance, he served the father of a former classmate whom he had met on several occasions. "I served him three times at his table, and he looked right at me . . . and did not recognize me. I was just someone to serve them, nothing more than that. And that was when I realized I was really invisible here." Steven Radwell, *Invisible Man Visits a Country Club,* S.F. EXAMINER, Aug. 23, 1992, at B8; *see also* Lawrence O. Graham, *Invisible Man,* N.Y. MAG., Aug. 17, 1992, at 26–34. While one can argue that any busboy could be treated as invisible, I cannot help but think that this African American's skin color contributed greatly to his treatment while in busboy uniform, particularly in light of his previous meetings with the white man he served. Studies confirm this correlation between race and disparate treatment suffered by well-dressed African Americans at the hands of landlords, retail merchants, and automobile salespersons. *See, e.g.,* Ian Ayres, *Fair Driving: Gender and Race Discrimination in Retail Car Negotiations,* 104 HARV. L. REV. 817 (1991).

Yet consider these words from a white author illustrating the opportunities for breaking down the distrust:

> As I walk down the street, mumbling to myself, I see an elderly black woman, toting two heavy bags. She's finished a day's work at the white lady's house. She is weary, frowning. I say, as a matter of course, "How's it goin'?" She looks up. Her face brightens. "Fine. And you?"
>
> Three young black kids are swaggering along. As they come toward me, I say, "How's it goin'?" The tall one in the middle is startled. "Fine. And you?"
>
> A presence was acknowledged. That was all.
>
> I am not suggesting a twilight stroll through the walkways of a

public housing project. The danger is not so much black hostility as a stray bullet fired by one black kid at another. What I am suggesting is something else: Affirmative Civility.

STUDS TERKEL, RACE: HOW BLACKS AND WHITES THINK AND FEEL ABOUT THE AMERICAN OBSESSION 17–18 (1992).

As David Mura states,

> To dig out the roots of racial resentment, Americans must come to terms with their subjective vision of race. If someone of another color gets a job you're applying for, is your resentment more than if a person of your own color won the job? When you hear the word American, whose face flashes before your mind?

David Mura, *Bashed in the U.S.A.*, N.Y. TIMES, Apr. 29, 1992, at A17.

4. Consider this description of the San Francisco Bay Area:

> Forty-two [San Francisco] Bay Area cities and towns now have nonwhite and Hispanic communities that form at least a third of their populations—a dramatic increase over the 22 recorded in 1980. . . .
> "What we are seeing here is the appearance of a new kind of American metropolis."
> [The Bay Area] is not an urban region where immigrants are concentrated exclusively in aging inner cities.
> It is not a region that has grown more desperate as it has grown less white.
> And it is not a region where perfect English, European descent and an American birthplace sum up the chief formula for success.
> "The familiar image of distressed, nonwhite, declining core cities surrounded by white suburbs simply doesn't apply to the Bay Area."

Frank Viviano, *A Rich Ethnic Mix in the Suburbs*, SAN FRANCISCO CHRONICLE, May 11, 1991, at A1, A1, A15 (quoting Richard LeGates, Director of Urban Studies at San Francisco State University).

5. Similarly, early commitments of the Clinton administration to overhaul the health care system were labelled "ambitious" and were expected to represent "a vast change in the way medical care is organized and delivered." Robert Pear, *Clinton Health-Care Planners Are Facing Delicate Decisions*, N.Y. TIMES, Mar. 23, 1993, at A1. A special lexicon in this regard has developed as well: employer mandate, fee for service, global budget, health insurance purchasing cooperative, health maintenance organization, managed care, managed competition, Medicaid, Medicare, tax cap.

6. I realize that an enormous difference exists between how people feel about newspapers and bottles versus race relations. Interaction and dealings

with real people are obviously far more complex. For many, less emotion and volatility attach to aluminum cans and recycled paper than to a street encounter with someone of a different race, language, or ethnic background. The point, however, is that society has invested a great deal of time and effort in the environmental movement to the betterment of our environment. While racial issues are more personal and even more difficult for many people, we have yet to invest the same commitment to race relations.

7. Professor Charles Lawrence points out,

> Americans share a common historical and cultural heritage in which racism has played and still plays a dominant role. Because of this shared experience, we also inevitably share many ideas, attitudes, and beliefs that attach significance to an individual's race and induce negative feelings and opinions about nonwhites. To the extent that this cultural belief system has influenced all of us, we are all racists. At the same time, most of us are unaware of our racism.

Charles R. Lawrence III, *The Id, The Ego, and Equal Protection: Reckoning With Unconscious Racism*, 39 STAN. L. REV. 317, 322 (1987).

His reminder also enables us to see that even the cultural assimilationist perspective may very well be racial at its core.

8. This idea was expressed in King's famous "I Have a Dream" speech: "I have a dream my four little children will one day live in a nation where they will not be judged by the color of their skin but by content of their character. I have a dream today!" MARTIN LUTHER KING, JR., A TESTAMENT OF HOPE: THE ESSENTIAL WRITINGS AND SPEECHES OF MARTIN LUTHER KING, JR., EDITED BY JAMES M. WASHINGTON 219 (1986).

9. For example, the poor state of education for African Americans—in terms of grades, and dropout and suspension rates—has led some African American leaders in San Francisco, Detroit, New York, Milwaukee, and Baltimore to call for the creation of all-black schools with an Afrocentric curriculum. However, segments of the African American community, including the NAACP, resist such proposals as anti-integrationist. *See* David L. Kirp, *School Idea Splits Black Community*, S.F. EXAMINER, May 2, 1992, at A15.

Elitism among people of color, based on educational or economic privilege, can threaten the solidarity necessary to make a thriving multiculturalism possible. For example, it has never been clear whether integration is the solution desired by the majority of the black community in all circumstances. *See, e.g.,* Brief for CORE as *amicus curiae, Swann v. Charlotte-Mecklenburg Bd. of Educ.,* 402 U.S. 1 (1971), arguing against a school integration plan. Young urban African Americans' thorough rejection of both "black mainstream culture" as well as "white mainstream culture" further exposes the rifts. *See Young Blacks Reject Black, White Mainstream Culture,* S. F. EXAMINER, May 27, 1992, at A2.

10. TODD GITLIN, THE TWILIGHT OF COMMON DREAMS 126–28 (1995).

11. Of course, filtering the media through cultural representatives can be

dangerous if it leads those outside the community to identify the entire community by the standard of the cultural representative, or if the cultural representative's own biases in interpretation are not made clear. However, the problem can be minimized if we are alert to the danger.

12. My intent is that the core leave room for civil disobedience. If people engage in civil disobedience to challenge a law that violates the human values I have listed, their behavior would be consistent with my vision of an American who has accepted the common core values. I realize that including respect for the country's democratic political and economic system as an element of the core is a controversial idea. Many people of color have, with good reason, given up on these institutions as being unjust and racist. I include the qualifier "democratic," in the hope that change will occur through the democratic process.

13. As Henry Louis Gates has pointed out:

> Ours is a late-twentieth-century world profoundly fissured by nationality, ethnicity, race, class, and gender. And the only way to transcend those divisions—to forge, for once, a civic culture that respects both differences and commonalities—is through education that seeks to comprehend the diversity of human culture. Beyond the hype and the high-flown rhetoric is a pretty homely truth: There is no tolerance without respect—and no respect without knowledge. Any human being sufficiently curious and motivated can fully possess another culture, no matter how "alien" it may appear to be.

Henry Louis Gates, Jr., Loose Canons: Notes on the Culture Wars xv (1992).

14. As James Baldwin wrote over thirty years ago:

> Do I really want to be integrated into a burning house?
>
> White Americans find it as difficult as white people elsewhere do to divest themselves of the notion that they are in possession of some intrinsic value that black people need, or want. And this assumption—which, for example, makes the solution to the Negro problem depend on the speed with which Negroes accept and adopt white standards—is revealed in all kinds of striking ways, from Bobby Kennedy's assurance that a Negro can become President in forty years to the unfortunate tone of warm congratulation with which so many liberals address their Negro equals. It is the Negro, of course, who is presumed to have become equal—an achievement that not only proves the comforting fact that perseverance has no color but also overwhelmingly corroborates the white man's sense of his own value.

James Baldwin, The Fire Next Time 94–95 (1963).

15. In addition, I urge immigrant friends and relatives to learn English, respect the environment, and attend school or find a job.

NOTES TO CHAPTER 11

1. Reports indicate that in spite of lagging wages, the economic situation of the middle class is not all gloom. For upper-middle-class households ($75,000–$100,000 annual income), spending is up over the past decade. For those earning $25,000 to $40,000, home ownership is up 4 percent since 1984 and the number of cars per family is up as well. Buying power for all is actually increasing, and living standards are on the upswing. Marc Levinson, *Hey, You're Doing Great,* NEWSWEEK, Jan. 30, 1995, at 42.

2. For example, Esther Taira, a Los Angeles schoolteacher who spearheaded a high school multicultural curriculum in 1986, said that she would design her course differently today. "We do have ethnic-specific courses, but they do not create the bridges we need. . . . [We cannot ignore] the problems in the streets." Sharon Bernstein, *Multiculturalism: Building Bridges or Burning Them?* L.A. TIMES, Nov. 30, 1992, at A1, A16 (quoting Esther Taira).

3. *See Gangs, Shopowners Reach L.A. Detente,* S.F. EXAMINER, May 26, 1992, at A4: "The Korean merchants representing the Korean American Grocers Association agreed to consider gang members for jobs. Initially, four gang members, two each from the Bloods and the Crips, would be hired in managerial or other professional positions in Korean-owned businesses."

4. *Listening to America with Bill Moyers* (Public Affairs television broadcast, July 2, 1992).

5. Prominent Chinese American activist and coalition builder Stewart Kwoh noted in the Rodney King aftermath, "An African American attorney who is working with us to try to heal the wounds told a group of Asians just a few weeks ago that for her to promote pluralism in her community puts her on the lunatic fringe. Nationalism and ethnocentrism is definitely on the upswing in Los Angeles." AT&T National Asian American Leadership Video Conference, New York, Chicago, Houston, San Francisco, and Los Angeles, June 24, 1992 (videotape on file with author).

6. Somehow we must grapple with the fact, for example, that while whites generally support the concept of equal opportunity, they have tended to avoid African Americans "in those institutions in which equal treatment is most needed." ELLIS COSE, A NATION OF STRANGERS: PREJUDICE, POLITICS, AND THE POPULATING OF AMERICA 216 (1992), quoting conclusion of the National Research Council.

7. For example, bilingual education programs have long been attacked by English-only reformers as fostering separatism. *See* Rachel F. Moran, *The Politics of Discretion: Federal Intervention in Bilingual Education,* 76 CALIF. L. REV. 1249, 1301–2 (1988). In my view, this type of stridency ignores the central issue: how to educate non-native speakers of English in a manner that values and respects their cultures, but also teaches them our nation's common values.

Index

Abbey, Edward, 219 n. 15
Acculturation, 152–54, 167
Act of February 5, 1917, 23
Affirmative action, 169
AFL-CIO, 73; California Immigrant Workers Association, 73; and concerns about GATT and NAFTA, 21; Labor Immigrant Assistant Project, 73; Organizing Institute, 73
African American, 2, 4, 15, 54, 75; and beef packing industry, 70; in Chicago, 57–58, 138; and construction industry, 68–69; and effects of inner city abandonment on employment levels, 133–35; in Los Angeles, 55, 67, 162; and low wage immigrants, 129–45; and reliance on public sector employment, 55; and separatism, 165
African American-owned businesses, 135
"Aggregate-benefit-to-all" argument, 50
Agriculture, 71–72, 120

Aid to Families with Dependent Children (AFDC), 98–99, 101
Alexis de Tocqueville Institution, study of public sector costs of immigrants, 53, 185
Ambach v. Norwick, 27
American, 153–54, 176, 188, 190; as defined by Buchanan and Duke, 149; and separatism, 167
Americanization, 15, 176; of Mexicans, 19–20; of Native Americans, 20–22
Americans for Immigration Control (AIC), 148–49, 161
Amnesty, 29, 37, 51
Angel Island, 34
Anticoolie clubs, 17
Aponte, Robert, 57–58, 139
Asia, and economic diversity, 157
Asian, 4, 97, 153; and culture-based arguments, 150; demographics, 2, 3, 51; and discrimination, 172; employment, 51,

237